D O W N T O

Earth

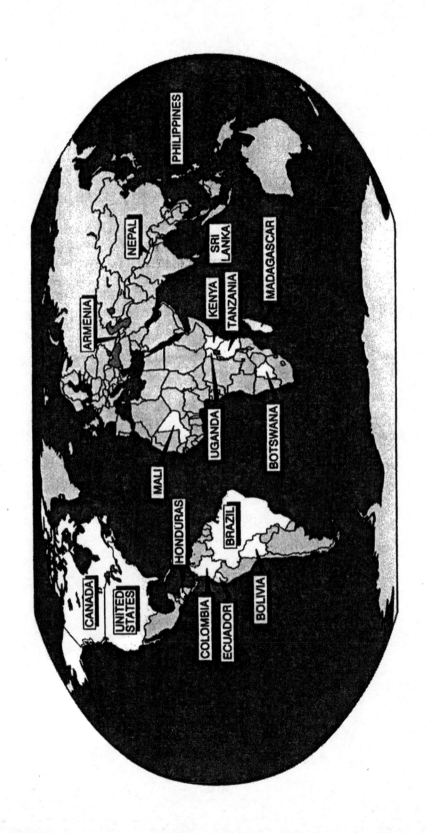

D o **E**w n t o **Earth**

Community Perspectives on
Health, Development, and the Environment

editors
BONNIE BRADFORD
MARGARET A. GWYNNE

Prepared under the auspices of the
National Council for International Health

Kumarian Press

Down to Earth: Community Perspectives on Health, Development, and the Environment. Published 1995 in the United States of America by Kumarian Press, Inc., 630 Oakwood Avenue, Suite 119, West Hartford, Connecticut 06110-1529 USA.

Production supervised by Jenna Dixon
Copyedited by Linda Faillace   Proofread by Beth Richards
Text designed by Jenna Dixon   Map by Christopher L. Brest
Index prepared by Barbara DeGennaro

Printed in the United States of America on recycled acid-free paper by Thomson-Shore, Inc. Text printed with soy-based ink.

Library of Congress Cataloging-in-Publication Data
Down to Earth : community perspectives on health, development, and the environment / editors, Bonnie Bradford, Margaret A. Gwynne.
     p.   cm. — (Kumarian Press library of management for development)
    Includes bibliographic references and index.
    ISBN 1-56549-050-9 (pbk. : alk. paper)
    1. Economic development—Health aspects. 2. Environmental health.
3. Economic development—Environmental aspects. 4. Environmental policy.
I. Bradford, Bonnie.   II. Gwynne, Margaret A.   III. Series.
RA566.D68   1995
362.1'042—dc20
                                              95-17307

04 03 02 01   10 9 8 7 6 5 4 3   1st Printing 1995

Contents

Foreword

All over the world, health problems, poverty, and environmental degradation are increasing. The trend underscores the development paradox: even as many societies witness unprecedented advances in scientific, economic, or technological fields, more people are living in extreme poverty, their access to basic health and social services diminishing more rapidly than at any time in the world's history. At the same time there are signs everywhere of the decreasing capacity of ecosystems to provide human subsistence or even to sustain life, and of political systems and economies to meet the basic human needs of their populations.

To date, too much emphasis has been placed on economic development and too little on human development or social progress. The two are intimately related; economic development is necessary if the quality of life of people everywhere is to improve. However, economic development alone is not enough. Human development, through sustained and equitable investment in education, health, and higher living standards, plays a vital part in achieving quality of life improvements. Economic development should be a means by which human development can be attained, not an end in itself.

To raise awareness about the relationship between economic and human development and to generate the kind of political commitment needed to achieve both, alternative development strategies are needed. Their paramount goal should be to support healthy lives and sustainable livelihoods. If they are to address the challenge of human development successfully, these new strategies must foster partnerships among individuals and institutions.

In June 1993, the National Council for International Health (NCIH), to encourage dialogue among policy makers and professionals in the interrelated fields of health, development, and the environment, convened a conference entitled "Health and the Environment: Meeting the Challenge for Human Development." Some of the rich case materials presented at the conference are assembled in this book. The cases selected for inclusion encompass a wide range of health and environmental problems from around the world, identifying their root causes, and describing how they were addressed.

Two messages reverberate through the book, and indeed through most of the presentations and discussions at the conference: first, that concerns surrounding health, the environment, and sustainable development must be addressed in an integrated manner; and second, that policy makers must identify innovative ideas and strategies that are responsive to local communities' needs and grounded in the involvement, participation, and empowerment of all members of a given community.

Formulating new insights and then putting them into action is perhaps the major challenge of human development today. This book responds to the challenge by presenting actual, down to earth cases from the field, each of which offers concrete, useful observations on what works, how, and why. Based on these cases, it is evident that the most promising path to sustainable, equitable human development is one based on emerging approaches that are primarily dependent on local (and often community) resources; that are sensitive to gender roles and relationships in local and/or community settings; and that are implemented through local institutions.

Additionally, the cases presented in this book provide cogent examples of how integrated approaches to human development can help to:

- foster self-reliance within communities, by encouraging community members to identify their own problems and priorities;
- sensitize community members to environmental, health, and development issues and the interrelationships among them;
- support, affirm, and encourage local leadership (one author calls this "leading from behind" another, "letting government do the steering, not the rowing"); and
- promote viable local institutions, especially through dialogue among community groups and by leveraging scarce financial resources.

The 1993 NCIH conference broke new ground by directing attention to the interrelated roles of health and environmental concerns in human development. The multidisciplinary mix of participants and the richness of their dialogue were testimony to the appropriateness of this holistic approach. In an increasingly interdependent world, such multidisciplinary dialogues and approaches will surely prove to be a sine qua non of sustainable, equitable development. It is our hope that the development efforts described in these pages will inspire others to take heart, to learn, and to replicate successes, and that the innovative approaches on which these efforts are based will become the norm for policy and decision making, planning, and implementation at all levels and in all sectors.

On behalf of the National Council for International Health, we thank the coeditors of this book, Bonnie Bradford and Margaret A. Gwynne, whose strong belief in the importance of the manuscript inspired extraordinary dedication. Their efforts on the book began during the conference in 1993 and continued through 1994 as they worked closely with each of the contributors to produce these chapters. NCIH applauds their untiring commitment to assisting NCIH as it continues with its work of stimulating new partnerships and linkages for the future.

George Alleyne
Cochairperson
1993 NCIH Conference

Waafas Ofosu-Amaah
Cochairperson
1993 NCIH Conference

Acknowledgments

The editors would like to express their sincere thanks to each of the contributors to *Down to Earth*. All of them spent significant time and effort working with us to transform transcripts of their 1993 NCIH Annual International Health Conference presentations into a chapter, and to update us through 1994. Their chapters are the heart and soul of this book.

We also thank Frank Lostumbo, president of the National Council for International Health (NCIH), who provided us with guidance, support, and encouragement throughout the process of preparing this book; the cochairs of the 1993 NCIH conference, George Alleyne and Waafas Ofosu-Amaah; and the members of the advisory committee for the 1993 conference, who helped guide the content and structure of the conference.

The Pan American Health Organization generously provided financial support to complete the background paper for the 1993 conference. Ray Eby, our coeditor on this paper, contributed much during its preparation. The general introduction and part introductions in this book draw upon many of the ideas and concepts initially developed in the background paper. Julie Bomengen of NCIH contributed valuable research assistance in preparing the manuscript, and the rest of the staff at NCIH provided ongoing support during this project.

We would like to thank the Governing Board of NCIH, as well as the organizations that provided grants and other support for the 1993 conference and long-term investments in NCIH's activities, including: the Aga Khan Foundation, USA; Camp Dresser and McKee International, Inc.; the Carnegie Corporation of New York; The Centre for Development and Population Activities; The Ford Foundation; The Health Foundation; The William and Flora Hewlett Foundation; the John D. and Catherine T. McArthur Foundation; Merck and Company, Inc.; the Pan American Health Organization; Pathfinder International; The Pew Charitable Trusts; The Rockefeller Foundation; the U.S. Agency for International Development; and World Vision Relief and Development.

Funding to help complete the manuscript was provided by the U.S. Agency for International Development (USAID), with funds and technical support channeled through the Environmental Health Project (EHP). The editors wish to express their appreciation to Dennis Carroll of USAID, who provided vision and valuable input to the 1993 conference as a member of the advisory committee and who supported our efforts to complete the manuscript. Our thanks also to John Austin of USAID for his insights and advice, and to Barbara Crane and Julie Klement, both of USAID, for their assistance during the conference preparations.

Craig Hafner of EHP contributed useful insights as a member of the 1993 conference advisory committee, and continued to support our efforts on the book. Special thanks to Diane Bendahmane, our activity manager at EHP; to Jonathan Darling, who provided essential logistical and administrative support; and to Rob Varley, Helen Murphy, and Steven K. Ault of EHP, all of whom were part of the brainstorming session at which the concepts and issues addressed in this book were defined and clarified. Dan Campbell and Sharon Gillespie at EHP provided excellent research and information services support.

Rosalia Rodriguez-Garcia, director of the George Washington Center for International Health, helpfully put us in contact with graduate students Carrie Ingalls, Ruth Mabry, Curtis Noonan, and Liz Weist, who provided research assistance for several chapters of the book.

Thanks also to Carl Bartone of the World Bank; Barry Levy of Tufts University; and David Satterthwaite of the International Institute for Environment and Development for their useful comments, input, and/or feedback on the background paper for the 1993 conference.

We are especially grateful for the time, effort, and advice we received from Trish Reynolds, our editor at Kumarian Press, and Jenna Dixon, who supervised the production of this book.

We acknowledge and thank the reviewers of the draft manuscript of the book: Diane Bendahmane, Helen Murphy, and Rob Varley of the Environmental Health Project; Josef Leitmann of the Urban Development Division of the World Bank; Waafas Ofosu-Amaah, consultant and cochair of the 1993 conference; and Diana Silimperi of BASICS, Management Sciences for Health, and member of the 1993 conference advisory committee.

Finally, we express our heartfelt appreciation to our families for their encouragement and support during the preparation of this book. Thank you from Bonnie Bradford to Eddy, Susana, and David; and from Margaret A. Gwynne to Tom, Cathy, Ellen, and Meg.

Introduction

There is a Midrashic story: A man is on a boat. He is not alone, but acts as if he were. One night, he begins to cut a hole under his seat. His neighbors shriek: "Have you gone mad? Do you want to sink us all?" Calmly, he answers them, "What I am doing is none of your business. I paid my own way. I'm only cutting a hole under my own seat." What the man will not accept, what you and I cannot forget, is that all of us are in the same boat.

—Elie Wiesel, winner of the
1986 Nobel Peace Prize

Elie Wiesel's words simply and eloquently convey how our actions—as individuals, communities, or nations—can profoundly affect others. Nowhere is this reflected more pressingly than in the care and respect with which we treat our environment. At the local level, the actions of the few who overconsume, waste, mismanage, or pollute impact the many. Globally, the effects of environmental degradation in one region of the world are often suffered in another. Differing points of view on health, development, and environmental issues in the North and South and in developed and developing countries[1] are now overlaid with new opinions and challenges as the boundaries between East and West continue to change.

At the same time, there is increasing awareness of the complicated linkages among health, development, and the environment.[2] These topics can no longer be viewed in isolation from one another, any more than the relationships among them can be explained in simple cause-and-effect terms. The main goal of *Down to Earth* is to illuminate these linkages through a series of stories contributed by concerned individuals—public servants, social scientists, health professionals, environmentalists, and activists—each of whom contributes a unique and personal point of view. By cutting across a number of disciplines and by presenting complex issues in the form of readable case studies, the book aims to raise awareness, promote critical thinking, and encourage debate in an interdisciplinary, practical, and meaningful way.

Defining "The Environment"

The word *environment* is often used to refer to our physical surroundings: the air and water, flora and fauna, soil and rock of which the ecosphere is constituted. In this book, we are concerned not so much with these natural

1

phenomena as with the numerous, complex, and interactive relationships of human beings to them. If we conceive of nature as separate from human behavior, we cannot hope to understand the relationships among natural phenomena and human health and development, for human and natural causative agents go hand-in-hand. Nearly one half of the world's population suffers from diseases associated with insufficient or contaminated water—mostly the poor and nearly all in developing countries (WHO 1992). Up to 85 percent of all cases of cancer can be attributed to environmental and human-made factors (UNEP 1992).

We are not the first to recognize that what human beings do (or do not do) helps to create "the environment." The term is seldom any longer equated with, or limited to, the "green" environmental agenda of natural resource management and biodiversity conservation; today it is increasingly understood to include the humanly caused "brown" environmental problems so troublesome in most of the world, such as air and water pollution, land degradation, and the use and misuse of energy resources.

In this book, however, we take the term one step further. For us, the environment refers not only to our physical, natural surroundings and the concerns of the green agenda, not only to human beings' pollution and degradation of natural resources and brown environmental concerns, but also to the environment we as human beings have created, the social and cultural climate in which we live, whether it be clean or polluted, affluent or impoverished, safe or dangerous. Sociocultural phenomena, such as poverty, discrimination, and interpersonal violence, negatively affect our environment even as industrial pollution, nuclear waste, and untreated wastewater do. We believe viewing the environment in such broad terms helps us understand not only what environmental problems human beings face, now and in the future, but also what we as a species can and must do about them.

Linking Health, Development, and the Environment

The major, overarching issues addressed in the chapters of this book—poverty, the excessive and unsustainable use of resources by the privileged and affluent, the growth of local populations beyond the ability of available resources to sustain them, the hazardous and unjust disposal of nuclear and industrial wastes—seem to be getting worse, not better. Poverty is increasing in many countries, and it is the poor who are invariably the hardest hit by the most common health and environmental problems. Gaps between rich and poor continue to widen in nearly all countries of the world, as does the poverty gap between developed and developing countries. Overconsumption by the rich and survival practices by the poor are both endangering the environment in all regions of the world. Social unrest and violence resulting from social and cultural conditions continue to rise. Increasing population pressures and inequitable distribution of natural resources fuel conflicts in many parts of the world.

These problems are related, but the linkages among them have tended to be unrecognized, misunderstood, or overlooked. An important reason may be that so many different professions and disciplines are involved in identifying these linkages and exploring the web of causes and effects that connects them. Finding solutions for the negative health consequences of environmental degradation, for example, may involve experts in the areas of public health, environmental conservation, energy management, reproductive health, women's issues, nutrition, migration, housing, water and sanitation, population, medicine, law, economics, sociology, and cultural anthropology.

Unfortunately, representatives of these various disciplines have few opportunities to work together. Moreover, traditional approaches to problem solving among development professionals tend to be discipline-specific and sectoral. The importance of these linkages as essential elements in problem solving is only now being recognized. Consensus is emerging that to develop and implement effective action plans, an interdisciplinary, integrated approach, fostering an active exchange of perspectives, expertise, and experiences, is required.

Background

Developing holistic, effective, and equitable strategies that address these complex and interrelated issues at community, national, and international levels requires not only the involvement and commitment of individuals and organizations from many different disciplines and sectors, but also solid partnerships between the public and private sectors. In recognition of this, the National Council for International Health (NCIH) brought together over thirteen hundred national and international representatives from dozens of different disciplines and both the public and private sectors at its 20th Annual International Health Conference, held near Washington, D.C., in June 1993. The conference, entitled "Health and the Environment: Meeting the Challenge for Human Development," provided participants with the opportunity to spend three days debating, exploring, and defining the linkages among their many separate areas of interest and expertise.

The fourteen chapters of this book, each of which explores a different aspect of the interconnections among health, environment, and development, were selected from among nearly two hundred presentations delivered at the conference, and developed from taped transcripts of these presentations. In every case the editors have attempted to reproduce, to the extent possible, not only the individual presenters' actual words, but also their unique voices.[3]

The chapters are similar only in that they all incorporate a community-based approach and convey firsthand experiences. Otherwise, quite intentionally, the perceptions and ideologies they reflect vary widely. They were selected on the basis of several specific criteria. The first was their distribution by topical area, since we wanted to represent as broad a spectrum of topics as possible. Second, we considered the innovativeness and activism of the authors and the organizations they represent. Third, we chose to develop chapters around experiences and programs that had not already received wide coverage in either the academic or popular press. Fourth, the chapters were selected with regard to their worldwide geographical distribution, in order to provide insights from distinct regions of the world.[4] Finally, we chose presentations that we felt reflected new, workable approaches or that could help advance the integration of different approaches to problems of health, development, and the environment.

One of the most compelling aspects of the 1993 NCIH International Conference on Health and the Environment was the powerful impact made by the presenters as they related their stories of success and failure in their continuing work for better health, safer communities, environmental preservation, and environmental justice. We felt strongly that the presenters' personal experiences, observations, and messages needed to be heard by a much wider audience. This book, which represents the collective efforts not only of the fourteen conference presenters but also their many colleagues, is the result.

Organization

The book is divided into five parts, each focusing on a broad topic area. Part I, "Urbanization, Health, and the Environment," addresses a range of issues, many attributable to poverty, often encountered in urban environments, including crowding, poor sanitation, and violence. Part II, "Implications of Industrialization for Health and the Environment," explores the risks and benefits of industrial processes. Part III, "Exploring Gender Roles in Environmental Management, Health, and Development," focuses on the role of women in environmental management and family and community health.

Part IV, "Environmental Politics: Grassroots Activism and the Search for Environmental Justice," reflects both the struggles and the dedicated activism of those whose right to live and work in a healthy environment has been abridged. Part V, "Creating Responsive Institutions," illustrates how multisectoral collaboration, education, community participation, and infrastructure investment can all contribute to workable solutions to local, regional, and global problems.

For each of the five parts, the editors—sometimes in collaboration with the chapter authors and with help from students and colleagues— have prepared an introduction which provides a general overview of some of the larger issues raised in the part's chapters. Because each topic addressed could be the basis for an entire book, the editors have also included compilations of Additional Readings and Resource Organizations (see end of book). While not all-inclusive, these lists are meant to be useful to readers who want to know more about, or who want to become actively involved in, any of the issues discussed.

Themes

A number of themes cut across chapters. Perhaps the most pervasive, and by now the most familiar in the field of development, is the importance of community participation. Thus in chapter 7, Kenyans come together to improve their water supplies and secure basic sanitation systems; in chapter 8, local Sri Lankans become involved in designing a new kind of stove; in chapter 9 community activists form a grassroots environmental protection organization to combat industrial pollution. Indeed, community-level awareness, action, commitment, and sustained involvement characterize every chapter. Taken together, the chapters show, beyond doubt, that sustainable improvements in the well-being of local communities demand the active and continued participation of the people those improvements are intended to benefit, and further that such participation is empowering, fostering increased self-reliance. A feedback cycle develops: greater participation, greater empowerment.

While continuous community involvement is a necessary prerequisite for a healthy environment, it is the rare community that can achieve this on its own. Health and environmental problems are generally complex, and the many elements that contribute to sustainable solutions are seldom found entirely within the boundaries of any one community.

A second theme that links the chapters of this book is the need for responsive institutions that can provide capital, technical assistance, building materials, and professional planning—not to replace, but rather to augment, the local expertise, human resources, and insights into community values and habits that local communities can contribute to the solutions of their own environmental health problems.

Responsive institutions can link long-term goals, aimed at altering the underlying forces that cause unhealthy environments and empowering people to take control over their own lives, to services that meet more immediate and pressing needs. The point is illustrated in chapters 1 (on innovative programs to help the urban poor help themselves in Colombia), 2 (on the financing of an urban sanitation loan program in Honduras), 7 (on providing clean water and sanitation in Kenya), 12 (on linking population and environmental conservation in Uganda), 13 (on controlling Chagas disease in Bolivia), and 14 (on the concept of primary environmental care), all of which illustrate the importance not only of community involvement but also of creating institutions that are responsive to the needs of communities.

A third theme that unites these chapters is the strength, ability, and dedication of local people in the face of daunting environmental problems. The message is perhaps most cogently expressed in chapters 1 (about the urban poor in Colombia), 6 (on community involvement in family planning in Mali), 9 (on community activism in Kentucky), and 10 (on the efforts of Native peoples to restore and protect their natural environment), but virtually every chapter illustrates that no one is more aware of local problems, more knowledgeable about local customs, or better able to help design and implement local strategies to combat specific environmental problems than local people themselves. Collectively the personal experiences relayed in these chapters add up to an incontestable case for the awareness, intelligence, and commitment of local people in the face of threats to their environment and health.

The fundamental but frequently violated right of every human being to live in a healthy environment, both physical and sociocultural, is a fourth thread that weaves these chapters together. Some believe the abrogation of this right stems from race or ethnicity (see chapters 3, 10, and 11), socioeconomic status (chapters 3 and 9), or gender (chapter 8). Whatever the cause, threats to this basic right are both grave and frequent. Taken together, the stories presented in *Down to Earth* do not suggest that responsibility for environmental inequality based on racism, sexism, classism, or sheer ignorance lies either in the North or the South. Indeed, there is no part of the world that is not characterized by these problems. Chapters 3, 8, 9, 10, and 11 give us a glimpse of how environmental justice is slowly—often painfully slowly—being achieved by communities that have until now been disenfranchised or merely overlooked.

A fifth theme is the crucial role of women in protecting both the environment and the health of families, communities, and nations. Women carry out productive, reproductive, and community management roles, and all these are linked to environmental concerns. From the Earth Summit in Rio de Janeiro to the International Conference on Population and Development in Cairo to the 1995 women's conference in Beijing, China,[5] the recognition that women's economic, social, and political empowerment and access to economic and educational opportunities are absolutely necessary for the health and well-being of communities and nations is drawing ever wider attention. The point is made most forcefully in chapters 6, 7, and 8, as well as in chapters 2 and 14. The value of empowerment for all disenfranchised people, male or female, is brought out in chapters 1, 9, 10, and 11.

A sixth theme is urbanization, the unrelenting growth of the world's cities. By the year 2005, one half the population of the world will be urban. Chapters 1, 2, 3, and 5 describe many characteristics of cities that affect the health and well-being of the urban poor. These characteristics manifest themselves not only in terms of the physical environmental hardships that often plague the urban poor, but also the social and cultural environmental characteristics—poverty, lack of economic opportunity, and violence—that are apt to typify their lives. Chapters 7, 11, 13, and 14 also offer insights into urban conditions.

Collectively, the solutions proposed in the chapters of this book are outnumbered by the problems raised. Not only are there no easy answers; there is no consensus on what constitutes an environmental problem, much less a solution. Thus a seventh theme that emerges throughout the book is conflict, of several different kinds. Chapter 4 addresses the conflict between economic growth and the health of the natural environment; and chapter 10 the conflict between economic development and cultural survival. Chapter 5 raises the potential for conflict between those who rely on traditional methods of assessing environmental risks and proponents of new methodologies that elicit and value insights and opinions from communities affected by these risks. Chapters 6 and 12 illustrate the conflicts engendered when population growth adversely impacts the environment. Chapters 9 and 10 highlight conflicts between environmental activists and the scientific community. Indeed, conflicts between differing ideologies and interests pervade virtually all these chapters.

Alternative ways to achieve sustainable livelihoods—all the coping strategies, outside of formal employment, that the poor use to respond to problems caused by the lack of resources—is an eighth theme characterizing these chapters. Chapters 1 and 2 highlight the reliance of the urban poor in Colombia and Honduras on the informal sector for their livelihoods, but the theme is most strongly brought out in chapter 14, in which primary environmental care is described, through examples from several different parts of the world, as an approach to helping the poor to achieve sustainable livelihoods.

Other themes also emerge. These include the tendency of people all over the world to behave like "environmental ostriches" and the consequent need for education and consciousness-raising; the adverse economic impact of environmental health problems; the problem of energy management (and, in particular, what to do with the undesirable by-products of energy use); children as victims of environmental degradation; the role of racism in environmental issues; women's time as a critical feature in the health of families and communities; violence as both a public health and an environmental issue; family planning as an environmental issue, and one that involves men as much as it does women; and the negative impact of both the rich and the poor on the environment.

Future Challenges

Today, all of us—individuals, communities, multinational corporations, donor organizations, and nations—face a series of daunting challenges.

First, we must choose wisely among competing models. Developing an environmental perspective on health and development is a necessary step toward the goal of improving the quality of human life, but there is no agreement on how best to approach the complex web of problems at the intersection of health, development, and the environment. Some specialists argue that economic progress is key; some champion technological innovations; others find solutions in greater community participation and empowerment or in greater coordination among institutions, or in feminism, or in political options. Still others believe that a focus on equity holds the most promise. The case studies collected here suggest a number of approaches that are available at the local, regional, and national levels to help people set priorities, given limited financial resources.

In addition, we must learn to think more holistically about progress and development, and more critically about industrialization and economic growth; create a healthy balance between environmental conservation and economic and political interests; replace arrogance with humility in our relationship with the earth; communicate and cooperate with one another rather than focusing on narrow local or regional interests; forge mechanisms for coordinated planning and decision making between sectors and institutions; and consider future generations, in addition to our own. The sustainability of the planet rests on the successful achievement of these goals.

Workable solutions do exist. With the commitment of individuals and many disciplines and sectors, it is possible to make significant strides toward improving health, human development, and the quality of life by ensuring a healthier environment for ourselves and for the generations that will follow. We hope the eclectic mix of hard and soft data, descriptive and analytical styles, and subjective and objective observations in this book will encourage dialogue, debate, and the germination and exchange of ideas as we grapple with some of the most difficult and complex problems of our time. Meeting the challenge of protecting and improving the environment depends on the actions of each one of us. The future is in our hands.

Notes

1. There is no general agreement within the international development community on a single, universally acceptable term by which to designate those countries and regions of the world often collectively referred to as "the Third World," "less developed countries (LDCs)" or "the South," and individually designated "developing" or "less developed" countries or regions. With the full knowledge that no term will please all readers, we have chosen to use the commonly encountered adjective "developing" throughout this book.
2. These linkages were given heightened visibility by the well-publicized June 1992 United Nations Conference on Environment and Development (UNCED, also known as the Earth Summit), which brought together representatives from

the North and South, world leaders and grassroots activists, industrialists and conservationists, and population control advocates and opponents.

3. In coauthored chapters, the name of the person who made the 1993 NCIH conference presentation is listed first.

4. The distribution of the chapters by geographical region is as follows:
   - Africa, chapters 6 (Mali), 7 (Kenya), 12 (Uganda), and 14 (Botswana, Madagascar, Tanzania);
   - Asia, chapters 8 (Sri Lanka), and 14 (Nepal, Philippines);
   - the former Soviet Union, chapter 4 (Armenia);
   - Latin America, chapters 1 (Colombia), 2 (Honduras), 5 (Ecuador), 13 (Bolivia) and 14 (Brazil);
   - North America, chapters 9, 10, and 11 (United States), and 10 (United States and Canada).

5. "Fourth World Conference on Women: Action for Equality, Development and Peace."

References

United Nations Environment Programme (UNEP). 1992. *Saving Our Planet: Challenges and Hopes, The State of the Environment (1972–1992)*. UNEP/GCSS.111/2:140–41. New York.

World Health Organization (WHO). 1992. *Our Planet, Our Health: Report of the WHO Commission on Health and Environment*. Geneva.

Part I

Urbanization, Health, and the Environment

Tegucigalpa, Honduras

Part I

Introduction

The world is becoming increasingly urban. In 1950, there were only two megacities with populations over 8 million, London and New York, and the world's total urban population was 737 million. In the span of just forty-five years, the number of people living in urban areas has more than tripled, growing from 737 million in 1950 to about 2.6 billion in 1995. Most of this increase has taken place in developing countries. By the year 2010, at current rates of growth, there will be twenty-six megacities with populations over 10 million, twenty-one of them in developing countries. By 2005, for the first time in human history, over half the world's population will be living in urban areas. By the year 2025, it is expected that there will be 4 billion urban residents in developing countries, compared with 1.2 billion in developed countries.[1]

This rapid urban growth is largely the result of natural increases in resident populations, but also of rural-to-urban migration. The search for better economic opportunities often leads to such migration in both developed and developing countries. Increasing numbers of people relocate in urban areas because environmental degradation, natural catastrophes, or warfare are driving them from their rural homes. Many new immigrants, especially in developing countries, join the ranks of the urban poor, who most often live in crowded and unhealthy conditions in peri-urban neighborhoods built on commercially undesirable or abandoned lands usually located on the outskirts of cities. These fast-growing neighborhoods are typically home to between 30 and 60 percent of the population in developing country cities.

While cities offer hope of a better life, they often do not provide the wealth, security, and happiness that draw people to them. The urban poor in both developed and developing countries are usually the most disenfranchised, with weak ties to many of the formal sectors of society, such as local government. Typically they lack employment opportunities in the formal economic sector, lack adequate access to social services (including health and educational opportunities), and live in overcrowded conditions lacking in privacy and basic amenities such as electricity, clean water, and waste disposal systems. These living conditions of the urban poor are strongly linked with ill health and diseases of poverty, including malnutrition, diarrheal diseases, acute respiratory infections, tuberculosis, and a number of vector-borne diseases. The frustrations of the urban poor, and

13

their daily struggle to survive, are factors increasingly linked with alcohol and drug abuse, domestic violence and homicide, as well as other forms of violence that plague many major cities in both developed and developing countries.

The chapters in Part I describe the challenges of life faced by the urban poor. Together they illustrate a number of salient points: the importance of understanding not only the physical environment but also the social and cultural environment in which the urban poor live; the necessity of involving urban residents as active participants in clarifying their needs and developing strategies for meeting them; the need to strengthen individuals and institutions by building skills, capabilities, and confidence; and the urgent requirement to devise multidisciplinary, multisectoral approaches that will lead to cost-effective and sustainable solutions in increasingly complex urban environments.

Devising Strategies for Helping the Urban Poor

In chapter 1, Rodrigo Guerrero, the mayor of Cali, Colombia, describes life in his city's poor neighborhoods. Cali is perhaps best known outside Colombia for its active drug cartel and the violence associated with the drug trade, but its poor neighborhoods are in many ways typical of many peri-urban settlements. Cali's municipal government has taken a number of innovative steps to help the residents of peri-urban neighborhoods to improve their quality of life. Mayor Guerrero relates how measures such as microenterprise development, linked with training, counseling, and access to credit, and an innovative waste recycling program are contributing to a healthier, more productive environment in peri-urban areas. In discussing strategic interventions to encourage self-help and self-reliance and to generate employment opportunities, Guerrero pays tribute to the energy, resourcefulness, and intelligence of Cali's urban poor.

Strengthening Institutions and Financing Improvements

Chapter 2 by Raymond Ocasio, Theresa A. Kilbane, and Judith A. Hermanson describes an innovative urban sanitation loan program in Honduras. Many residents of peri-urban communities in Tegucigalpa, the capital city, lack adequate bathing, laundry, and waste disposal facilities. Through participating nongovernmental organizations (NGOs), residents are able to obtain access to credit and technical assistance to improve environmental sanitation. Through this program they also learn, in practical ways, about the linkages between environmental problems and health. The model used in this program incorporates two elements crucial for its long-term success: cost recovery, so that the program can cover its operating costs while expanding its reach to additional communities, and building the capacity of local NGOs to manage credit programs effectively.

Reducing Urban Violence

Mexico City has an estimated fifteen hundred urban youth gangs. In Washington, D.C., there are as many as 250 to 350 shootings and stabbings reported each month. In Dakar, Senegal, gratuitous violence has become a way of life for the members of youth groups, which adopt their names from television shows and movies imported from the United States. In New Delhi and most other large Indian cities, murder, theft, burglaries, and rape are on the rise, with violence against women increasing most rapidly.[2] Violence in cities has become a worldwide problem, with profound effects on the quality of urban life. An especially disturbing trend is the effect of urban violence on young people, who—unable to see hope for the future—are increasingly joining street gangs, participating in the drug trade, and resolving conflicts with guns and other deadly weapons.

In chapter 3, Caswell A. Evans Jr. and Billie Phyllis Weiss describe how public health professionals in a homicide-ravaged U.S. metropolitan area, Los Angeles County, California, are addressing the problem of escalating rates of violent injury and death, especially among the young. The new Los Angeles County Violence Prevention Coalition is a consortium of public and private agencies whose forward-thinking, innovative, community-based strategy to reduce violent injury and death takes a public health approach to violence. Recognizing that the problem of reducing violence can be overwhelming when organizations attempt to tackle it alone, coalition members, working together, have implemented an eclectic approach with a community-wide focus, which has a much greater chance of creating positive changes.

Long-standing debates—whether people are better off in cities or rural areas; whether urbanization trends will continue—are being superseded by the urgent need to develop proactive strategies to deal with the unprecedented changes in population dynamics and the unstoppable growth of urban areas. The chapters in Part I offer diverse insights into urban problems and suggest innovative strategies for developing workable solutions and sustainable programs with which to confront the needs of urban residents.

Several common themes emerge. First, urban service delivery programs must include effective cost-recovery components, since no government or institution can possibly meet all the basic needs of growing urban populations through give-away programs. Second, human development, education, training, and capacity building are also essential elements in effecting long-lasting changes and improvements in urban areas. Finally, public and private institutions and governments must forge new alliances, and refine multidimensional, multisectoral approaches, to develop sustainable solutions to the complex, and interconnected, health and environmental problems in an increasingly urban world.

Notes

1. The figures in this paragraph are drawn from the best available data and projections from the United Nations. See United Nations, *World Urbanization Prospects: The 1992 Revision* (New York: United Nations, 1993).
2. The information about Mexico City, Washington, D.C., Senegal, and India is drawn from articles in *The Urban Age* 1(4), a journal issue devoted entirely to urban violence.

Chapter 1

Innovative Programs for the Urban Poor in Cali, Colombia

Rodrigo Guerrero

There is no question that among urban dwellers the most important environmental threat, as well as the strongest predictor of ill health, is poverty. I say this as a physician who has spent most of his life trying to do the traditional things that doctors do to help the poor—things like working in health centers or advising people on nutrition. Poverty is more important than the numbers of physicians or hospital beds or nurses—it is always poverty that has the greatest impact on the health of urban dwellers. So the best way to improve the health of the urban poor is to fight poverty.

There has been a lot of discussion among economists about the definition of "absolute" poverty. To me, the definition is very simple: for an urban dweller, unemployment means absolute poverty. Unemployment is more important than health, education, or environmental sanitation. The poor have to live, and to live they need to earn money. You don't have to search, as many people have done, for other measures of absolute poverty, such as daily caloric intake vis-à-vis the number of calories needed to live. An unemployed person in a city is a person in absolute poverty.

To help its unemployed and impoverished residents to improve their quality of life, the city of Cali, Colombia, has managed—through measures such as developing microentrepreneurial activities and encouraging waste recycling—to create employment opportunities while simultaneously contributing to a healthier environment in poor neighborhoods. In part thanks to immigration from rural areas, Cali is the third largest city in Colombia, with nearly two million people. It is perhaps best known outside of Colombia for its active drug cartel and the violence associated with illegal drug activity.[1] Despite this image, Cali—with its crowded slums and squatter settlements, high rates of morbidity and mortality, large informal sector, and extreme poverty—is in many ways typical of large urban centers in Latin America and elsewhere.

Cali's urban poor may be illiterate, but they are also extremely intelligent, hardworking, creative, and resourceful people. They are adept at solving their own problems and fulfilling their own needs. In most cases, this is despite governmental efforts, which—to be generous about it—tend to be either inadequate or nonexistent. The urban poor avoid unemployment every day of their lives by finding self-employment.

It has been only a few years since people began to recognize the importance of this kind of employment. Economists previously neglected this area, calling the poor in our cities members of the "informal" sector of the economy, in contrast to the "formal" sector in which employees work a fixed number of hours per week, receive regular compensation, pay taxes, contribute to mandatory social insurance schemes, and save for retirement. It so happens that in Latin America, at least, the informal sector employs more than 50 percent of the total urban workforce. In some cases— in Peru, for example—this figure may be 70 percent or higher. So the most important kind of employment for the urban poor is informal self-employment, and the urban poor find this kind of employment themselves, with little or no governmental help.

What do they do? In the slums of Cali, you might find somebody selling chickens one day and giving injections the next. Or you might see a woman making clothing on a primitive sewing machine; her whole family lives on what she can make with this machine. Or you'll see a street-corner food-selling operation—these little shops and stalls are a very popular institution in Latin America. The vendor employs her or his whole family, and they all live on the income that food selling provides. Another popular microbusiness, though somewhat more complex, is shoemaking. In the slums of Cali you can see people manufacturing shoes with Adidas or Nike labels. These examples show how very resourceful poor people are; they'll do anything to make enough money to live on. In the slums of Cali, there is some kind of economic microentrepreneurial activity going on in more than 50 percent of all households. In all those households, people are doing something "informal" to make money to live on.

Some years ago in Colombia, it was traditional for the government to try to solve the problems of the poor by offering them employment. But the government is now unable to do this. So the question can no longer be "How can we solve the problems of the poor people of Cali?" Instead, it must be "How can we help the poor people of Cali solve their own problems?" To do this, whether at the level of the individual, the neighborhood, the city, or the country, work must begin with the positive aspects, not the negative. The focus must be on what is already happening, not on what is not happening or what is lacking. You have to look for the positive. Problems are a frequent topic of international academic discussions. A better idea is to work on solutions rather than on problems.

I'll give two examples of how the city of Cali has helped its urban poor to help themselves.

First, having discovered that the poor of Cali are among the best microentrepreneurs in the world, we devised a program of small business development based on three pillars: training, counseling, and credit. To train Cali's poor people, who have all the virtues of entrepreneurs except that they lack knowledge of business administration, we developed a simplified master's program in business administration, so that these people could learn personnel management, cost estimation, accounting, marketing, production principles, project analysis, quality control, and so on. Whether you're managing a big business or running a street-corner food store, the same principles apply.

The second pillar of our business development program is individual tutoring and counseling. After going through the training process, microentrepreneurs can go to individual counselors to get help in applying the theoretical principles they've learned to their own specific business situations.

The third and final pillar, long-term credit, is made available to microentrepreneurs only after they have taken the first two steps. Credit is never extended before training and counseling, because people need to learn how to use it properly. They must be able to pay it back, which in turn means that their earnings must be sufficient to do so. How can they achieve this level of earnings? A frequent complaint of microentrepreneurs is that they lack accurate ways of estimating the true costs of what they produce, which they need to know in order to price their products appropriately and not lose money on them. Without accurate information they may price their products simply by multiplying the price of their raw materials by three, or by making a survey of their competitors' prices and cutting these prices by 10 percent. The result is that they often sell their products below their real cost. So you have to train microentrepreneurs in cost estimation before making loans available; otherwise you run the risk of losing your money.

This package of training, counseling, and credit has been used extensively in Cali and is now being used elsewhere in Colombia. More than 100,000 microentrepreneurs have gone through the process, and more than U.S.$30 million has been made available in loans. The default rate is less than 1 percent. Each U.S.$1,000 in loans creates another stable job opening—a success rate that compares very favorably with other kinds of investments in entrepreneurship.

And the beneficiaries of our three-part package really do go on and develop successful businesses. Ten years ago, I became acquainted with one of the first people to go through the training/counseling/credit process. Today he has two businesses, neither of which is "micro" any longer. One business makes mattresses, and the other, in which he employs his family and all his children, makes beds and household furniture. I'll give you another example, one of the most successful cases I've seen. As a young man, this entrepreneur saw his father go broke after investing all his money in a small scale-making business. The father lacked basic business administration skills. The son, at that time a seventeen-year-old who hadn't finished high school, went through our training course, and received a loan of about U.S.$2,000. Today he has more than one hundred employees assembling electronic scales.

Another example of the kind of businesses people start are little corner food shops. In the impoverished neighborhoods of Cali, there are several of these on every block. Supermarkets aren't really appropriate in communities where people need to eat now and pay later, but corner food stores are a natural kind of food distribution system in these communities. For one thing, they cater to people who buy their daily food in very small amounts—a couple of tablespoons of oil, half a pound of rice, three tablespoons of coffee, one plantain.

The owners of these corner stores are yet another kind of entrepreneur for whom a special program has been designed in Cali. In this case, it is a course in business administration for small merchants in which entrepreneurs can get individual tutoring, credit, and access to wholesale prices through special food distribution warehouses. The warehouses are places where food producers rent space inexpensively and sell their produce to corner food store owners at wholesale prices. The nongovernmental organization (NGO) running the program provides the warehouse space, insurance, and cleaning services, covering its costs by charging producers a very small percentage of their sales volume for these services. Only corner food store owners who have been trained have access to the warehouse and its services. By gathering a large number of small customers in the same outlet, these warehouses help to solve everyone's needs; food producers can sell large quantities of their products for cash, small merchants have access to wholesale prices, corner food store owners make more money, and poor people pay less for their food. Even the NGO running the program sometimes makes money, with which it subsidizes more training and tutoring for its beneficiaries.

My second example of how the city of Cali has helped its urban poor to help themselves involves recycling. Cali is a very nice town, despite what you've heard about the Cali cartel. It is very modern—above average, in terms of the usual health and economic indicators. But still there are parts of the city where you'll find slums, parts of the city that do not have running water, where water is distributed in closed carts. And the quality of the streets and roads in these parts of Cali is very poor.

The city doesn't do a very good job of collecting waste in these poor neighborhoods. The people in these areas complain about it. Because waste isn't collected, they normally throw their trash—plastic, metal, glass, everything—into holes in the ground, or into the river that runs close to where they live.

So, with the same idea in mind on which our three-part entrepreneurial development process was based—that the problems of the poor should be viewed as opportunities and that the people involved should be part of the solution—we recommended to these people that they collect their recyclable materials and use them to pay for paving their streets. We established recycling centers where people can take recyclable materials and receive credit for them. They are credited with the market price of each item they bring in. They can spend the credit that they earn either to help pave the streets or for their own individual purposes—improving their houses, paying for doctor visits, even buying things for the family at the central warehouses described earlier.

Bottle caps, for example, are considered scrap iron, so some people bring in 55-gallon drums filled with bottle caps for recycling. This starts the process of improving the quality of the unpaved streets in Cali's squatter neighborhoods. The credits they earn can be used to purchase cobblestones; we prefer cobblestones because they can be manufactured by hand and put in place by members of the community. This helps to unite people, to bring them together. When a street paving job is finished, the group dynamic remains, ready to be channelled toward another goal.

Two principles underlie these examples. First, poor people are intelligent. Second, they are hardworking. What those who wish to help should do is liberate that energy and channel it. I recently read a book that I'm sure most of you know, *Reinventing Government* by David Osborne. One of the key ideas in this book is that government should do the steering, not the rowing. That is exactly what we've tried to do in Cali: to channel people, to indicate the direction, to liberate the energy that is inside individuals, communities, private organizations, and nongovernmental organizations.

Here is an example of how applying this principle at the city level has helped to solve a particular problem. Last year in Cali, the cost of bus transportation was eighty-five pesos. Most people paid with one hundred-peso notes, and often the bus driver had no change to give them. We estimated that this might be costing the people of Cali as much as five to ten million dollars a year, so we instituted the use of transportation tokens instead of cash. What is unique about our new token system is that recyclable materials can be exchanged for tokens. In the city of Cali there are now forty places where people can take twenty-two beer cans and have them exchanged for a bus token. Or they can bring in two and one-half kilos of newspapers or two kilos of scrap iron to exchange for tokens.

These innovations show how the poor people of Cali, instead of creating a problem by throwing garbage into the streets, are now part of the solution. We're putting them to work for the city, cleaning up the streets. Glass, metal, plastic—all these things are now taken to what we call "eco-centers." We've hired kids, former street toughs, as garbage collectors and cleaners of streets, parks, and marketplaces in the areas of the city where many people won't dare to go. They have also received training as microentrepreneurs.

Housing provides another example. We had a government two terms ago that made a huge investment in public housing. The project was a failure because poor people couldn't afford to pay for the finished houses. They didn't have the economic capacity. So they continued to solve their housing needs by doing what they have always done—building and improving their own houses. Now we have a new housing strategy, based on people solving their own housing needs as they have always done. City government has developed twenty-five thousand building lots complete with basic services for poor families. Eventually, when houses are built on these lots, this will be the largest public housing project ever created in Colombia.

Our work in Cali is illustrative of several points that have broad implications for solving the interlaced problems of urbanization, health, and environmental quality in other areas of the world:

- Among urban dwellers, poverty is both the strongest predictor of ill health and the most important environmental threat.

- The root cause of poverty is unemployment. To alleviate poverty and improve health, income-producing work for the poor is fundamental.

- The urban poor are intelligent, resourceful, and hardworking. However, providing them with needed resources directly, from the top down, may give them a sense of powerlessness and helplessness. If, on the other hand, the help that is offered allows people to utilize their energy and intelligence, they will ultimately become their own benefactors.

The basic principle behind Cali's programs to help the urban poor is something I learned at the school of public health I attended in the United States. It was the principle that Walter Reed applied when he was working to control yellow fever and malaria during the construction of the Panama Canal. He said, "If you want to control mosquitos, you have to learn to think like a mosquito." And what I always say is, "If you want to help the poor, you have to learn to think like the poor." Unless you do that, you are bound to fail.

Note

1. Mayor Guerrero has been actively involved in developing innovative approaches to preventing violence. As part of this process, the municipality of Cali has created a program called DESEPAZ (Development, Security, and Peace) to reduce crime rates in the city of Cali (Guerrero 1993). In addition, the municipality of Cali and the Latin American and Caribbean Urban Management Programme (UMP/LAC) have coordinated workshops and national conferences on urban violence (Urban Management Programme 1994). For additional information, contact the Urban Management Programme, Regional Office for Latin America and the Caribbean (listed in Resource Organizations). —Ed.

References

Guerrero, Rodrigo. 1993. "Cali's Innovative Approach to Urban Violence." *The Urban Age* 1(4):12, 13, 17.

Osborne, David E. 1992. *Reinventing Government*. Reading, MA: Addison-Wesley.

Urban Management Programme, Regional Office for Latin America and the Caribbean (UMP/LAC). 1994. "Tackling Urban Violence: An Update." *The Urban Age* 2(2):9.

Chapter 2

An Urban Environmental Sanitation Loan Program in Honduras

Raymond Ocasio, Theresa A. Kilbane, and Judith A. Hermanson

The Cooperative Housing Foundation (CHF), a private, nonprofit, U.S.-based organization, has been working in Honduras since 1985. CHF has placed special emphasis on providing assistance to people living in marginal neighborhoods in urban areas in the development of housing, sanitation, and community services. Through its work with low-income communities around the world, CHF has been able to see firsthand the extent to which densely populated, poorly planned settlements negatively affect the natural environment, as well as the negative effects of degraded environmental conditions on the health and standard of living of the people in such communities.

Honduras, along with most other developing countries in the world, is struggling to react to, and recover from, large-scale rural-to-urban migration and natural increases in population growth in densely populated urban areas. Tegucigalpa, the capital city, has doubled its population size in the past decade. In 1991, the population of Tegucigalpa was estimated to be 738,500 (SECPLAN/OIT/FNUAP 1994). Increases in urban population, especially among the poor, have placed tremendous demands for public services and affordable shelter on both national governments and individual municipalities.

The population growth rate of 4.6 percent in Tegucigalpa is significantly higher than the rate of 3.3 percent for Honduras as a whole (SECPLAN/OIT/FNUAP 1994). According to World Bank estimates, the percent of population that is urban continues to climb steadily: from 32 percent (1970–75), to 40 percent (1980–85), up to 45 percent (1987–92) (World Bank 1994).

In major cities and large towns in Honduras, many families live in unhealthy and crowded conditions in sprawling, haphazardly built informal sector settlements known as *barrios marginales* (marginal neighborhoods). They are characterized by poor-quality shelter and a lack of services such as sanitary waste disposal, garbage collection, running water, roads, walk-

23

ways, electricity, and health care services. Nevertheless, they are home to a vast and ever-increasing number of poor Hondurans, and their populations are growing faster than the populations of Honduran cities themselves. The shortage of affordable housing and public services has forced many poor urban families to take matters into their own hands.

Over 60 percent of the people who live in Tegucigalpa live in barrios marginales (CHF/Presidencia/UNICEF 1991). Access to potable water in Tegucigalpa is estimated at 34 percent, and 42 percent of the population lacks access to any type of sanitation services (CHF/UNICEF 1991).[1]

In March of 1990, urban pressures in Honduras escalated when the country's newly elected government introduced sweeping economic reforms as part of a structural adjustment program. While deemed necessary by the government, these reforms have had a disproportionate impact on the poor as real costs have risen. And today, four years later, Honduras remains one of the poorest countries in Central America, second only to Nicaragua. From 1989 to 1990, inflation climbed from 10 percent to 36 percent, and fell to 21 percent in 1990 following the introduction of structural adjustments (Secretaría 1992). In 1988, 53 percent of households in Honduras were considered to be below the poverty line; this figure rose to 56 percent in 1989. By 1990, 63 percent of households were considered to be below the poverty line (CHF/Presidencia/UNICEF 1991).

Barrios marginales may not be served by municipal water, sanitation or sewer systems for years; indeed, they may never be reached by these services. The families living in these communities cope as best they can with an inadequate water supply, limited trash collection, and sanitary facilities that are rudimentary at best. Simply carrying out the necessities of daily living often places residents' health, as well as their environment, at risk.

As part of the response to this situation, the Honduran government, multilateral and bilateral agencies, and private and nongovernmental organizations (NGOs) have identified the delivery of infrastructure and social services to poor Honduran families as a high priority. There are a variety of approaches being used. This chapter describes one collaborative effort which is successfully using market mechanisms to improve the living conditions of the urban poor and help alleviate environmental health problems in marginal neighborhoods.

One of Tegucigalpa's barrios marginales is Las Torres, home to 11,600 people. Las Torres was founded in 1980 in an invasion (also known as "recuperation") of privately held land. It is built on the site of an old lumber mill, and the most recent arrivals have taken up residence on the steep slopes of the mill's dumping ground. The location of the community reflects the increased desirability of land not used by traditional development in the process of land invasions.

The average household size in Las Torres is six people, a typical family size in many peri-urban areas. Most of the economically active residents are employed in the informal sector. Family incomes range from approximately U.S.$53 to U.S.$372 per month, with an average household income of U.S.$138 per month.

Like other such communities in Tegucigalpa, Las Torres has been plagued with substandard conditions that threaten residents' health and have a negative impact on the natural environment. Throughout the community, wastewater stands in stagnant puddles due to poor soil conditions and lack of adequate drainage. Rainwater is collected and stored in uncovered 55-gallon metal drums, most of which have been recycled after industrial use. These are relatively cheap and easy to obtain, but since they are usually left open without lids or screens, stagnant and uncovered water creates breeding grounds for disease-carrying insects such as those that transmit dengue fever, a major problem in Honduras.

Until recently, the residents of Las Torres had to purchase their water from water vendors; residents then store the water in metal drums or plastic containers. Water deliveries were unreliable, prices were high, and the water often highly contaminated with disease-carrying organisms. SANAA (the national water and sewage agency), with assistance from the government of Germany and self-help within the community, recently installed a water distribution system, but this system is constrained by the limited capacity of Tegucigalpa's municipal water system. The 60 percent of households fortunate enough to have taps cannot be assured of an adequate supply of potable water because of intermittent and unscheduled rationing by SANAA.

Although water was introduced as part of service expansion, the community of Las Torres does not have a sewage system. Many families have simple pit latrines, which often prove inadequate—raw sewage overflows from them during heavy rains, and residents' small plots of land provide few opportunities to build new latrines once a pit becomes full. Conditions are even worse for families lacking latrines. Their options are limited to using a neighbor's latrine, defecating in the yard or nearby areas hidden from public view, or walking longer distances to use ravines or wooded areas.

In Tegucigalpa, as elsewhere, the greatest contributions to the alleviation of environmental problems in low-income settlements result from the efforts of community members themselves. Yet most low-income families in Tegucigalpa lack the technical expertise or resources (human as well as financial) they need to build water, sanitation, or waste disposal systems, and to manage their natural resources.

CHF has assisted in the development of two cooperative federations, and nine Honduran NGOs throughout the country. The Credit Union Federation of Honduras (FACACH), which was founded in 1966, represents thirty-seven credit unions with over 135,000 members nationwide. The Honduran Federation of Housing Cooperatives (FEHCOVIL), founded in 1963, represents fourteen housing cooperatives, and provides technical assistance, training, and financing to its member cooperatives to assist them in housing development.

The nine NGOs are located throughout urban areas of the country and each works in a variety of development areas including small business development, training programs, women-run businesses, legal assistance to women, health education, child welfare, and housing and infrastructure programs. Many of the NGOs had not worked in the housing or infrastructure sector prior to their relationship with CHF, and none of them had worked with a cost recovery component.[2]

Building on its positive experience with short-term lending for shelter improvements through NGOs, and as part of its work to promote environmentally sound practices in urban informal settlements, CHF, in partnership with the United Nations Children's Fund (UNICEF) and local NGOs, initiated the Urban Family Sanitation Program in Honduras in 1991. This project is based on a community mobilization strategy that introduces affordable and appropriate technologies to help alleviate household and community environmental problems through a well-managed urban sanitation loan program. The program, which addresses many of the problems that threaten health and the environment in the barrios marginales of Tegucigalpa, is designed to reach low-income families. The sanitation loan program has provided short-term loans to residents of twelve neighborhoods in Tegucigalpa.

A key element of CHF's Honduran urban sanitation loan program is its collaborative arrangement with a network of local nonprofit organizations. Short-term loans under the program are offered in collaboration with local NGOs. Currently, three community-based organizations are participating in the sanitation loan program in Tegucigalpa.

The research stage of the sanitation loan program began in October 1990. A worldwide literature search, conducted with technical assistance from the Water and Sanitation for Health (WASH) Project, sponsored by the U.S. Agency for International Development (USAID), was carried out to discover small-scale, low-cost human waste management technologies, and strategies for community organizing and hygiene education appropriate for urban informal sector settlements. Little information was found about technologies designed or adapted for urban settings; more than 90 percent of the literature about latrines focused on rural areas.

CHF and UNICEF jointly conducted a baseline study in two low-income urban neighborhoods in Tegucigalpa in February 1991 (CHF/Honduras 1991a, 1991b, 1991c). In addition to questions about knowledge, attitudes, and practices, residents were asked about their ability and willingness to pay for improved human waste disposal. It was found that there was a broad range of needs and capacity and willingness to pay among residents of these urban informal settlements. At the same time, sanitary engineers assessed the physical environment to determine what kinds of sanitation systems could be built in the two neighborhoods.

The socioeconomic survey information and engineering assessment results were used to develop a menu of possible sanitation technologies. They also helped project planners identify potential social marketing strategies and hygiene education techniques. For example, the survey results suggested that responding to social concerns would be more effective than citing health benefits in promoting sanitation improvements. These concerns included safety, privacy, and the ability to use a sanitary facility, wash clothes, or bathe in the home, without bothering neighbors or leaving young children unattended.

In April 1991, a multidisciplinary CHF/UNICEF team began working with two local Honduran NGOs to develop the sanitation loan program. The loans are designed to cover the costs calculated for materials and labor to build the sanitation options selected, as well as to cover the costs to the NGO of generating the loan, providing technical assistance, construction supervision, and hygiene education.

In contrast to other loan programs, loans made by CHF cover labor, in addition to materials. The CHF program does not assume that people living in peri-urban areas simply need a loan to help pay for materials, and can do the work themselves. Most people feel they could use their time more productively by pursuing their traditional line of work rather than taking on technical construction work, which is something new and for which they have had little or no experience. The poor usually do not have reserve funds to pay for labor, are often working several jobs without "free" time, and some cannot physically do the work.

Program participants can generally contract workers at very competitive prices, because the loan gives them the ability to pay and provide materials in a timely fashion. In other instances, relatives and neighbors with the appropriate skills can be contracted at bargain rates. This process generates employment, often within the community, and makes the program attractive to people in low-income communities since it takes into consideration their time availability and financial constraints.

The sanitation loan program contains two important and complementary components: education and financing.

Education

Research carried out by CHF/Honduras found that many residents of Tegucigalpa's informal settlements are not aware of the linkages between inadequate sanitation, disease, and environmental degradation (CHF/Honduras 1991a, 1991b, 1991c). CHF developed an innovative marketing and educational program that includes community gatherings, seminars, and a variety of printed materials, including pamphlets, posters, and comic books. These materials are used to promote interest in education programs, develop the linkages between hygiene and health, and convey information on the correct use and maintenance of sanitary facilities.

Much of the program's marketing and promotional efforts take place in the homes, yards, stores, and streets of the neighborhoods. The program's promoters know their neighbors, and when project staff members come from outside the community, contacts are made first with the local leadership. In the course of conversations about family, friends, and the neighborhood, the promoter can easily bring up the opportunities available in the sanitation loan program. Once a loan is made, the promoter continues to provide useful information.

The poor are very aware of their own needs, but often lack the opportunities to resolve even the most basic needs. The loan program is an opportunity to take action to satisfy some of these necessities. Options are presented as a "menu" from which the family can select the desired elements and, more important, the appropriate technology. This built-in flexibility is extremely attractive to most people; it does not force a family to build a latrine if it wants a flush toilet, and does not insist on high standards, so, for example, a plastic curtain rather than a door would be an acceptable option and more affordable for some families. In addition, attention is given to discussing each "solution" so facilities are strategically selected, designed, and located within the property to allow integration with the rest of the house and plot of land.

When families express interest in participating in the loan program, a loan application is completed. This is followed by an on-site consultation with the construction technician from the participating NGO. With this technical assistance provided by the participating institutions, families determine which sanitation improvements they want, based on their needs and economic circumstances.

They learn that sanitation loans can be used to make connections to the city's water pipes or sewer system, when this is technically possible; to construct ventilated improved pit latrines, dry compost latrines, or pour-flush toilets; and/or to build shower stalls, *pilas* (a combination water storage tank and washboard), and improved rainwater collection systems. Physical factors related to the proposed site, including soil composition and topography are also considered. Promoters and NGO personnel help families weigh their options, but ultimately family members themselves choose the sanitation methods they want and can afford, although inappropriate technologies would not be funded.

Once the loan is approved, the family is invited to attend a two-hour seminar. They receive information and instructions about the loan and about the construction process. The seminar also provides the opportunity to bring in the health education component of the program, with the discussion of health and sanitation issues. Promoters discuss the problems that result from inadequate sanitation and explain the connections between poor health and environmental sanitation.

During the construction process, the promoter visits the house and provides support, as well as delivers and reinforces the health and sanitation messages. The comic book and other educational materials are used here and in subsequent encounters. These are particularly useful, because they provide the material in a simple and comprehensible fashion and can be used with both adults and children, and with both literate and illiterate members of the participating families.

Upon completion of the construction of the sanitation facilities, the NGO staff congratulates the family for achieving their initial goal of completing the sanitation facilities. The promoter continues their education about sanitation. This includes instruction in how to use, clean, and maintain the facility. Once a month for the next six months, the promoter visits the family at home to check for signs of proper and improper use and maintenance, to answer any questions or concerns, and to reinforce the health and sanitation messages. This activity is continued as needed on a case-by-case basis.

These follow-up activities also have a financial side. During the regular visits, the promoter is able to establish and reinforce good financial practices. Payment dates and procedures are clarified, and follow-up on delinquent accounts can be managed in a more timely way by the NGO.

Women are actively involved in the program: more than 60 percent of all loan recipients are women. It has been estimated that 37 percent of households in barrios marginales in Tegucigalpa are headed by women (Kawas and Zuniga 1991). And even when women are not considered the head of household, they are usually responsible for managing the water, sanitation, and home maintenance, in addition to their other child-bearing, child-raising, and income-earning responsibilities. Most of the health promoters who have worked in the program have been women. The health promoters are generally recruited from the community, and receive a stipend for the site visits they complete. This stipend, which is built into the interest charged on the loans, helps these women generate income for their own families, and at the same time provides a vital service to other residents of the community.

Financing

The second component of CHF's program provides residents with market rate credit, channeled through participating NGOs, to be used for specific sanitation improvements. In Las Torres, the household head may have relatively low and unstable earnings working as a street vendor, janitor, cook, seamstress, driver, or unskilled laborer. Residents are often unable to save enough money to pay up front for needed improvements, and are considered undesirable credit risks by commercial banks. Some governmental sanitation programs define the poor as a monolithic group, all of whom are unable to afford desirable solutions. As a consequence, many sanitation programs provide or allow a single, simple technology or modest facilities which are neither appropriate nor wanted by many residents.

As of 1994, loans in the program ranged from U.S.$250 to U.S.$430. In most cases, families contribute materials or personal funds to complement the loan monies they borrow, and often some labor as well. The loans are provided at near-market interest rates so that on repayment, the funds go back into a capital fund which can roll over the monies and provide credit to other families without decapitalization. The program is self-sufficient, sustainable, and able to reach increasing numbers of families. An essential and innovative aspect of the program is that the costs of providing technical assistance and hygiene education to participating families are incorporated into the loans, within the established interest rate and as a surcharge.

Completed loan applications are usually reviewed and decided upon within one week. Repayments are generally spread over a one- to three-year period. Each borrower's payments are calculated so as to be affordable, and the average loan payment is U.S.$12 per month for a three-year period. Careful attention is paid to each family's income and living expenses to be sure borrowers are not assuming too much debt. Each loan is considered a personal obligation, and is guaranteed by a friend or family member who agrees to repay the loan in case of default.

To date, most of the loans have financed combinations of either a sewer connection, septic system, or a latrine; along with a pila and a shower. A loan of U.S.$430, for example, will typically build a twin-chamber, aboveground, dry compost latrine; a pila; and a shower. Every effort is made to build in drainage systems to remove wastewater from the loan recipient's property by channeling wastewater to sewer pipes, storm drains, or soak pits.

Such improvements yield a variety of health and environmental advantages and benefits. The latrines provide for the proper management of human waste and help eliminate odors; pilas and showers ensure that family members can wash clothes and bathe regularly and in privacy. There are economic advantages as well: for example, a rainwater collection system, often using the pila for storage, allows families to collect, store, and use rainwater for domestic purposes such as laundry, bathing, and housecleaning. This means that when rainwater is available, families are not completely dependent on the municipal water schedule, or on buying water from water vendors for all their household needs.

There are other important impacts of the CHF urban sanitation loan program in addition to sanitation improvements at the household and community levels. With technical assistance from CHF, each of the participating NGOs has acquired the skills to implement and manage sanitation loan programs reinforced by community education. These institutions are now trained and experienced in the various aspects of credit programs, including program design, loan evaluation, disbursement of funds, monitoring and construction of sanitary facilities, conduct of educational programs, and loan repayment collection.

Since the program began in 1991, almost one thousand loans have been made to low-income families in Tegucigalpa. Repayment rates have been strong, despite the fact that at the same time, and often in the same barrio, the government has offered donated materials for pit latrines. This has created difficulties for the NGOs involved in cost-recovery programs, but the NGOs have persevered, and have played an important role in the strength of repayment rates because of their community ties and because the loan program more adequately addresses the communities' needs. Give-away programs will continue to create problems for cost-recovery programs until actions are taken at a higher policy level by government and international agencies.

The sanitation loan fund has an investment portfolio of U.S.$271,658 (the funds are held in local currency), which represents a 54 percent increase over the volume of funds initially donated. Though inflation has somewhat lowered the real value of the fund because of the worsening Honduran economy, the fund continues to revolve to other communities and has provided a viable credit option for low-income families lacking such an option on the private market, such as through commercial banks. Loans repaid into the revolving fund thus enable the program to be self-sustaining and to expand its reach. As borrowers repay their loans, participating institutions are able to offer credit to additional families in the community for these much-needed sanitation improvements.

Program Evaluation

Evaluations conducted after the first six and twelve months of the program showed that the program has succeeded in altering unsanitary behavior and improving community health and environmental conditions. The last formal evaluation of the program was carried out by CHF in October 1992. The program is currently being evaluated, and the results of this evaluation are expected in early 1995.

The 1992 evaluation was conducted in two of the neighborhoods where the program has been implemented. There was a marked increase in awareness of issues related to health and hygiene. For example, on hygiene issues, knowledge about washing hands after using a latrine or toilet increased from 10 to 40 percent; knowledge of the importance of washing hands before eating increased from 18 to 55 percent; and knowledge of the importance of maintaining the sanitation unit and keeping it clean increased from 18 to nearly 80 percent.

In most households surveyed in 1992, the sanitation unit was found to be well maintained. The evaluation stressed the value and importance of the follow-up site visits. Most of the project beneficiaries stated they would not have been able to construct the improved facilities without access to credit, and expressed satisfaction with having participated in the program.

The following are among the lessons learned in the ongoing CHF/UNICEF sanitation loan program:

- Prior to program interventions, the urban poor had limited knowledge and understanding of the relationships between health and sanitation, or of the range of potential technology options.

- Social factors, and the general desire to improve their lives, homes, and general conditions, were very appropriate vehicles to market sanitation and health improvements.

- Meaningful and appropriate financial alternatives, when offered to the poor, are viable means of supporting their own initiatives and maximizing scarce resources.

- No single technology is suitable, even within one community, so that a variety of technology options needs to be developed and suited to the needs and wants of the participants.

- Grassroots, practical, and focused intervention strategies and educational programs can alter the comprehension, circumstances, and behavior of low-income families related to basic sanitation and health.

Based on the positive results achieved so far in the urban sanitation loan program, CHF/Honduras received a U.S.$407,915 grant from USAID in May 1994 to expand the program to areas outside Tegucigalpa. These funds will be programmed through five or six local counterparts in Tegucigalpa, San Pedro Sula, and elsewhere in the country. With the initial investment of these funds, CHF will be able to support about 800 additional sanitation improvements during the next one to two years. In the coming year, approximately 250 sanitation improvements will be financed through the CHF/UNICEF revolving sanitation loan fund.

CHF's urban environmental sanitation loan program in informal settlements is a replicable model for sustainable community-based improvements. It illustrates how a well-targeted community education campaign, combined with training, technical assistance, and financing, can successfully alleviate household and community environmental problems in low-income urban areas through low-cost and appropriate technologies. It also demonstrates that low-income families are good credit risks and they are willing and able to invest in improving their living conditions. The program is also helping to develop and increase the capacity of local organizations to plan, implement, and monitor sanitation improvement projects. This institutional strengthening should enable these organizations to work even more effectively to the benefit of low-income families, and the environment, both now and in the future.

Notes

1. These figures are for Tegucigalpa as a whole, including middle- and upper-income households. The percentage of the population without access to water and sanitation in the barrios marginales is therefore much higher than these figures suggest.
2. Since 1985, CHF has helped finance more than five thousand loans throughout the country in the areas of housing, water, sanitation, community-level

improvements, and shelter-related small business loans. Nearly all the loans have been to families in Tegucigalpa, San Pedro Sula (the other major urban center in Honduras), and several of the smaller, secondary cities of Honduras.

References

Banco Central de Honduras. 1993. *Honduras en cifras 1991–1993.* Tegucigalpa, Honduras: Dept. de Estudios Económicos, Banco Central de Honduras.

Brand, Anthony, and Bonnie Bradford. 1991. "Rainwater Harvesting and Water Use in the *Barrios* of Tegucigalpa." Tegucigalpa, Honduras: United Nations Children's Fund and Agua para el Pueblo.

Castaldi, Juan Carlos, Herman Felstehausen, and David Stanfield. 1991. "Access to Urban Land and Housing by Informal Sector Households in Honduras." Madison, Wisconsin: Land Tenure Center.

Cooperative Housing Foundation (CHF). 1988. "Banking on the *Barrios*: Financing Shelter and Jobs for Low-Income Families in Honduras." *CHF Fact Sheet* 3. Washington D.C.

————. 1992. "A Livable Environment: Financing Sanitation Improvements in the Urban Settlements of Honduras." *CHF Fact Sheet* 6. Washington, D.C.

————. 1993a. "CHF Continues to Offer Shelter and Sanitation Loans in Honduras." *CHF Newsbriefs* 6. Washington, D.C.

————. 1993b. "Supporting Shelter and Community Improvements for Low-Income Families in Central America." *Environment and Urbanization* 5(1): 38–51 (London).

Cooperative Housing Foundation (CHF)/Honduras. 1991a. *El saneamiento ambiental y la estrategia de la participación comunitaria para asegurar un sistema de disposición de excreto en los barrios marginales de Tegucigalpa utilizando como medio a las organizaciones privadas de desarrollo.* By Enrique Gil. Tegucigalpa, Honduras.

————. 1991b. *Encuesta sobre conocimientos, creencias y prácticas generales sobre eliminación de excreto en el Sector Uno, Barrio San Francisco, Tegucigalpa.* By Enrique Gil. Tegucigalpa, Honduras.

————. 1991c. *Informe preliminar sobre saneamiento urbano en los barrios marginales.* By Xiomara del Rosario Torres A. Tegucigalpa, Honduras.

Cooperative Housing Foundation, Presidencia de la República de Honduras, and United Nations Children's Fund (CHF/Presidencia/UNICEF). 1991. *Honduras: Crisis urbana actores y políticas.* Tegucigalpa, Honduras.

Cooperative Housing Foundation and United Nations Children's Fund (CHF/UNICEF). 1991. *Llegando al pobre desde el sector informal urbano: Ejemplos Hondureños.* Edited by Mario Martin. Tegucigalpa, Honduras.

Grupo Colaborativo de Agua y Saneamiento en Honduras. 1993. *Encuesta sobre el uso, operación y mantenimiento de letrinas en Honduras.* Tegucigalpa, Honduras.

Kawas, M. Celina, and Melba L. Zúniga. 1991. *Profile of Honduran Women.* Prepared for the Canadian International Development Agency, Tegucigalpa, Honduras. Unpublished.

Programa de las Naciones Unidas para el Desarrollo (PNUD) and Centro de Naciones Unidas para los Asentamientos Humanos (CNUAH/HABITAT). 1993. *Lineamientos preliminares para una política nacional de asentamientos humanos y vivienda en Honduras—Documento básico.* Tegucigalpa, Honduras.

SANAA and United Nations Children's Fund. 1991. *El gasto familiar para la compra de agua en los barrios marginales de Tegucigalpa, Honduras.* Tegucigalpa, Honduras.

Secretaría de Planificación, Coordinación y Presupuesto para el Proyecto (SECPLAN). 1991. *Urgencias y esperanzas.* Tegucigalpa, Honduras.

————, Organización Internacional del Trabajo, and Fondo de Naciones Unidas para Actividades de Población (SECPLAN/OIT/FNUAP). 1994. *Potencialidad y focalización de Honduras.* Libro Q, Pobreza Municipal. Segunda Edición. Tegucigalpa, Honduras.

————, United Nations Children's Fund, and Programa de las Naciones Unidas para el Desarrollo (SECPLAN/UNICEF/PNUD). 1994. *Desarrollo humano, infancia y juventud, primer informe de seguimiento y evaluación del Plan de Acción Nacional.* Tegucigalpa, Honduras.

Secretaría Ejecutiva del Gabinete Social. 1992. *Plan de Acción Nacional: Desarrollo humano, infancia y juventud 1992–2000.* Tegucigalpa, Honduras.

United Nations Children's Fund/Honduras. 1990. *Análisis de la situación de la infancia y de la mujer en Honduras.* Tegucigalpa, Honduras.

———— and Junta Nacional de Bienestar Social. 1992. *Children in Especially Difficult Circumstances in Honduras.* Tegucigalpa, Honduras.

Water for Sanitation and Health (WASH) Project. 1992. "Spotlight from the Field: CHF and UNICEF Provide Options for Improved Urban Sanitation in Honduras." *Peri-Urban News* 4–5 (Arlington, VA).

World Bank. 1994. *Social Indicators of Development.* Baltimore, MD: Johns Hopkins University Press.

Chapter 3

Developing a Violence Prevention Coalition in Los Angeles

Caswell A. Evans Jr. and Billie Phyllis Weiss

Cities as diverse as Los Angeles, São Paulo, Dakar, and Moscow share a common scourge: although not officially at war, these are cities under siege. The culprit in each case is interpersonal violence.[1] Over the last thirty years, this kind of violence has become an increasingly significant part of city life. Today it seems to erupt as a response to a variety of urban frustrations, prominent among them overcrowding, personal animosity, and—particularly for young people—disempowerment and a lack of positive community interaction and healthy entertainment.

In Los Angeles County, California, with a population of almost nine million people[2] in an area of about four thousand square miles, the leading cause of death for the population under the age of forty-five is injury, and homicides account for close to 30 percent of all deaths resulting from injuries. Homicides surpass even motor vehicle accidents as the leading cause of injury deaths for Los Angeles residents. The homicide rate is recognized as a relatively reliable indicator of the level of violence in a community, despite the fact that it does not reflect nonfatal violent injuries. In 1988, the homicide rate in the United States as a whole was 9 per 100,000 thousand population. In the State of California.it was 10.9 per 100,000, but in Los Angeles, it was 19.4 per 100,000—over twice the national average.

The homicide rate in Los Angeles varies by location, sex, age, and race.[3] It is highest in the South Central section of the city, an area that also has the highest rates of infectious diseases and other conditions associated with poverty and overcrowding. It is also highest among males between the ages of fifteen and thirty-four, and much higher for African Americans than members of other ethnic groups. The absolute number of homicides among African Americans and Hispanics in Los Angeles is similar, but Hispanics represent almost a third of the population, and African Americans less than one-twelfth. In 1990, the homicide rate per 100,000 for white males aged fifteen to thirty-four was 27.8, while for Hispanics of the same age and sex it was 88.3. But for the corresponding

35

group of African Americans, it was 263 per 100,000—a rate that reflects the special vulnerability of African American males.[4]

Children and adolescents often bear the brunt of the urban violence problem. Surrounded from birth by an atmosphere of violence, spawned by poverty and discord, they may become inured to it, and in addition may lack opportunities to learn alternative ways of behaving and communicating beyond the use of violence. To fulfill their need for acceptance and personal defense, those born into fractured or powerless families may turn to street gangs as surrogate families. Los Angeles has 900 of them, and has been labeled the gang capital of the world. It is estimated that there are more than 100,000 gang members in the county. About 30 to 37 percent of the homicides are gang related, as defined by law enforcement. In 1993, there were 2,067 homicides countywide, of which 720 were attributed to the activities of known gang members. The issue of violence as a public health problem has become more focused in Los Angeles as a result of this carnage, and it is becoming increasingly apparent that law enforcement alone cannot manage the problem.

In 1992 there was a widely publicized gang truce in Los Angeles, which had a positive impact on gang violence, especially in the South Central section of the city. Gang-related homicides in South Central decreased. However, the truce primarily affected African-American gangs; it was not acknowledged by members of the more numerous Hispanic gangs and the Asian gangs. Thus, although the total number of gang-related killings in South Central decreased, the rate among ethnic groups other than African American actually increased. This trend continued in 1993; the decrease in the homicide rate among African Americans was offset by the dramatic and escalating increase among Hispanics. In 1993, there were 720 homicides among African Americans, compared to 886 among Hispanics. The result was a stable countywide homicide rate for 1993. Data for 1994 are still preliminary, but suggest that the trend is continuing.

Over the years, a number of community-based agencies and programs have addressed the problem of urban violence in Los Angeles. Under a program called Teens on Target, for example, teens who have been injured by gang violence, some of whom are paraplegics or quadriplegics, work with youths in schools to help them understand the consequences of gang membership. Other efforts have included mentoring programs, employment training, self-esteem building, conflict resolution, dispute mediation, parenting skills education, and support for families of victims of violence. In general, however, the people involved in these programs have not been aware of the work of others in the same general area.

In 1990 the Los Angeles County Department of Health Services received a grant to begin a project devoted to the epidemiology and prevention of intentional and unintentional injury.[5] It was decided that part of the project should be to establish a network to exchange ideas and resources and to examine the problem and its potential solutions from a multidisciplinary perspective. Other objectives of the project included developing an enhanced injury-surveillance system to describe the epidemiology of specific injuries, designing and implementing a program to reduce preschool pedestrian injuries in five health districts with higher-than-expected injury rates, and conducting a study of gang-related homicides and assaults.

In March 1991, in order to bring violence prevention experts from various disciplines together, we sent out some forty letters of invitation to a meeting where the formation of a "Violence Prevention Coalition" would be discussed. Recipients of these invitations included police departments; school districts; community-based agencies ranging from boys' and girls' clubs to parenting programs for teenaged parents; researchers; rehabilitation programs; the office of the coroner; hospitals; child health providers (both public and private); representatives of the emergency medical system, trauma network, and victim assistance programs; mental health workers; and agencies dealing with domestic violence. Gang members or former gang members were included.

At the first meeting of the group, the public health model of primary, secondary, and tertiary violence prevention was presented,[6] and we asked for input regarding interest in building an eclectic, multidisciplinary coalition to pool our knowledge and pursue our mutual goal of preventing violence and reducing and controlling the injuries that result. Among the group's goals would be developing a focused approach to reducing the level of violence in Los Angeles, encouraging the development and promotion of prevention and intervention programs, sharing information, providing a forum for influencing public policy regarding violence prevention, and increasing community awareness of existing prevention programs.

Representatives of the different disciplines acknowledged that their various groups, working alone, viewed the problem of reducing violence as overwhelming, and were becoming discouraged. It was agreed that the problem requires a more generalized community approach. The group decided to go forward and to meet again, in the belief that an eclectic approach had the potential to change Los Angeles County's distressing statistics on violence.

Subsequently this group, called the Violence Prevention Coalition of Greater Los Angeles, formulated a mission statement. The coalition's collective goal would be to "reduce violence and its impact on the health of the citizens of Los Angeles County by measuring and describing the conditions which promote violence, and by recommending strategies, methods, and means to reverse the conditions which promote violence, and prevent the injuries and adverse outcomes that result from violence."[7]

This mission presented some challenges, beginning with the need for the coalition to define its terms. For instance, the term *surveillance* can have quite different meanings, depending on whether it is used in a public health or law enforcement context. Another problem was that many of the community-based agencies represented in the coalition were topic-specific, addressing, for example, gangs or domestic violence. After lengthy discussion, it was decided not to focus on any single topic, since many experts are convinced that the root causes of all forms of violent behavior are likely to be similar.

Representatives of both the judicial system and law enforcement expressed gratitude for the entry of public health into the violence prevention arena. Both police departments and the prosecutors agreed that previous efforts at violence containment had been ineffective, and welcomed the new multidisciplinary, public health approach.

The job of establishing a structure for the coalition was delegated to a small, representative group of volunteers. The design for the coalition they drew up included a number of committees, each of which would address some specific area of concern. Gang members and former gang members were represented both on committees and in youth forums.

One committee, for example, investigates the media's role in violence, tracks related legislation, identifies key legislators, and recommends positions related to the media's role in violence. Much of this committee's work is carried out through the preparation and distribution of "Fact Sheets," which are distributed to policymakers, state and local legislators, and the media. The fact sheets present information on specific forms of violence and are produced by committee members with experience in particular fields such as domestic, gang, or drug and alcohol-related violence.

Another committee works with the public schools, and is responsible for determining which violence prevention curricula, if any, are in use in which schools. This group has also undertaken a comprehensive community education campaign focusing on the effects of violence on the entire community. Additionally, the committee provides training in specific curricula for schools and community-based organizations. For example, a special training seminar was held for representatives of sixty school districts and forty community-based organizations on "Best Friends for Life," the curriculum developed by Deborah Prothrow-Stith, a leading proponent of addressing violence as a public health issue, on violence prevention for adolescents.[8] Training and materials on the STAR (Straight Talk About Risks) curriculum, developed by the Center to Prevent Handgun Violence, were also provided. This curriculum teaches alternative methods of dealing with anger and how to remain safe in the presence of a gun.

The epidemiology committee is currently exploring sources of data to help quantify the magnitude of the problem, establishing standard definitions, and developing potential methods for linking data sets. In addition to providing epidemiological information, such data linkages will enable a more realistic estimate of the costs of violence in Los Angeles.

The community mobilization committee investigates community resources and community programs and facilitates interactions between community-based organizations, in an effort to expand available resources to all segments of the community. Currently, this committee is mobilizing communities around specific topics such as domestic violence.

Meanwhile, the resource identification committee has compiled a countywide directory of all resources identified by the other committees. This group is also responsible for identifying potential sources of funds for coalition member organizations, and for research and program evaluation activities.

The Violence Prevention Coalition conducted its first conference, entitled "Our Violent Society: Causes, Consequences, Interventions, and Prevention," in May 1993 in Los Angeles. It received financial support from the California State Department of Health Services, and was attended by representatives of state, national, and international agencies. The conference was very successful: it stimulated the formation of violence prevention coalitions in six additional communities across the country.

The coalition has had to deal with immediate and critical funding issues. Funding for community-based agencies in Los Angeles County has been severely curtailed due to strained economic conditions in the State of California and the county, and many agencies are operating with inadequate funding. Coalition members have collaborated on at least nine grant proposals, each of which involved a minimum of three member agencies. To date, at least seven of these proposals have been successful.

One area in which the eclectic nature of the coalition has been particularly helpful is evaluation. The community-based organizations involved in the coalition do not have the technical expertise to develop systematic evaluations, and although many of their programs appear to be effective, none has been evaluated systematically. The coalition's public health and academic members have developed evaluations that rely on epidemiologic methods to systematically evaluate the effectiveness of community-based programs. In the area of education, for example, fourteen separate violence prevention curricula are being used in Los Angeles schools, but none had been systematically evaluated for effectiveness. The schools are now evaluating their curricula; preliminary results should be available by the end of 1995.

The availability of firearms is a primary concern to all Violence Prevention Coalition members, including the law enforcement agencies. In fact, the district attorney was the first to suggest that the coalition membership focus on this concern. Not only is the number of firearm homicides in Los Angeles increasing, but suicides and unintended shootings are also rising at an alarming rate. Coalition advocacy of the control and/or confiscation of weapons is an issue on which coalition members have been working with legislators, although no state laws have yet been changed as a result.

We have also established a speakers' bureau to talk to parents and community groups, and have facilitated the formation, in smaller communities in Los Angeles County such as Pasadena and Englewood, of coalitions whose goal is to empower communities to reclaim their streets from the youth gangs that have terrorized residents and kept them captive in their own homes. These smaller coalitions are built on the Los Angeles model, but are at a more grassroots level. We have compiled a resource directory that will permit small communities to locate the services and programs they need. For example, although after-school programs are provided by a number of community-based organizations, many neighborhoods do not yet have such programs. The resource directory helps communities to establish after-school programs, train the participants, implement them, and evaluate their effectiveness. It has been distributed throughout the county.

The activities of the Violence Prevention Coalition have taken on greater urgency since the events that took place in the spring of 1992. On April 29, the streets of Los Angeles, particularly in the Central and South Central sections of the city, erupted in violent rage. More than two thousand visits to emergency departments occurred as a result of civil unrest in the streets of Los Angeles between April 29th and May 1st, 1992. During this time, both victims and perpetrators were more likely to be minority males fifteen to thirty-four years of age than members of any other group. As is the case with homicides and suicides in Los Angeles generally, most of the injuries were due to firearms.

Violence is not a normal way of life, but in Los Angeles it is often viewed this way. Change is necessary to reduce the acceptance of violence as a fact of life, and this requires community-wide commitment. We believe that bringing a community-wide focus to the problem, creating awareness, sharing the resources we have available to us, and exploring potential solutions together represent our best hope of creating change. Other kinds of destructive behaviors—smoking and certain kinds of sexual behavior, for example—have been changed, largely through the efforts of single-issue coalitions whose emphasis has been community-wide involvement and dedication.

The epidemic of violence in Los Angeles County is far from spent, but we think our model, which places ownership of the problem in the hands of the entire community, is beginning to have an effect in South Central, which is reflected in the decreasing homicide rate. We believe that by replicating the model in other sections of the county, similar reductions in the level of violence can be achieved. We hope that other communities will adopt similar strategies to change community norms and reduce violent deaths and injuries.

Notes

The editors thank Liz Weist for her contributions to this chapter.

An earlier version of this material was presented at a meeting of the American Public Health Association, held in San Francisco, California, in November 1993. In addition, the information presented here is included in a paper entitled "The Violence Prevention Coalition of Greater Los Angeles," forthcoming in *Public Health Reports*.

1. The epidemiological statistics on violent injury and death show that in the United States this was the leading cause of mortality among fifteen- to twenty-four-year-olds as early as 1985 ("Public Health Problem" 1985:882); gunshot wounds cause the most deaths in both black and white teenaged boys in America (Koop and Lundberg 1992:3075). The problem is not unique to the United States; according to WHO, violent injury is now the leading cause of death for children and young adults in virtually all countries ("The Cutting Edge" 1993:2:5). —Ed.

2. Population Estimation and Projection System of the Los Angeles County Department of Data Processing, Urban Research Division. Projections are based on the United States Census.

3. A number of risk factors for violent injury have been identified. In one U.S. study, low socioeconomic status, a history of physical abuse, and school problems were found to be highly correlated with the risk of violent injury (Schubiner et al. 1993:216). (Individuals characterized by these risk factors were also at high risk of sexually transmitted diseases, adolescent parenthood, alcohol and substance abuse, difficulties at school and work, family conflicts, and depression.) Other U.S. studies have pinpointed some of the factors that seem to predispose individuals to commit violent acts. One cites youth, male sex, nonwhite race, unemployment, and a "disorganized family background" (Ford and Rushforth 1983:238); another adds alcohol use and a paranoid and impulsive personality (Shepherd and Farrington 1993:91). Environmental determinants such as overcrowding or exposure to media violence have often been faulted as well.

4. Los Angeles County is one of the most ethnically diverse communities in the United States. Its current population is estimated to be 47 percent non-Hispanic white, 30 percent Hispanic, 12 percent African American, 7 percent Asian, and 3 percent other racial groups. Only about half of all Los Angeles County households report they speak English as the predominant language at home. More than ninety languages have been officially recognized and are spoken within the Los Angeles Unified School District (Los Angeles Unified School District, Annual Ethnic Survey Report, 1992).

5. Funding was provided by the California State Department of Health Services, Emergency Preparedness and Injury Control Branch.

6. The three levels of medical services—primary, secondary, and tertiary—can also be applied to violence prevention. Primary violence prevention focuses on preventing aggressive behavior before it occurs (for example, teaching parenting skills at prenatal clinics). The role of parents is pivotal at this level, and pediatric health practitioners can also help at this stage by providing families with guidance on nonviolent disciplinary methods and resolution of intersibling conflict (Spivak et al. 1988:1343). Secondary level prevention aims at precluding violence, once it has occurred, from escalating or spreading, by identifying individuals who are at high risk of violent behavior and addressing their need for alternate methods of resolving conflict or expressing their emotions through educational, mental health, and other support services. The goal of tertiary level prevention is the rehabilitation of already violent individuals, such as those imprisoned for violent assault or hospitalized for violent injury, who (unless they are innocent victims) may be intent upon revenge against their adversaries. These individuals are identified and targeted, usually in institutional settings, by a combination of criminal justice, human service, mental health, and public health workers. Retraining them in how to use peaceful means to resolve future conflicts is particularly difficult.

7. The Violence Prevention Coalition of Greater Los Angeles, Mission Statement, June 1991.
8. Deborah Prothrow-Stith is associated with Harvard's School of Public Health and has served as Boston's Public Health Commissioner.

References

"The Cutting Edge: Vital Statistics—World's Toll from Injuries." 1993. *Washington Post* (February 23), section 2:5.

Ford, Amasa B., and Norman B. Rushforth. 1983. "Urban Violence in the United States—Implications for Health and for Britain in the Future: Discussion Paper." *Journal of the Royal Society of Medicine* 76(4):283–88.

Koop, C. Everett, and George D. Lundberg. 1992. "Violence in America: A Public Health Emergency (editorial)." *Journal of the American Medical Association* 267:3075–76.

"Public Health Problem of Violence Receives Epidemiologic Attention." 1985. *Journal of the American Medical Association* 254:881–83.

Schubiner, Howard, Richard Scott, and Angela Tzelepis. 1993. "Exposure to Violence Among Inner-City Youth." *Society for Adolescent Medicine* 14:214-19.

Shepherd, Jonathan P., and David P. Farrington. 1993. "Assault as a Public Health Problem." *Journal of the Royal Society of Medicine* 86(2):89–92.

Spivak, Howard, Deborah Prothrow-Stith, and Alice J. Hausman. 1988. "Dying is No Accident: Adolescents, Violence, and Intentional Injury." *Pediatric Clinics of North America* 35:1339–47.

Part II

Implications of Industrialization for Health and the Environment

Medzamor nuclear power station,
Armenia

Part II

Introduction

The health and environmental problems faced by countries worldwide vary greatly depending on each country's stage of development; the structure of its economic, political, and social welfare systems; and its policies on economic growth, industrial development and environment protection, among other factors. Some environmental problems and their health consequences are associated with a lack of economic and human development. Inadequate supplies of potable water, inadequate sanitation, lack of social services, poor quality housing, land degradation, and overcrowding are all generally associated with poverty and the lack of economic opportunities. But many other environmental problems and disease patterns are related to increased economic growth. For example, pollution of air and water by industries, deforestation to accommodate fuel and building needs of growing populations and from commercial logging, and the use of pesticides for increased agricultural production are often associated with economic development and industrialization.

Economic growth and industrialization continue to be goals sought after by national governments in all parts of the world, especially those struggling to achieve higher standards of living for their people. However, from a public health and environmental point of view, these goals carry with them complex new challenges, difficult choices, and ethical dilemmas. Diseases associated with poverty and underdevelopment, such as malnutrition, diarrheal diseases, and acute respiratory infections, are likely to decrease with increased levels of employment and other kinds of improved economic growth. And without adequate economic resources, adequate investments in environmental protection and safety at local, regional, or national levels are unlikely to occur.

While economic growth and the industrialization that generally accompanies it can help to alleviate poverty and increase living standards, both also have negative aspects. For example, many of the by-products of industrialization—including toxic emissions and hazardous waste products—have the potential to endanger workers and the general public. Many governments and institutions, especially in developing and industrializing countries, are poorly equipped to address adequately the public health hazards associated with the industrialization process. Industrialization, especially when it is uncontrolled, often brings with it a corresponding increase in diseases such as lead poisoning, central nervous system

45

disorders, asthma, cancers, birth defects, and other acute and chronic conditions.

The decades ahead will present enormous challenges on a scale much greater than has ever been experienced in human history. Between 1990 and 2030, as the world's population grows by an estimated 3.7 billion people, the need for food production is expected to double, and industrial output and energy use will likely triple worldwide and increase five-fold in developing countries (World Bank 1992:2). If current trends continue, the magnitude and scale of potential risks to human health and the environment due to unchecked industrialization are enormous. Policy decisions at the local, national, and international levels will largely determine the quality of life and environmental conditions for our own and future generations.

Many countries in both the developing and industrialized world lack experience in designing and implementing strategies to promote and regulate positive industrial growth. The need to attract industry and capital investment is a powerful disincentive for many governments to regulate and enforce health and safety standards. As seen in chapter 4, heavy dependency on existing industries often makes strengthening existing health and safety regulations difficult, especially in times of national economic crisis. Without enforced safety standards, few industries are likely to invest in measures to protect the health and safety of workers or people living in close enough proximity to be affected by these industries.

The chapters in Part II explore some of the implications of economic development and industrialization for people's health and the health of their environment. A common theme in these chapters is the need to make difficult choices, as well as to recognize and deal with the trade-offs among economic growth, industrial development, and sustainable human development. The chapters clearly illustrate that these kinds of choices, whether made by local communities or national governments, are not easy. On the positive side, workable strategies and approaches, some of which are described in these chapters, are being developed to help tackle these issues. And as these chapters show, recognizing that major health and environmental problems exist at all is often the first, most difficult, and yet most vital step on the way to developing solutions.

Unregulated Industrial Growth in the Former Soviet Union

In chapter 4, Kim Hekimian provides insights into the role of public health and environmental concerns in events leading up to and following the dramatic breakup of the Soviet Union. Although Armenia is the focus of the chapter, it provides many widely applicable lessons on how people's health, and environmental integrity, have been abridged in the name of economic and military production. The experiences in Armenia and the lessons being learned there offer important insights and warnings to the rest of the world as nations continue to weigh their options and make decisions about their future growth and development. In Armenia, and elsewhere in the former Soviet Union, rapid, mismanaged, and unregulated industrial growth has led to environmental degradation and chemical pollution of monumental proportions. The government and the people of Armenia are now faced with deciding between short-term economic survival and the increasingly recognized long-term environmental and public health needs of the population.

Developing New Approaches for Assessing Environmental Health Risks

Most developing countries are simultaneously experiencing both rapid urbanization and industrialization. In terms of public health, this means that their citizens, especially the poor, are at risk from both the infectious diseases common to peri-urban areas and diseases related to industrialization, such as heart disease and cancers. Local and national governments must set priorities and make decisions among competing demands, each of which requires the commitment of human and financial resources. There is an increasingly urgent need for policymakers to be able to make sound and informed decisions on public health and environmental issues.

In chapter 5, Eugene P. Brantly Jr. describes an innovative new methodology for assisting communities, local governments, and national governments to assess environmental health risks and to help them prioritize public health and environmental problems. Traditional risk assessments are limited by their dependence on quantifiable scientific and clinical data—the kinds of data that many countries lack. The new methodology represents a very different approach: it incorporates and values the perceptions of people who are affected by public health and environmental problems. Chapter 5 describes the use of this methodology in Quito, Ecuador, a city in a developing country, but the approach is also being used to help assess risks and prioritize problems in industrialized countries, such as countries in the former Soviet Union.

A number of common themes emerge in the chapters of Part II—themes that are linked to others found throughout this book. One is the essential need to develop interdisciplinary approaches to address health and environmental problems. Another is the need for new tools to assess the benefits and risks of economic growth and industrialization, as well as for making wise decisions among competing needs, for assessing the short- and long-term effects of these decisions, and for making these decisions within financial constraints.

While chapter 4 is set in an industrial country and chapter 5 in a city in a developing country, many of the lessons to be learned from these chapters, and the issues they raise, are also important for the United States and other industrialized, Western countries. This is despite the fact that the United States is often cited as an example of an industrialized country that has been able to develop and enforce regulations and standards for industries, worker safety, and environmental protection. The chapters in Part IV of this book provide illustrations of the public health hazards and environmental contamination caused by industrial pollution and toxic waste dumping that have occurred, and are continuing to occur, within the borders of the United States. No country can lay claim to having achieved an acceptable and just balance between economic growth with industrialization and sustainable development. Clearly, the dilemmas and decisions raised in these chapters will become increasingly important to all people and nations in an increasingly urbanizing and industrializing world.

Reference

World Bank. 1992. *World Development Report 1992: Development and the Environment*. New York: Oxford University Press.

Chapter 4

The Post-Soviet Legacy of Industrial Pollution in Armenia

Kim Hekimian

Prior to the tumultuous breakup of the Soviet Union, the USSR was the largest country in the world in terms of land mass, and the third largest country in population. It was among the world's largest producers of oil, steel, and military technology. And yet, in recent years, the world has learned that during the seventy years of communist rule, the environment and public health of the population were sacrificed for the sake of economic and military production. Environmental degradation occurred as a result of rapid, mismanaged, and unregulated industrial growth, intensive cultivation, and mining.

The Soviet public was rarely informed of the environmental disasters that occurred. Most health and contaminant statistics were never made available to the population. Even when the information was disseminated, the lack of democratization prevented people from openly protesting. The general public could therefore not put pressures on the government to regulate the destructive forces of industrial growth, which were allowed to continue without regard for natural resources.

The Republic of Armenia, like many of the former Soviet republics, is experiencing an environmental disaster of monumental proportions. The explosive impact of unrestrained, poorly managed economic growth in the past half-century, combined with increases in population size, have severely polluted the nation's air, water, and soil. As a result, numerous public health problems have been associated with this pollution, including increased incidence of cancer, respiratory, and congenital diseases.

During the openness of the glasnost era in the 1980s, community leaders in Armenia and in other Soviet republics began to publicly discuss the compelling evidence of their country's environmental disasters. In Armenia, underground documents began circulating. They discussed, in particular, the effects of chemical, metallurgical, and energy-producing industries on public health. The unprecedented, massive public protest which ensued served as a forum for change. However, due to the economic and political breakdown of the former Soviet Union, the democratically elected, noncommunist government of Armenia found itself without sufficient capital and technical support to correct the overwhelming problems. In fact, the government was faced with the choice of short-term economic survival versus the long-term public health needs of its population.

The Armenian people have lived in the Anatolian and Armenian plateaus for millennia. The Armenian kingdom once spanned the vast area from the Mediterranean to the south, the Black Sea to the north and the Caspian Sea to the east. From the sixteenth to nineteenth centuries, Armenia was divided by the Persian, Ottoman, and Russian empires. After a brief time as an independent republic, from 1918 to 1920, Armenia was annexed by the Soviet Union.

Armenia is the smallest republic of the former Soviet Union in terms of its geographical area. Landlocked, it is bordered to the west by Turkey, to the east by Azerbaijan, to the south by Iran, and to the north by the Republic of Georgia. At the beginning of 1993, the government of Armenia estimated the population to be 3.7 million. Two-thirds of the population is reported to live in urban areas, and one-third in rural areas.

Armed conflict between the Armenian-populated region of Karabagh and the republic of Azerbaijan began in 1988 and continues today. This conflict resulted in the Azeri-blockade of all rail lines, as well as all oil and natural gas pipelines, into Armenia from other former Soviet republics. Armenia's only remaining source of fuel, through a single natural gas pipeline from the Republic of Georgia, is sporadic due to numerous explosions and attacks during the fighting.

As a result of an almost complete lack of fuel and ground transport, Armenia's highly industrialized economy has been paralyzed, and the standard of living for all Armenians has declined dramatically. For the last four winters, there has been a lack of heat or cooking fuel throughout the nation, and electricity has been severely rationed. Now, in 1994, most families in Yerevan receive one to three hours of electricity per day. Many hospitals and clinics have been forced to close during the winter months due to the lack of fuel. Hyperinflation has caused food prices to soar beyond the reach of most of the population. As of March 1994, the cost of a minimally nutritious food basket for one person was forty-five times greater than the minimum monthly salary.

The conflict in Azerbaijan has also produced hundreds of thousands of refugees who now reside in Armenia. The majority of refugees are women, children, and elderly, many of whom now live in poorly equipped, unsanitary, and overcrowded shelters throughout the country. The Armenian population also experienced the stress of a major earthquake in late 1988, which devastated one-third of the nation of Armenia, killing 25,000 people, injuring thousands of others, and displacing nearly 250,000 residents.

Armenia has thus entered the post-Soviet era of scientific and technological progress as a country characterized by complete economic destruction and plundered resources. When Armenia was annexed to the Soviet Union in 1921, it entered a period of rapidly paced, centrally designed economic development and industrialization that characterized the Soviet Union during the period between the two World Wars. This growth continued in the postwar era. Industrial output grew 146-fold in the fifty years between 1920 and 1970. Armenia became one of the principal suppliers of high-technology products to the former Soviet Union, including computers, semiconductors, and laser technology. In addition, large chemical, construction, and mining industries were created.

The economic development strategy proved to be environmentally shortsighted and destructive, as heavy industries were located in Armenia without regard to the country's resources and ability to sustain those industries. Armenia's water, energy, and land resources were scarce. Approximately 90 percent of the country is over 1,000 meters above sea level, over half the territory is covered by mountain ranges, and forest covers less than 12 percent of the land. Almost the entire republic is seismically active, as manifested by the 1988 earthquake. Water sources are limited since the country is landlocked, has few lakes, and few significant rivers. The average surface flow of water is reported to be eight times less per person in Armenia as compared with the other former Soviet republics (Valesyan 1990). There are no proven reserves of fossil fuels in Armenia. All fossil fuel supplies for Armenia's industry, energy production, and central residential heating were received from other Soviet republics, primarily through transport routes in neighboring Azerbaijan.

Despite these geographic characteristics, industries that were extremely high in water and energy consumption were developed. Most heavy industry facilities were under the direct control of ministries headquartered in Moscow. This not only led to a lack of decision-making power in Armenia, but also resulted in policies that did not appropriately match production capacity with local natural resources. The industrial complexes in Armenia were built without safety buffer zones and often without antipolluting equipment. The result was nothing short of environmental disaster, in the form of air pollution, soil erosion, and water contamination from pesticides and untreated industrial wastewater.

The environmental neglect reportedly led to an alarming increase in public health problems and a drop in the life expectancy of the population. Reports from the ministry of health indicate a high incidence of cardiovascular, gastrointestinal, lung and other respiratory diseases, as well as birth defects and infertility. In 1979, the incidence of lung and larynx cancers in Armenia, as well as lymphomas and leukemias, was the highest of any country in the former Soviet Union (Morabia and Levshin 1992:157). The geographic variation reported in these diseases suggests a strong role played by environmental factors. In fact, the capital city of Yerevan, where over one-third of Armenia's population resides, and where the majority of industrial facilities are located, had the highest incidence in the Soviet Union of lymphoma, myeloma, and leukemia among males in 1979.

Within the last decade, Armenians began to publicly discuss the compelling evidence of the country's environmental disasters. The era of glasnost and perestroika, which began under Gorbachev during the 1980s, created an openness which had not been previously allowed. Public protests, speeches, and newspaper reports resulted in the Armenian population's awareness that it was unsafe to breathe the air, drink the water, and eat locally produced foods. However, in the wake of the economic and political breakdown of the former Soviet Union, Armenia has found itself without sufficient capital and technical support to correct its overwhelming environmental problems.

The blockade imposed by Azerbaijan in the early 1990s has caused the almost total paralysis of industrial functioning. As a result, those factories and industrial enterprises which are most harmful to the environment and to public health have been forced to operate at minimal capacity, due to the severe lack of fuel. Because of this situation, the public's sense of urgency about environmental problems has decreased. This does not, however, indicate that the crises have been resolved, and these concerns will emerge again when the economy revives.

While the correlation between pollution and ill health in the Republic of Armenia has not yet been properly researched and documented, the level of air and water pollution has been relatively well examined. Intensive and unregulated production and high population density, when combined with complex climatic conditions, have put the natural environment of the Yerevan basin under considerable stress. The greatest stress has been on the region's atmosphere.

Prior to the blockade, the basic pollutants were: (1) carbon monoxide, largely from the exhaust fumes of automobile engines; (2) sulfur dioxide, formed during the process of fuel combustion, especially at electric power stations; (3) soot and ashes from electric power stations, cement factories, and other industrial enterprises; and (4) nitrogen oxides, hydrocarbons, lead, mercury, and radioactive isotopes. The prevalence of these pollutants has presumably decreased in the last few years due to fuel shortages and power rationing which have resulted largely from the blockade by Azerbaijan.

In early 1990, the air quality of the Yerevan basin was found to be very poor based on observations by the Hydrometeorological Service of Armenia and periodic observations at the central public health station of the republic's ministry of health. The content of certain substances was found to exceed the maximum permissible concentrations by several times (Valesyan 1990:574).

Until the near-total shutdown of industry due to the blockade, the annual pollutant discharges into the republic's air basin by stationary sources was on the order of 255,000 tons, including sulfur anhydrite (45 percent), nitrogen oxides (11.5 percent), hydrocarbons (8 percent), carbon oxide (11 percent), and chloroprene (Abovian 1989:13). These levels have decreased significantly as a result of the current lack of energy.

Many industrial enterprises are not fully equipped with pollution control devices for trapping noxious gasses or removing particles, and most of the existing gas and dust removing equipment does not work satisfactorily. Compared with other former Soviet capitals, Yerevan has the lowest removal level of noxious material from stationary source emission—only 34 percent of the total amount. In 1990, Murray Feshbach, an American expert on Soviet health affairs, discussed health problems in Armenia during testimony for the United States Congressional Joint Economic Committee. He described the difficulty of trying to improve environmental conditions:

> The Nairit combine [a large industrial plant producing a variety of chemicals] in Yerevan, Armenia is a prime example. The rate of leukemia, respiratory illness, and many [other diseases] are much higher among the population residing in the immediate district where the combine is located than for the city as a whole or for relatively clean small districts. But the medicines or basic chemicals produced by this combine are essential to help improve the health of the population, if not treat them in the future. Nonetheless, there seems to be relatively little or no understanding that scrubbers and filters for various sources of pollution actually need to be installed, and if installed, to be maintained. . . . But as far as cleaning up their act without closing plants, one of the problems is that there is not a single specialized plant for the production of scrubbers in the whole Soviet Union. (Feshbach 1990)

The air pollution situation is aggravated by the fact that the republic's most polluted cities, Yerevan, Vanadzor (Kirovakan), Alaverdi, Hrazdan, and Ararat, are located in basins with fairly high potential for atmospheric pollution, due to surrounding mountains, dry weather, and temperature inversions which prevent the natural process of purifying the air. Higher rates of respiratory disease have been reported in these cities compared with the rest of the country.

In addition to the air pollution problems, water pollution has also reached crisis levels. According to data of the State Committee for Statistics of Armenia, over one-fourth of the approximately 580 million cubic meters of wastewater discharged in 1986 into natural surface reservoirs within the Yerevan basin was not treated. The amount of wastewater satisfying norms for water treatment was less than 45 percent. The capacity of treatment facilities was not adequate to ensure treatment of even 50 percent of the volume of wastewater discharged.

In five of the basin's eleven districts, wastewater treatment installations are completely lacking. More than forty industrial plants discharge untreated and undisinfected sewage into the most important river basin, the Razdan. The director of the Nairit compound admits that wastewater dumped from this plant into the Araks river is not suitably treated (Melkumyau 1992:62).

In addition to industrial water pollution, the problem of water contamination from sewage backflows into municipal water supplies and inadequate treatment has recently emerged. During the last three winters, there were numerous breaks in sewer lines that have not been repaired due to lack of government financial and technical resources. Moreover, many water treatment stations have deteriorated and lack both the proper chemicals as well as sufficient electricity to ensure a safe water supply. As a result, there have been numerous outbreaks of dysentery over the past three years. During the summer of 1992, three epidemics of dysentery broke out in three separate districts of Yerevan, due to the crossing of sewer and water lines. Although chlorinators were installed in the municipal water supply, there was an outbreak of shigellosis (bacterial dysentery) in Yerevan during the summer of 1994, with five hundred cases reported from one district alone.

Armenia also suffers from a history of pesticide use. In particular, the levels of DDT found in Armenian soil samples in 1988 were two to eight times higher than established norms, despite the supposed outlawing of DDT in the Soviet Union in 1970 (Peterson 1993:105). An Armenian physician and researcher documented an association between rural areas in Armenia with high DDT use and incidence of congenital abnormalities and various tumors (Feshbach 1992:65). The degraded environment has taken a heavy toll on human health and biological productivity.

After decades of government-imposed silence and suppression of political discourse, the democratization and decentralization that came with glasnost and perestroika provided an opportunity for people to bring environmental issues to the forefront of public attention during the mid-1980s. The environmental movement became a powerful force on its own. Both in Armenia and elsewhere in the USSR, it also served as a cover for a variety of protests against the one-party regime. In fact, many of the leaders of environmental movements in Armenia, Ukraine, and the Baltics emerged as national leaders during the subsequent moves for independence.

In March 1986, a month before the nuclear disaster at Chernobyl (Ukraine) focused the attention of the Western press on the Soviet Union's environmental problems, 350 Armenian intellectuals, including writers, scientists, and academicians, sent an open letter to Soviet leader Mikhail Gorbachev protesting environmental pollution in Armenia. They claimed the problem had reached horrific proportions, and attributed severe health problems to toxic emissions from the republic's numerous chemical plants and radiation leaks from the Medzamor nuclear power plant in the capital city of Yerevan.

The letter outlined many of the major environmental issues that were of primary concern to people in Armenia during the mid- to late 1980s. It also presented a very disturbing picture of the health hazards that were due in large part to Armenia's unregulated industrial development. Some of the allegations of the letter have since been corroborated by the Soviet and Armenian press, which for years had denied the existence of pollution and health hazards.

The letter detailed the causes, extent, and effects of air pollution, which those who wrote the letter believed to be the most serious ecological problem facing the republic. The authors of the samizdat (underground or dissident) document claimed that toxic pollutants from chemical and industrial plants in and around Yerevan and the Ararat valley, were leading to disastrous consequences for human health. Two-thirds of Armenia's 3.5 million residents live in this area. In 1987, the Yerevan basin accounted for 23 percent of Armenia's land area, 58 percent of its population, and 68 percent of its urban population. The Yerevan basin also contains over 60 percent of the republic's industrial facilities, including chemical industries, heat and power engineering, metallurgy, non-ferrous metals, and industries related to construction materials.

The samizdat authors linked toxic pollutants from these industries with a massive increase in the incidence of stomach cancer, cardiac and respiratory diseases, and congenital defects. They cited official statistics from the ministry of health's cancer registry which showed that from 1965 to 1985, the number of cancer cases per 10,000 people living in this area quadrupled. They further claimed that during the previous fifteen years, the number of mentally retarded children had risen five-fold, the incidence of leukemia four-fold, and abnormal and premature births seven-fold (Fuller 1986).

The 1986 letter to Gorbachev had an enormous impact. It is true that the scientific validity of the document, and the extent to which it may or may not have exaggerated health hazards related to environmental pollution, have not been determined. However, politically, the publication of this document was an impetus for grassroots mobilization throughout the urban centers of Armenia. This movement manifested itself by public protests that received media attention throughout the Soviet Union, and around the world. Public demonstrations were held in front of the Nairit Scientific Production Association, a large chemical producing facility situated in residential Yerevan, and the Medzamor nuclear plant, which lies 20 kilometers from the same city. The letter and protests also helped draw the attention of public health officials in Armenia, and elsewhere in the Soviet Union, to the need for further research in this field.

A month after the letter, in April 1986, the explosion at Chernobyl occurred. The result was the release of more radioactive material into the air than had occurred from the atomic bombings of Hiroshima and Nagasaki (Feshbach 1992:12). The West, particularly those countries that felt the effects from the radioactive gas and particles that reached their environments, reacted with anger, outrage, and anxiety. Western pressure prodded the Gorbachev government to begin publishing data on its environment for the first time.

In 1990, the Armenian people democratically elected a non-Communist Party president and a parliament in which the majority of members were not from the Communist Party. One year later, in September 1991, the country declared its independence. As a result of these political changes, and intense public pressure, the new government took some immediate measures in response to concerns about environmental pollution. The Medzamor nuclear power station, reportedly built without maximum containment, situated on an earthquake fault line, and leaking radiation, was one of the first enterprises shut down by the new government. The

Nairit combine, the only manufacturer of chloroprene-based rubber and latex in the whole former Soviet Union, was also closed down, along with the Alaverdi copper smelter, the Kanaz aluminum plant, and the Kirovakan chemical plant, which produced mineral fertilizers.

These measures compounded the already troubled economy of the fledgling nation. The closing of so many plants put thousands of Armenian laborers out of work. The blockade of rail transport, oil, and natural gas pipelines by Azerbaijan, which occurred after the decisions to close various industrial facilities, began in 1990 and continues today. The result has been severe energy shortages. Without fossil fuel being transported through Azerbaijan, and with the nuclear power plant being closed, Armenia is forced to rely on limited hydroelectric power resources as its sole mechanism for producing electricity. This has taken a toll on the already limited water resources. The consequent rationing of limited energy supplies has affected homes, schools, and hospitals, as well as industrial productivity, leading to further unemployment.

The population of Armenia has endured the past four winters without heat or cooking fuel and with severely rationed electricity. Deforestation has emerged as yet another ecological crisis, as numerous forests have been cut for fuel in the last few years. The dramatic change in socioeconomic conditions has caused both the government and the population of Armenia to review and, in many instances, reverse the decisions taken by the new government in its infancy.

For example, the Armenian government currently has plans to reopen at least one unit of the Medzamor nuclear power station, which would supply the country with approximately 400 megawatts of electricity. This would provide an increase of nearly 80 percent in Armenia's current supply of electricity. The reopening of both units of the nuclear power plant could provide 800 megawatts of electricity, 1.6 times the amount now available.

Most Armenians now support such action, despite remaining concerns for seismic risk and radiation leakage. The opening of Medzamor has become an economic necessity, and one of the few viable means for survival, at least in the short run. The Russian government has made a commitment of 110 billion rubles to use toward the refurbishing of the plant, and the International Atomic Energy Association has approved the plant's reopening with additional safeguards. Although there has been some dissension from neighboring countries, who would be affected in the event of a major nuclear accident, Armenia is anticipating bringing the first unit on-line by the winter of 1995–96.

The government also reversed its decision to close the Nairit compound, which reopened in April 1991, since the products it manufactures, including chloroprene, ammonia, fertilizer, and chemicals included in heart medicines, painkillers, and vitamins bring in much needed hard currency revenue (Peterson 1993:245). In addition, Nairit employs thousands of workers. However, the government does not have enough capital to invest in the compound to ensure its environmental safety. When the Nairit facility reopened, wastewater was again dumped untreated, and toxic wastes were again emitted into the air. Nairit is also the sole producer of sodium hypochloride, a chemical desperately needed in the water treatment process throughout Armenia.

It is clear that decontaminating the Republic of Armenia is a precondition to improving public health. However, it is also clear that cleaning up the region will cause substantial economic and social dislocations. High rates of unemployment and continued energy shortages will also have adverse effects on public health in Armenia. Thus, the challenge is to design cleanup programs that offer maximum long-term gains at minimum costs in the short term.

Because of Armenia's economic crisis and plummeting standard of living, the environmental agenda, once a high priority for the new government, has been relegated to the back burner. As a result, alternative ways to encourage the protection of the environment are needed. At the present time, there are a handful of local nongovernmental organizations (NGOs) working on issues pertaining to the environment. Donor agencies have paid some attention to issues such as water, sanitation, and deforestation, and some have conducted assessments in the energy sector, namely the Medzamor nuclear plant and hydroelectric power. However, the resources that have been appropriated to environmental issues are minimal given the competing needs of issues related to survival, such as food, heating fuel, and medicines.

The Armenian government has begun the process of establishing monitoring and regulatory agencies such as a ministry of environment and a nuclear regulatory agency. However, as might be expected given the conditions in Armenia, these entities are not well funded and appear to have little power to implement major policy change.

Training and education are essential for the measurement of health effects, exposure assessment, environmental engineering, risk communication, and policy development. Efforts in this area have been made by the American University of Armenia, affiliated with the University of California state university system, which opened in Yerevan in 1991. The university offers graduate coursework in earthquake engineering and environmental engineering. This year, a graduate program in public health will begin, in which students will be able to study epidemiology, health policy, environmental health, and other topics.

The Armenian government, NGOs, donor agencies, and training institutions should aim not only to address the current environmental issues in Armenia, but also those that will reappear as the economy recovers. Armenia is in the process of developing its strategies for future economic development. This is an extremely complex task, given the uncertainty of when and if the blockade will ever be lifted and if Armenia will be able to import the amount of fossil fuels its industrial structure consumed during the Soviet period.

There is overwhelming consensus that Armenia's number one concern is to secure sources of energy for the republic. The pressures to reopen the nuclear power plant and to exploit the limited existing natural resources for the production of electricity have superseded environmental concerns. Armenia's population is asking the question whether it is better to risk nuclear radiation leaks for some heat and electricity, or struggle to survive yet another cold, dark winter.

The transition to an environmentally safe economy will no doubt be a long and arduous one. This transition can be accomplished by restructuring the economy away from heavy and polluting industries, toward an emphasis on industries that are more appropriate for the size, location, and resources of Armenia. Graduated environmental reforms are possible if they are not too costly in the short term. While Armenia's populace may not demand such reforms as integral parts of an economic development plan, lending institutions such as the World Bank and the European Bank for Reconstruction and Development could encourage economic policies that address environmental needs.

The case of Armenia demonstrates the complexity and difficulty of balancing environmental and economic concerns, especially during such a dramatic era of political change. When Armenia was given an opportunity for more autonomous, democratic reforms, its government made hasty decisions responding to population demands. These decisions were made without thorough policy analysis of the potential negative consequences. However, Armenia probably could not have anticipated the rapid demise of the Soviet Union, the eruption of ethnic conflict in Azerbaijan and subsequent blockade of fuel and transport, and the abrupt entrance into the world market economy. The challenge for Armenia is to reconcile long-term goals for public health and ecology while meeting immediate economic and energy needs.

References

Abovian, Yurias. 1989. "The Ecological Situation of the Armenian SSR and Concept of Mature Preservation." Presented at The Ecological Situation in Armenia: Problems and Solutions Conference in Moscow, May 31, 1989. Reprinted in *Asbarez* (June 30):13–17.

Feshbach, Murray. 1990. "Social Change in the USSR Under Gorbachev: Population, Health, and Environmental Issues." Testimony for the Joint Economic Committee, Congress of the United States.

———— and Alfred Friendly Jr. 1992. *Ecocide in the USSR*. New York: Basic Books.

French, Hilary F. 1990. "Green Revolutions: Environmental Reconstruction in Eastern Europe and the Soviet Union." *Worldwatch Paper 99*. Washington, D.C.: Worldwatch Institute.

Frumkin, Bernard, Barry S. Levy, and Charles Levenstein. 1991. "Occupational and Environmental Health in Eastern Europe: Challenges and Opportunities." *American Journal of Industrial Medicine* 20:265–70.

Fuller, Elizabeth. 1986. "Is Armenia on the Brink of an Ecological Disaster?" *Radio Liberty Research Bulletin* RL306/86.

Ketchian, Philip P. 1990. "The Environment in Armenia: Problems and Analysis." *Armenian Weekly* (November 10):4–7.

Melkumyau, Evelina. 1992. "How Are You Doing, Nairit?" Report no. USR-92-013, 60–63. Washington, D.C.: Foreign Broadcast Information Service.

Morabia, Alfredo, and Vladimir F. Levshin. 1992. "Geographic Variation in Cancer Incidence in the USSR: Estimating the Proportion of Avoidable Cancer." *Preventive Medicine* 21:151–61.

Peel, Quentin. 1990. "Energy Crisis May Force Armenia Nuclear Power Plant to Reopen." *Financial Times* 31.

Peterson, D. J. 1993. *Troubled Lands: The Legacy of Soviet Environmental Destruction.* Boulder, CO: Westview Press.

Sagers, Matthew J. 1987. "News Notes: Commission Proposes Measures to Reduce Air Pollution In Yerevan." *Soviet Geography* 28:608–9.

Schultz, Daniel S., and Michael P. Rafferty. 1990. "Soviet Health Care and Perestroika." *American Journal of Public Health* 80:193–97.

Valesyan, A. 1990. "Environmental Problems in the Yerevan Region." *Soviet Geography* 31:573–86.

Chapter 5

Assessing Environmental Health Risks in Quito, Ecuador

Eugene P. Brantly Jr.

U rban areas in developing countries face an increasingly complex set of environmental health problems. Rapid growth, particularly in peri-urban areas, brings with it a high incidence of diarrheal diseases, vector-borne diseases, respiratory diseases, and other health problems associated with inadequate sanitation, contaminated water supplies, poor housing and ventilation, and overcrowded living conditions. At the same time, increases in industrial employment, use of hazardous materials in small-scale industry, traffic congestion, air pollution, and cigarette smoking, among other changes, are increasing the occurrence of diseases such as cancer and heart disease, and work- and traffic-related injuries.

Environmental health problems must compete for attention and resources with many other types of problems and priorities, in the health and environment sectors and beyond. Local and national governments in developing countries need better data and practical analytical tools that will help them set priorities among environmental health problems, so they can make wise decisions about where to invest public resources. Environmental health risk assessment is such a tool. This chapter describes how environmental health risk assessment is being used in developing countries and presents results from a risk assessment study conducted in Quito, Ecuador. It is based on my experience as a staff member of the Environmental Health Project (EHP), and its precursor, the Water and Sanitation for Health (WASH) Project. EHP provides technical assistance in specialties such as risk assessment to the U.S. Agency for International Development (USAID).

Background on Environmental Health Risk Assessment

In the 1970s and 1980s, the U.S. Congress passed over twenty major environmental laws that required the U.S. Environmental Protection Agency (EPA) to regulate various types of environmental contaminants. Some of the laws were designed to protect the quality of air and water; others were designed to regulate toxic substances, solid wastes, and hazardous wastes. Some laws required that the EPA set environmental standards at a level that would protect human health, with an adequate margin of safety; others required that standards be based on best available technology, without reference to health impacts; and still others required that regulators set standards at a level that would balance health protection with the economic impacts of controlling pollution. Offices were established in the EPA to implement each new law, and each regulatory program developed methods for performing the analyses that Congress required.

Over time, three things happened. First, environmental scientists and toxicologists developed various methods for predicting the long-term effects that environmental pollutants would have on public health. These were the first "health risk assessment" methods. Regulators needed these methods because they had to predict the long-term impacts of environmental pollution, and then set standards at a level that they thought would avoid some or all of the worst impacts.

Second, industries that were subject to environmental regulations began complaining that different regulatory programs were using different methods for calculating health effects and were, therefore, producing standards that did not reflect the same levels of stringency. Environmental professionals in EPA also noticed these differences and sought to reconcile them. Eventually, the National Academy of Sciences and the EPA defined standard methods for health risk assessment (National Research Council 1983, U.S. Environmental Protection Agency 1987a).

Third, once the practice of health risk assessment was fairly well accepted, risk estimates were used not only to justify specific regulatory standards, but also to compare the severity of the health problems being addressed by different regulatory programs and reexamine the priorities that are reflected implicitly in the laws passed by Congress. Environmental professionals developed methods that would enable them to evaluate and compare a broad range of environmental problems in terms of their human health, economic, and ecological impacts. These methods are referred to as "comparative risk assessment."[1]

Comparative risk assessment can be used to examine whether the current levels of spending on certain environmental problems are justified by the risks that they present to public health, ecological integrity, and quality of life, or alternatively, to identify environmental conditions that may have large adverse impacts now or in the future and are not receiving a commensurate level of attention and funding.

In the United States, the need for comparative risk assessment became clear as people began to realize that certain environmental health problems were absorbing a large proportion of environmental budgets, yet presented low or moderate public health risks. For example, a substantial share of the environmental protection budget has been spent on abandoned hazardous waste sites (such as Love Canal) under the Superfund program. In contrast, comparatively little has been spent on reducing toxic air pollutants or on public education regarding radon contamination in indoor air, both of which present significant health risks to larger numbers of people.[2]

Methods Used in Environmental Health Risk Assessment

The assessment carried out in Quito, Ecuador, used three different approaches for investigating and evaluating health risks from environmental problems: (1) health risk assessment, as developed and practiced by environmental scientists and toxicologists; (2) health effects (outcome) assessment, as developed and practiced by epidemiologists; and (3) ethnographic investigations of health-related behavior, as developed and practiced by medical anthropologists.

Health risk assessment is a procedure used to characterize the potential adverse health effects of human exposure to toxic agents.[3] The U.S. National Academy of Sciences has defined four components of risk assessment: hazard identification, exposure assessment, dose-response assessment, and risk characterization. Hazard identification is a qualitative determination of whether human exposure to an agent has the potential to produce adverse effects. Exposure assessment involves identifying populations that are exposed to a toxic agent and estimating the intensity and duration of their exposure. Dose-response assessment evaluates the relationship between exposure to a toxic agent and the probability that adverse health effects will occur. The relationship is described in a dose-response model. Risk characterization uses the exposure estimate and the dose response model to estimate the health risks experienced by exposed individuals and populations.

Health effects assessment uses public health data (such as mortality and morbidity rates organized by type of illness or cause of death), information on known cause-and-effect relationships between specific environmental pollutants and health problems, and the analytical methods of epidemiology to estimate the proportion of current mortality and morbidity rates that may be attributable to environmental causes. Data are used to identify and describe the type and magnitude of health problems that occur in the subject population according to time, place, and other descriptors (such as occupation, gender, age, etc.); identify which of the health problems observed in the population may be related to environmental factors; and if possible, estimate the proportion of observed mortality and morbidity that is plausibly attributable to environmental causes.

Ethnographic investigations are used to collect original data on environmental conditions and health conditions in poor urban areas, and to gain a better understanding of people's knowledge, attitudes, and behaviors that are relevant to environmental health. Going to peri-urban neighborhoods and interviewing people who live there is the best way of filling in the gaps in official data and discovering the environmental health problems that have the greatest impact on the poor. Ethnographic investigations use a variety of methods to collect information. Three techniques were used in the Quito study: focus groups, key informant interviews, and direct observations. Focus groups are carefully planned discussions with a preselected group of people (usually seven to ten) designed to obtain information on specific topics. Key informant interviews are used to obtain information that may be too complex to acquire during a focus group. Direct observations are firsthand, on-site observations by the researcher—they provide a necessary reliability check on information gathered through other techniques.[4]

Using Environmental Health Risk Assessment in Developing Countries

The lesson from the U.S. experience is that environmental problems should be ranked according to the seriousness of the risks they present, so that citizens, legislators, and government agencies can establish rational priorities. By identifying and comparing the environmental health problems in a particular town or region, an environmental health risk assessment can help communities, municipalities, national governments, and donor agencies identify appropriate emphases for environmental health programs.

Environmental health risk assessment is beginning to be used in developing countries, primarily through the sponsorship of the USAID and the EPA. USAID and EPA have conducted risk assessment studies in Bangkok, Thailand, Quito, Ecuador, Cairo, Egypt, Silesia (southern Poland and the Ostrava region of the Czech Republic), and several other locations. Each of these studies evaluated and ranked a range of environmental problems on the basis of their predicted impacts on public health.[5]

There are three major difficulties in applying risk assessment methods in developing countries:

1. There is a general lack of data on environmental conditions, exposures to toxic agents, and environmentally related health effects. This lack of data reflects the fact that environmental agencies are poorly developed and health-care delivery institutions do not address many environmental health conditions. The lack of data is particularly acute with regard to peri-urban areas.

2. Many of the assumptions used in the United States to estimate people's exposure to environmental contaminants—for example, assumptions about food consumption and the average diet, or the relative proportion of time people spend in their home, outdoors, and at work—are inappropriate for use in developing countries without modification.

3. Since most risk assessments in the United States concentrate on the risk of cancer from exposure to toxic chemicals, dose-response models have not been developed for most biological hazards and infectious diseases. These hazards constitute the largest proportion of the environmentally related disease burden in developing countries.

The collection and use of additional data helps address each of these difficulties during a risk assessment study, particularly in peri-urban areas. The study in Quito collected original data from people living in peri-urban areas through the use of ethnographic investigative techniques. The focus groups and key informant interviews were used to gather information from neighborhood residents on the environmental conditions to which they were exposed, which of these conditions they thought were most harmful to their health, and which diseases or health problems they thought were environmentally related and most important. Direct observations were used to confirm some of the information obtained from focus groups and interviews regarding food hygiene, collection and disposal of garbage, and disposal of human wastes.

The information collected in peri-urban neighborhoods helped the risk assessment study team in three ways:

1. It helped the team understand the context of environmental health problems and interpret information gathered through official sources. For example, official data indicated that the quality of drinking water in Quito is good, that food is frequently found to be contaminated with bacteria and other microbes, and that rates of diarrheal diseases are modest. Interviews in the neighborhoods indicated that diarrheal diseases are a larger problem than indicated by official statistics. This is not an unusual finding, since many cases of diarrhea do not require treatment in a clinic and therefore go unreported. Observations revealed practices in markets and households that promote biological contamination of food. Taken together, all of this information led the team to conclude that food contamination is an important health risk in Quito—a conclusion that could not have been reached using official data alone.

2. Qualitative data helped the team understand how typically benign environmental conditions may be harmful in certain circumstances. For example, participants in the focus groups complained that airborne dust created by traffic on unpaved roads was one of the main problems in their neighborhoods, and that it caused frequent sore throats and respiratory infections. Data from toxicological research show that dust does not usually cause serious health problems, as long as the dust particles are large enough to be filtered by the lungs and the dust does not carry pathogens or toxins (such as lead). Further questioning of community residents revealed that at certain times, heavy rains cause the surface drains and latrines in the neighborhoods to overflow, creating an open sewer in the roadways. Once the water has dried, the dust left behind is laden with many pathogens, which could certainly cause respiratory infections if inhaled.

3. Qualitative information from focus groups and interviews helped the team identify environmental health risks that they might not have recognized otherwise. For example, focus group participants reported that many of the men in the community worked in construction trades, and that they were frequently injured in falls and accidents. These health problems show up in clinical statistics as broken limbs, puncture wounds, and burns, but are not attributed to work-related causes because the injured workers would be penalized for reporting on-the-job injuries. Since occupational health records were virtually nonexistent, or were not available to the team, such interviews were the only way the team could determine whether occupational injuries are a problem. Similarly, women who work as food vendors reported that the lack of public sanitation facilities in markets and along roadways caused them to urinate infrequently and in unsanitary conditions; they felt that this contributed to a high rate of urinary tract infections. Although other risk factors (such as sexual practices) may also have a role, the connection that these women noted is a potential contributing factor that might not otherwise have been considered by the team.

While not used in this manner in the Quito study, ethnographic investigations can also be used to develop profiles of food consumption patterns and activity patterns, that are in turn used to estimate people's exposure to various pollutants. In the Quito study, a previous study was available which described the typical diet of Quito residents.

Another challenge of conducting risk assessment studies in developing countries is involving local citizens and officials in the problem-ranking process. In the United States, risk assessment has been criticized as an undemocratic activity because, in many cases, technical "experts" have prepared rankings that were intended to influence public policy, without adequate input from the general public.

Public input is even more important in developing countries, because ranking environmental health problems involves many subjective judgements based on personal and societal values. Outside technical advisers cannot hope to discover and understand all of the values that are called into service to make such decisions. For example, to set priorities, one must judge whether diarrhea in children is more or less important than lead poisoning in children, or occupational injuries in working-age adults, or environmentally related cancers in older adults. These choices involve trade-offs among diseases (acute versus chronic, reversible versus permanent, one organ system versus another) and among different demographic groups (by gender, age, ethnicity, and economic level). Such choices must reflect local values and should be made by the people who will bear the benefits and the costs of the decision.

The following guidelines should be used in designing environmental health risk assessments in developing countries:

- Local people's experiences and observations, while inevitably subjective, are a legitimate input to research on environmental health risks. Risk assessments should include not only quantitative data from official sources but also qualitative data collected from local residents who are at risk of environmentally related health problems.

• Environmental health risk assessment provides information on the nature and magnitude of risks, but cannot provide purely objective conclusions about which risks are the most important. Deciding which risks deserve the highest priority attention involves value judgements that should be made by the people who experience those risks. Community residents are the best source of information about the environmental conditions that affect them and the health problems they experience, and have a legitimate role in determining how those problems should be prioritized.

• Value judgements on how to use information produced by risk assessments should not be made by scientific or technical advisors. Their job should be to provide the conceptual and methodological tools that are useful in risk assessment and to help build up local capacity to use these tools.

• Local institutions and communities should be involved in every stage of environmental risk assessment studies, from design through data collection to interpretation, evaluation, and priority setting.

Results of the Environmental Health Risk Assessment Study in Quito, Ecuador

Overview of Environmental and Socioeconomic Conditions in Quito

Quito, Ecuador, with a population of about one million people, lies on a narrow plateau high in the Andes mountains of South America. Over the last forty years, the city has seen phenomenal growth; in 1990, Quito was twenty times its 1950 size geographically, and home to six times its 1950 population. Much of this growth can be attributed to migration from rural areas of Ecuador. Immigrants typically establish homes in peri-urban areas located on hilly, rocky, ecologically fragile lands ill-suited to dense population concentrations. They are only poorly provided, if at all, with basic municipal services such as clean running water, electricity, and sanitary waste disposal systems. These neighborhoods, called *asentamientos populares*, are plagued by environmental problems such as airborne particles stirred up by vehicles traveling over unpaved streets and, in the rainy season, drainage backups that turn those streets into lagoons.

In addition to the problems primarily associated with its asentamientos populares, Quito also suffers the same environmental problems found in other densely populated cities. These include air pollution from motor vehicle exhaust, poor sanitation, polluted water, poor food hygiene, inadequate solid waste disposal, and unsafe workplaces.

In June 1992, a multidisciplinary research team, working in collaboration with USAID/Quito, undertook a three-week comparative environmental health risk assessment in Quito, focusing on the city's peri-urban neighborhoods. The five-person study team included an occupational health specialist, a risk assessment specialist, an economist, a medical doctor, and a medical anthropologist. The team's broad goal was to test and refine previously established methods for conducting environmental health assessments in developing country settings. More immediate goals were to identify the most significant environmental health problems facing the people of Quito and to generate information necessary for the city's public health officials to set priorities for addressing these problems.

Summary of Results

The results of the assessment of Quito's environmental health risks are summarized in Table 5.1. Environmental conditions in Quito have different human impacts in asentamientos populares than in the rest of the city. For Quito as a whole, food contamination with microorganisms appears to be

Table 5.1   Assessment of Environmental Health Risks in Quito

Risk	Quito as a whole	Asentamientos populares
High	food contamination: microorganisms	food contamination: microorganisms
	particulates in outdoor air	particulates in outdoor air
		occupational hazards
		drinking water
		wastewater
		indoor air pollution
Medium	traffic hazards	traffic hazards
	occupational hazards	solid waste
	drinking water	
	wastewater	
	indoor air pollution	
Low	solid waste	food contamination: pesticides
	food contamination: pesticides	
Not estimated	lead (air)	lead (air)
	toxic substances: pesticides (nonfood sources)	toxic substances: pesticides (nonfood sources)

the most common environmental health risk. The data collected indicate that gastrointestinal problems are the most frequent type of illness, as well as the most common cause of death. Since water quality seems to be adequate, and since 65 percent of all foods are contaminated, it appears that food contamination may be the principal source of gastrointestinal illnesses.

The second highest risk source is particulate matter in outdoor air. Analogous to food contamination, air pollution potentially affects everyone. The severity of most health problems caused by air pollution, however, is low when compared to other hazards, such as car accidents. Still, the evidence, both in terms of morbidity and mortality, indicates that it is a significant risk to human health. This risk is particularly high for those people—about 25 percent of the population—who live and work along the heavily used transportation corridors running from north to south throughout the city.

For asentamientos populares, the data show that contaminated food and polluted outdoor air are also the largest sources of risk. However, outdoor air quality problems in these areas are caused, at least in part, by dust from unpaved streets. Although respiratory ailments may come from several sources besides dust in the air, the site visits performed by the study team indicate that dust is such an overwhelming problem in these neighborhoods that trying to associate respiratory problems with other sources may be difficult.

In addition to food and outdoor air, people living in the asentamientos populares are more exposed to risks from indoor air contamination and occupational hazards than people living in other areas of the city. Cooking stoves and small-scale textile and metal industries are important risk sources. Although the anecdotal evidence also points toward the construction industry, data were not available to document its potential risks to human health.

The results also show two surprises: the relatively low risks associated with solid waste and with drinking water in Quito as a whole. Solid waste is less a source of pathogens than originally believed because of the cool weather and because of the relatively little contact that occurs between people and garbage. Even though there are many informal dumps around the city, the data show that almost 80 percent of the solid waste is disposed of properly. Moreover, direct observation and in-depth interviews indicate that the uncollected waste does not seem to account for much environmental health risk.

Water quality also seems to pose low risks to the general population in Quito. The data collected by the water company on a regular basis clearly show that network water is of good quality. Contamination seems to occur at the connection points in houses with septic tank problems, or in households with poor hygiene, which are primarily in the asentamientos populares.

Overall, the results show that there are significant differential health consequences related to access to infrastructure, such as paved roads and potable water. Hence, residents of asentamientos populares are more at risk of environmental health consequences than are those living in middle-class neighborhoods. Most striking is the health risk people are exposed to through food contamination and outdoor air pollution, and contact with waste water. There was not enough information available to evaluate health risks from exposure to lead.

The experience gained from this study shows that qualitative data need to be integrated into risk assessment studies conducted in developing countries. Without such data, quantitative data on environmental quality and health will be substantially less useful.

Although this study has its limitations, the evidence from secondary data—and the corroboration provided by qualitative data from focus groups—yield clear findings. The results of this study should be useful to the local government of Quito and to the national government of Ecuador, in setting priorities for new investments and allocating existing resources for environmental health programs.

Notes

This chapter is based on *Environmental Health Assessment: A Case Study in the City of Quito and the County of Pedro Moncayo, Pichincha Province, Ecuador*. 1993. WASH Field Report No. 401, Water and Sanitation for Health Project (WASH), Arlington, VA. The report was prepared by Gustavo Arcia, Eugene Brantly, and Robert Hetes of the Research Triangle Institute; Barry Levy and Clydette Powell of Management Sciences for Health; Jose Suárez-Torres, School of Medicine, Central University of Ecuador; and Linda Whiteford, University of South Florida. The original study and the preparation of this chapter were sponsored by the Office of Health and Nutrition, U.S. Agency for International Development. Reprints of the report are available from the Environmental Health Project (see Resource Organizations).

The Environmental Health Project continues and expands the work of the WASH Project and the Vector Biology Control Project, building upon the lessons that have been learned.

1. See U.S. Environmental Protection Agency 1993, Brantly et al. 1993, and Northeast Center for Comparative Risk 1994 for more information.
2. See U.S. Environmental Protection Agency 1987b and U.S. Environmental Protection Agency 1990 for more detailed information on U.S. experience in comparative risk assessment.
3. A basic premise underlying health risk assessment is that there is a predictable chain of events linking the production and release of environmental contaminants with public health problems, and that these events can be modeled. Links in this chain include the generation of a pollutant; its discharge into the environment; its transport through the environment via various physical, biological, and chemical processes (together referred to as "fate and transport"); an individual's exposure to the pollutant through his or her behavior; intake of the pollutant into the individual's body; its movement through the body; the resulting dose to one or more organs of the body; biological damage to organs; and finally, disease, disability, or death.

4. In an environmental health assessment, observations should focus on garbage dumps, household refuse removal systems, the use and condition of sanitation facilities, access to drinking water or other household patterns for water retrieval and storage, food handling, preparation, and storage, and family and household hygiene practices, such as handwashing and waste removal.

5. Comparative risk assessment studies conducted in the United States evaluate human health and ecological and economic impacts. To the author's knowledge, studies conducted in developing countries to date have evaluated only the potential health impacts of environmental problems, and have not included an assessment of ecological and economic impacts.

References

Brantly, Eugene, Robert Hetes, Barry Levy, Clydette Powell, and Linda Whiteford. 1993. *Environmental Health Assessment: An Integrated Methodology for Rating Environmental Health Problems. WASH Field Report* no. 436; *PRITECH Report* no. HSS-133IR. WASH Project and PRITECH Project, Arlington, VA. (Available from the Environmental Health Project; see Resource Organizations.)

National Research Council. 1983. *Risk Assessment in the Federal Government: Managing the Process.* Washington, D.C.: National Academy Press.

Northeast Center for Comparative Risk (NCCR). 1994. *The Resource Guide to Comparative Risk.* South Royalton, VT: NCCR.

U.S. Environmental Protection Agency (EPA). 1987a. *Risk Assessment Guidelines of 1986. EPA Report* no. 600-8-87/045. Office of Health and Environmental Assessment. Washington, D.C.

———. 1987b. *Unfinished Business: A Comparative Assessment of Environmental Problems.* Office of the Administrator. Washington, D.C.

———. 1990. *Reducing Risk: Setting Priorities and Strategies for Environmental Protection. EPA Report* no. SAB-EC-90-021. Science Advisory Board. Washington, D.C.

———. 1993. *A Guidebook to Comparing Risks and Setting Environmental Priorities. EPA Report* no. 230-B-93-003. Regional and State Planning Branch, Office of Policy, Planning, and Evaluation. Washington, D.C.

Part III

Exploring Gender Roles in Environmental Management, Health, and Development

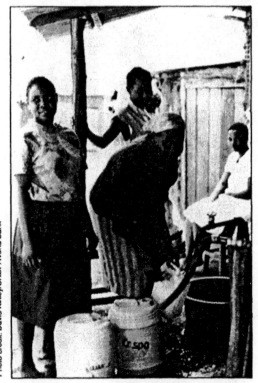

Kibera, Nairobi, Kenya

Part III

Introduction

P art III explores the multiple and expanding roles of individuals, especially women, working at the household and community levels toward improved management of their natural and cultural environments. The chapters address three distinct but interrelated environmental problems—population growth rates that threaten to exceed local environmental carrying capacities, the lack of sufficient clean water and adequate sanitation, and residential air pollution. The three are linked together by several themes: the traditional status of women, and how this affects environmental problems; the appropriateness of women as project planners and implementers and as household and community resource managers; and the crucial role of community participation and community education in effective environmental management.

Population Growth

Whether viewed in terms of absolute numbers, rate of growth, distribution in relation to resources, or impact on resources, population is central to any consideration of environmental health issues at any level—global, regional, or local. Ten thousand years ago, the planet was populated by only about ten million people, distributed for ready access to needed resources; today it is home to close to six billion (Jordan et al. 1994:46).

The inequitable distribution of global resources, the tremendous imbalances in resource consumption between the North and South, and the overuse of some resources and degradation of others, have critical impacts on environmental problems and global changes. However, population growth also plays a major role in environmental problems such as air and water pollution, deforestation, soil exhaustion, and erosion; and can be linked with global changes such as poverty, famine, increases in disease rates, and conflicts between groups over resources. Rapid population growth can and does negatively affect physical and cultural environments, and makes other environmental problems more difficult to solve.

Like many other environmental problems, overly rapid population growth cannot be halted or reversed without addressing the cultural factors responsible for it, including the values and practices associated with childbearing. While there is no effective yet still universally acceptable means of reducing population growth, there is general agreement that any solution must preserve the right of individuals to decide whether, when, and how many times to become a parent. Chapter 6, by Lily P. Kak and Marjorie B. Signer, describes a project in which individuals' voluntary acceptance of modern family planning methods was successfully won within the context of a culture with virtually no previous recourse to such methods. It highlights several important elements of effective services delivery in traditional communities that place a high value on fecundity.

Water and Sanitation

Only 3 percent of the earth's water is fresh, and over 2.9 percent of that is inaccessible, reducing the supply available for human use to less than one percent of the total. Globally, pollution from nondegrading wastes continues to reduce this small supply. Locally, 1.2 billion people (over one-fifth of the world's population) currently do not have adequate access to sufficient clean water, due to pollution, temporary drought, or population growth that has outstripped groundwater supplies. Worldwide population growth projections suggest that this number may reach 2 billion by the year 2000 (Miller 1994:336).

Of the thirty-seven major diseases that collectively most afflict developing countries, twenty-one are related to water and sanitation (Water and Sanitation for Health Project 1993). In addition, when water sources are distant from households, health problems are compounded by the toll in time, energy, injuries, and exhaustion associated with water procurement.

Access to clean water does not by itself guarantee good health. Appropriate siting and distribution of water sources, as well as community education about sanitation, are essential. To ensure that the placement of water sources is culturally appropriate and that water users understand how to keep water free of contamination, the full involvement of community members in water projects is critical.

In many developing countries, women, often aided by their children (particularly female children), are the main procurers, distributors, and managers of water at the household level, and are therefore best qualified to design and oversee water projects that meet household and community needs. At the same time, however, women's time and energy are usually already severely stretched among their roles as resource and income producers, reproducers, home managers, and caregivers. In addition, in some communities traditional restrictions are placed on women's community leadership or project management roles. If they are to be successfully involved in the planning, implementation, management, and evaluation of safe water projects, women must realize clear advantages, including savings in time, energy, and money, as well as social acceptance.

Chapter 7, by Margaret Wuganga Mwangola, illustrates the importance of community participation, community education, and the active involvement of women in successful water and sanitation projects. It also highlights the essential role indigenous nongovernmental organizations

(NGOs) can play by actively involving local residents and community leaders in the implementation, maintenance and repair of water sources and by incorporating women. The chapter points to a growing trend: the increasing attention paid by indigenous NGOS, once focused on rural environmental problems, to urban settings.

Residential Air Pollution

Particularly in the South, the household use of biomass fuels, such as wood or dung, causes a variety of serious physical ailments including heart, lung, and eye ailments from smoky pollution and injuries from burns and scalds. In addition, biomass fuel use incurs heavy costs in time and energy, mostly for women, the household members usually responsible for fuel procurement, cooking, and cleaning away the smoky residue that results.

Some of the problems associated with indoor air pollution can be mitigated easily and inexpensively through the introduction of simple and appropriate new technologies. In chapter 8, Emma Crewe describes the health and household environmental problems associated with the smoky cookstoves traditionally used in Sri Lanka, and how these problems have been alleviated by the introduction of new, improved, more appropriate stoves. The chapter lends strong support for three important notions. First, to be effective, appropriate technologies must "fit" into the local economic and social contexts. Second, women play a crucial role as designers of appropriate technologies for household use. Finally, developing appropriate technologies in consultation with those who will use them can go a long way toward protecting the environment and thus the health of poor people.

Together the three chapters in Part III help us better understand and appreciate the status and roles of women in traditional communities as these affect the natural and cultural environment in household and community settings. They make clear that the opinions and expertise of women are of paramount importance if development projects are to be appropriately planned, effective in reaching their intended beneficiaries, and, ultimately, sustainable. The chapters also suggest that project planners, at any level, should avoid relying on women's volunteerism for project success since women's time and energy are frequently already strained by household obligations. Effective projects tend to be those that provide local women with rewards—financial, social, or practical—that are acceptable within their sociocultural context.

International and national-level political and financial commitments to insuring access to family planning information and services, ample supplies of safe water, and appropriate technologies are important, but by themselves, such commitments are not enough. A central message of the chapters in Part III is that the ability of individuals and communities to change environmentally damaging behaviors and manage their environments more effectively can be enhanced if development projects: (1) take local cultural factors into account; (2) assiduously seek the opinions and active participation of women; (3) involve community members in every step of the development process; (4) include community education in project design; and (5) lay the groundwork for local communities to eventually claim full ownership of development projects.

References

Jordan, Terry G., Mona Domosh, and Lester Rowntree. 1994. *The Human Mosaic: A Thematic Introduction to Cultural Geography.* 6th ed. New York: HarperCollins.

Miller, G. Tyler, Jr. 1994. *Living in the Environment: Principles, Connections, and Solutions.* 8th ed. Belmont, CA: Wadsworth Publishing.

Water and Sanitation for Health (WASH) Project. 1993. *Lessons Learned in Water, Sanitation, and Health.* Updated edition. Arlington, VA: WASH Project and the U.S. Agency for International Development.

Chapter 6

Improving Access to Family Planning Services in Rural Mali

Lily P. Kak and Marjorie B. Signer

Bintou, fifteen years old on her last birthday, is an illiterate housewife living in a remote village of about four hundred people in Mali. The nearest health facility is 14 kilometers away by dirt road, and Bintou's only access to it is on foot. She was recently married to a farmer, also illiterate, who has three other wives;[1] Bintou now shares with them the responsibility for preparing food, chopping wood, and drawing water for a large household. Every day during the dry season, she walks 10 kilometers to the Niger River to draw water. If her life takes a typical course, Bintou will have at least one living child by the time she is seventeen, and by thirty-one she will have four, the result of six pregnancies. Two of her children will have died from measles, malaria, or diarrhea. More pregnancies will follow, and by the end of her reproductive years she will have seven living children.

In rural Mali, the total fertility rate (TFR) is 6.7 children per woman, among the highest in the world. This has resulted in a rate of natural population increase of about 3 percent per year. With a current (mid-1994) population of 9.1 million, Mali's population is expected to double in twenty-three years (Population Reference Bureau 1994). Although the environmental impact of such growth would be significant, through the mid-1970s the government of Mali remained unconcerned about the country's rates of fertility and natural population increase, in the belief that a larger population could easily be supported by the country's vast size and by what were considered substantially underutilized natural resources (van de Walle and Maiga 1991:84).

Mali's TFR, as high as it is, does not coincide with Malians' cultural preferences; seven children is seen as the ideal family size (Kak and Signer 1993:1). But the country's infant and child mortality rates are also among the highest in the world, and women are aware that close birth spacing is a factor here (DHS/Mali 1987). This may help to explain why, even though Malians value large families highly, many married women—for example, nearly half of those who participated in a 1987 demographic and health survey (DHS/Mali 1987)—say they want and need modern family planning services.[2] Some of these women (16 percent) said they already had all the children they wanted; but twice as many (32 percent) said they would like to be able to space their pregnancies two or three years apart in order to give their babies a better chance of surviving and preserve their own health. The most common reason given for not using modern contraceptives was a lack of information about them (Kak and Signer 1993:1).

Mali's weak and unevenly distributed health infrastructure has been unequal to the task of responding to the need for family planning services. Few local health centers offer such services, even though it is the government's policy to provide them;[3] and where family planning services are available through government-run programs, they are mostly delivered through centralized clinics that tend to be inaccessible to the nearly 80 percent of the population that lives in rural areas. Overall, Mali's contraceptive prevalence rate is just 1.3 percent, among the lowest in the world.

Some analysts have attributed the disappointing record of family planning efforts in rural Mali to deeply rooted sub-Saharan cultural traditions, where motherhood is viewed as women's most important role and a high value is placed on female fecundity. Family planning, family size, and child spacing are usually not openly discussed by spouses; instead, men—traditionally dominant in Malian society—make the decisions on these matters. The idea of sterilization is abhorrent, as is abortion. Virtually all women are married in this polygynous Moslem society. Households are large, averaging 12.7 people (Kak and Signer 1993:6). The average age of brides is sixteen, although many girls marry at thirteen or fourteen; a woman who is widowed is urged to remarry quickly.

Despite these cultural norms and values, however, rural Malians consider a relatively long interval between births to be desirable as a way of maximizing children's chances of survival and ensuring that mothers have a chance to regain their health after pregnancy. Traditionally, birth spacing is achieved by breastfeeding and by postpartum female sexual abstinence for up to three years after a birth. Villagers also rely for contraception on wearing a *tafo*, a belt made of animal skin and cotton that has been blessed by a traditional healer (Kak and Signer 1993:12).

The district of Katibougou, in Western Mali some 70 kilometers from the capital, Bamako, lies in a poor agricultural area where droughts frequently devastate the local economy, reducing agricultural production and decimating livestock herds. The primary economic activities of the largely illiterate Katibougou villagers are farming, fishing, animal husbandry, and craft production. Given a steadily growing population, the natural environment in Katibougou is neither rich enough nor reliable enough to provide the basic necessities of life indefinitely.

Katibougou district has a government-sponsored primary health center, the Katibougou PMI-Maternité (Protection Maternelle et Infantile-Maternité) which is the only provider of health services (including free family planning services) for some twenty thousand people in twenty villages. The PMI-Maternité was established in 1976 to provide integrated health and family planning services to the residents of the district. At that time, district residents had no knowledge of modern contraceptive methods, and there were no family planning acceptors.

In 1985, the Katibougou PMI-Maternité's midwife, after training by and with the support of CEDPA, designed the Katibougou Family Health Project.[4] Her intent was to augment the health center's clinic-based service delivery with community-based information, education, and communication (IEC) targeting six local villages with a combined population of three thousand. This new strategy, to be tested in a pilot project, was aimed at creating awareness of family planning, changing community attitudes toward contraception, generating demand for family planning services, and making those services accessible to community residents. Since the small-family norm—the crux of most family planning programs in other parts of the world—is unacceptable to many people in the sub-Saharan region, it was decided not to promote family planning as a means of limiting family size, but rather to stress how the temporary use of contraceptive methods improves the chances of infant survival and facilitates achieving the cultural norm of long birth spacing.

As the pilot project began, the Katibougou PMI-Maternité continued to provide clinic-based health and family planning services while project activities were slowly phased in. As its first intervention, the project trained female village health workers (VHWs) and traditional birth attendants (TBAs) to introduce community-based IEC to villagers in the project's catchment area. Villagers were informed that family planning can help improve maternal and child health through child spacing, and thus can help them achieve their desired family size. Given the extremely high infant and child mortality rates in Mali, this approach proved very appealing.

A year later, in November 1986, the pilot project ended and the Katibougou Family Health Project officially began, under a grant from the Office of Population, USAID/Bamako. The project targeted ten villages with a total population of 6,300 people. Services continued to be clinic based, but were supplemented by community-based IEC provided by teams of female VHWs and TBAs who made monthly visits to each village. However, two major problems combined to thwart villagers' demand for family planning services and to impede effective client recruitment. First, the clinic-centered outreach system restricted community members' access to information and services. It became increasingly clear that if awareness and acceptance of modern family planning methods were to be increased, it would be crucial to change the focus of family planning services in the district from the central clinic to the community. Second, the project included no men. Family planning was offered in conjunction with maternal and child health care, so the service delivery system was oriented toward women. Overlooking men ignored their influence in making contraceptive choices, and limited the acceptance of family planning by both women and men.

To address these problems, the project added two innovative interventions in September 1987. First, a community-based service delivery model was introduced under which the VHWs, in the role of outreach health and family planning motivators, began to distribute condoms and spermicides to new and continuing clients in the community and to provide appropriate follow-up. In addition, the VHWs began to distribute resupplies of oral contraceptives under the strict supervision of the project director. The initiative proved to be a breakthrough in making contraceptives more accessible in the target villages.

Second, because experience from other family planning programs had shown that the most successful community-based contraceptive distributors are those who are most similar to their target populations, male VHWs were recruited and trained to work alongside the project's female VHWs and TBAs in community-based teams—the first time this had been done in Mali. In the rural setting of the Katibougou project, sensitivities resulting from traditional gender roles discouraged men and women from communicating with each other about family planning, so project work was allocated by gender: the female VHWs worked with the community's women, providing them with spermicides and resupplies of oral contraceptives; the male VHWs worked among the men of the community, providing them with condoms. Gradually, men's resistance to the idea of family planning began to erode with their greater understanding of the health and economic advantages of birth spacing.

By November 1989, the project had grown to include a total of fourteen villages containing 10,200 people, and the VHWs were receiving literacy and numeric training to enable them to record data about their clients. Shortly thereafter, two income-generating activities, a cereal grinding business and a ferry service to provide transportation across the Niger River, were begun. These activities were intended to increase access to income among family planning acceptors and to provide monetary compensation to the VHWs; as is the case with many impoverished people around the world, the capacity of rural Malians for volunteerism is severely limited by their lack of time and need to generate income. At the same time, the management of the project was decentralized in order to empower project staff and enable them to make managerial decisions.

In mid-1991, the project provided its male VHWs with bicycles to increase their mobility and facilitate recruitment and follow-up of clients, and expanded yet again to include another five villages. By the end of the year, the project covered a total population of fourteen thousand in nineteen villages. Another income-generating activity for female family planning acceptors was added in January 1992: a women's textile cooperative, which proved to be a successful means of increasing women's economic options and promoting the use of family planning. By now the project had grown to include some twenty thousand residents in twenty villages.[5]

Today, the Katibougou PMI-Maternité, still the only health facility servicing Katibougou district, offers an integrated health and family planning program in a format that has been remarkably successful in increasing its clients' acceptance of family planning services. Health services include prenatal and postnatal care, tetanus immunization for pregnant women, deliveries, immunization, malaria prevention, oral rehydration to treat diarrhea, medical visits for both adults and children, referrals of complicated cases to the area hospital, and educational sessions on health, nutrition, environmental health, and safe drinking water. The family planning program conducts counseling sessions and provides oral contraceptives, IUDs, condoms, spermicides, and injectables, all obtained from the government.

The project team includes the project director/midwife, an assistant midwife, two matrons, and a male paramedical health aide, all on the staff of the Katibougou PMI-Maternité. In addition, each village in the project's catchment area has two male and two female VHWs, members of the community who have been nominated by the village chief and elders. The VHWs' main responsibilities are motivation, recruitment of new family planning clients, distribution of supplies, and follow-up of clients to identify side effects and complications. Completing each village's team are two local TBAs whose training in safe, hygienic birthing techniques has helped to win the confidence of villagers in the project. Since each member of each team is a resident of the village in which he or she works, team members are well known to their clients, and most are accorded new respect for their role in the program.

Regular monthly follow-up of clients to identify side effects and ensure client satisfaction has resulted in high family planning continuation rates. The follow-up system has been, by necessity, intensive. Through home visits and group meetings, each team of community-based workers tracks condom and spermicide clients for resupplies, and IUD and injectable clients for side effects and dissatisfaction. Clients using clinical methods are referred to the clinic team's monthly village visit. The linkage between the community-based team and the clinic team has been critical to the success of the follow-up and referral system.

To the project's grain milling business, ferry service, and textile cooperative, originally intended mainly to raise funds with which to compensate the VHWs, have been added a number of kiosks for the sale of miscellaneous items. Each village selects its own income-generating activities based on its perception of what kind of activity would most benefit its area. Funds to start the activity are provided either in cash or in kind, and project staff provide management and bookkeeping support. Residents of villages with successful ventures serve as technical advisors to new and growing projects.

The most successful small business associated with the project is the Katibougou Young Women's Textile Cooperative, funded through a USAID Women in Development grant. This differs from the other income-generating activities in that the product can be marketed to a broad range of clients. The cooperative members are young women of reproductive age who use modern contraceptive methods as a result of the project. All unemployed when they joined the cooperative, many were unmarried as well, and were looked down upon by the community as economic liabilities and social outcasts. Options for women in this position in Katibougou district have traditionally been very limited; typically, a woman would marry for economic reasons, then fall into a cycle of repeated unwanted pregnancies and further dependence.

The members of the Katibougou Young Women's Textile Cooperative, in contrast, have become role models for other young women in Katibougou, thanks not only to their entrepreneurial success but also to their visible freedom from repeated or unwanted pregnancies. The notion that family planning afforded them the opportunity to participate in a successful and profitable activity figures prominently in the way other women view them. Although cooperative members are not directly involved in service delivery or family planning education, the cooperative has become a powerful symbol of family planning as a means to free women for rewarding pursuits other than childrearing. Thanks in part to cooperative members, there has been a significant change in women's attitudes about the use of family planning: in general, they are more accepting of it.

Given the almost complete lack of knowledge about family planning in Katibougou district prior to the implementation of the Katibougou Family Health Project, and given also the medical and cultural barriers and lack of infrastructure that existed at its inception, the project has seen remarkable success. By the end of its fifth year, it had recruited a cumulative total of over five thousand clients and had provided a total of almost five thousand couple-years of protection (CYP), at a cost of U.S.$49 per CYP. Based on the results of a 1991 census in the catchment area, the contraceptive prevalence rate, in marked contrast to the very low national contraceptive prevalence rate of 1.3 percent, was estimated to be almost 58 percent. Focus groups among the beneficiaries revealed that residents of the project area had progressed from ignorance about family planning to a high degree of knowledge about the most common methods (oral contraceptives and condoms), and a general acceptance of the value of family planning. While clients' acceptance of modern contraceptives was based mainly on their desire to enhance infant and child survival, increased economic productivity and quality-of-life improvements were also cited as benefits.

The project has also increased communication about family planning between women and men, which may in the long run enable women to play a more active role in deciding matters related to their own fertility. Discussions in group meetings and between individual men and women about family planning and health issues indicate that the project has increased open communication about family planning, and enabled women to have a say in its practice for the first time. Not surprisingly, the villagers who have been served by the project for the longest period of time report more open discussion about family planning than villagers who have only recently been included in the coverage area.

A side benefit of the project has been its empowering effect on women who participated as VHWs. In a survey of the female VHWs, almost all reported that their lives had changed since they began to work. They believed they were more respected in the community as a result of being associated with the family planning project. Similarly, a large proportion reported that their relationships with their neighbors, husbands, and parents-in-law had improved. About half the VHWs felt that their decision-making power regarding their children's education and medical treatment and the management of their households, including household expenditures, had increased as a result of their employment. Over half said their mobility had increased and that they could leave the house without permission from husband or parents-in-law. They agreed that, in addition to their training in family planning and health, the community's respect and gratitude were important rewards of their work.

Within a cultural belief system that values large families, the Katibougou project, by moving away from clinic-centered services delivery, integrating family planning with income-producing opportunities, and including men, has found a niche for modern family planning methods as an effective way to promote child survival and thus enhance the quality of life. The project shows conclusively that generating demand for family planning services is possible when services are accessible, respond to clients' needs, and respect clients' cultural norms. Another benefit of the project, although not the one that is foremost in the concerns of rural Malians, is that it is serving as a model for family planning service delivery, having been replicated by the government in other areas of the country.[6] As such, it may, in the long run, help to mitigate the environmental consequences of unchecked population growth in Mali.

Notes

1. About 40 percent of married women in rural Mali are in polygynous unions.
2. This survey is the most recent one available.
3. In May 1991, almost five years after the project described here was initiated, the government of Mali, in recognition of the country's population problems, instituted an official population policy.
4. The Katibougou Family Health Project had its inception at a training workshop held by the Centre for Development and Population Activities (CEDPA), and was initially funded by the Population Crisis Committee and USA for Africa. Since 1985, funding has been provided by CEDPA through grants from the Office of Population, USAID/Bamako. Additional funding, earmarked for support of income-generating activities, has been provided by the USAID Office of Women in Development.
5. By this time the project was under the management of the ministry of public health and social affairs.
6. Since this chapter was originally prepared, funding for the Family Health Project was cut back by the government of Mali. In response, its initiator, Mme. Fatoumata Traore, has founded a new NGO, ASDAP (Association de Soutien

au Développement des Activités de Population), which will carry on and expand project activities.

References

Demographic and Health Survey (DHS)/Mali. 1987. *Demographic Health Survey of Mali.* Washington, D.C.: U.S. Agency for International Development.

Kak, Lily P., and Marjorie B. Signer. 1993. *The Introduction of Community-Based Family Planning Services in Rural Mali: The Katibougou Family Health Project. Working Paper* no. 2. Washington, D.C.: Centre for Development and Population Activities.

Population Reference Bureau. 1994. "1994 World Population Data Sheet." Washington, D.C.

van de Walle, Francine, and Mariam Maiga. 1991. "Family Planning in Bamako, Mali." *International Family Planning Perspectives* 17(3):84–90, 99.

Chapter 7

Bringing Clean Water to Kenyan Households

Margaret Wuganga Mwangola

I n 1975, in conjunction with a conference held in Mexico at the beginning
of the International Women's Decade (1975–85), the United Nations established a fund to support development projects to benefit women in the
developing world. Determined to take advantage of this opportunity, several Kenyan women's nongovernmental organizations (NGOs) with a particular concern for water and sanitation issues, working through the
United Nations Children's Fund (UNICEF) regional office in Nairobi,
joined together to design a pilot project that would benefit rural Kenyan
women by increasing their access to adequate supplies of safe water. If
successful, the project would be replicated in other developing countries.

There was a pressing need for a new attempt to improve access to safe
water and sanitation for rural Kenyans. Kenya is a dry country, despite its
geographical position astride the equator. Less than 15 percent of its land
is arable, and the amount of rainfall varies greatly, both seasonally and annually. Furthermore, the country's population was growing rapidly.[1]
Previous water and sanitation efforts had failed, due mainly to the fact
that communities had not been involved in discussing their needs or in
designing solutions to their water-related problems. As a result, sustainable water and sanitation programs had thus far remained unachievable.

Funded in 1976 under the UN program, the new project was named the
UNICEF/NGO Water for Health Project. It began as a grant-making program funding small water-for-health efforts, overseen by Kenya's National
Council of Women, which at the time was made up of some forty women's
NGOs. I joined the project in January 1980, as its coordinator. In 1983, I became its executive director, and the organization was registered by the government of Kenya as a full-fledged NGO. This new status allowed the
project to address directly the monumental challenge of providing sustainable community water supply and sanitation facilities throughout Kenya,
and also to apply for funding from national and international donors.

Renamed the Kenya Water for Health Organization (KWAHO), the organization soon grew to a full-scale program carrying out community-

85

based water and sanitation projects of its own. The staff swelled from 12 in 1984 to 56 in 1986, then to 94 in 1988, 124 in 1990, and 156 in 1993. Today, staff members include community development specialists, water engineers, anthropologists, sociologists, public health and information specialists, home economists, teachers, nurses, agricultural and health extension workers, and representatives of women's, church, and educational groups. Our functions include prospecting for water, disseminating information, undertaking socioeconomic baseline surveys, training staff and community leaders, conducting educational workshops, promoting low-cost appropriate technologies, and handling public relations. By 1989, we had supported over one hundred water-related projects and had benefited some 600,000 Kenyans, many of them women. Today we estimate that more than one million Kenyans have been served by KWAHO.

KWAHO's many activities are generated in several different ways. In some cases a community requests a specific project; in others, the government of Kenya or a donor agency invites KWAHO's collaboration in implementing a project. In either case, KWAHO staff, working closely with the Kenyan ministry of water development, visit the proposed project site to meet with community members and help them to identify, assess, and prioritize their water-related needs and problems. Invariably the community is urged to develop its own plan of action. KWAHO supplies trained fieldworkers, but is committed to building teams consisting of both experts and local people. Working together, these teams set specific goals, form committees, identify resources, collect funds, and select a specific technology (KWAHO advocates no specific type of water pump; the organization continually tests different models).

Next, a publicity campaign is mounted, and on-site training of field staff in the chosen technology begins. KWAHO provides the pump, but the community must maintain it. Community members are trained in leadership, management, health education, and bookkeeping, and training materials are developed so that community members will be prepared to care for their new facility and monitor and evaluate its use. Once the project is up and running, KWAHO's assistance is gradually phased out.

KWAHO's approach to water and sanitation is an integrated one. The organization's projects go well beyond the provision of safe, accessible water supplies, for a source of clean water only begins to answer communities' needs. So that a community can fully realize the health benefits of a new water system, numerous related projects are undertaken. Depending on the needs of the particular community, these may include workshops in personal hygiene (bathing, clothes washing and drying, and hand washing); environmental health (residential ventilation, lighting, and cleanliness); safe food preparation; household waste disposal; or drainage. KWAHO may also help the community to develop health education materials, start up a school health program, or establish community organizations for water-source cleaning and maintenance. A *harambee* (pull together) spirit develops, and often leads to still wider health and education efforts.

Women and children are the primary beneficiaries of KWAHO projects, since traditionally they are the community members who queue for, draw, and carry drinking water. Once a KWAHO water project is in place, the women of a beneficiary community enjoy more free time. With KWAHO training and support, many have become involved in income-generating activities (such as brick or tile making, handicrafts, or small farming); environmental activities (such as planting trees, terracing, or erecting fences to protect gardens from animals); or adult education. In addition, it is often a community's women who maintain and repair its water pump.

KWAHO has many partners. We are in partnership with the government of Kenya, which has set for itself a goal of safe water for all by the year 2000. We provide services, such as organizing community activities in support of the implementation and management of community projects, and the government provides technical and engineering services, mostly with the assistance of multilateral and bilateral donors such as the World Bank, UNICEF, the United Nations Development Program (UNDP), the United Nations Fund for Women (UNIFEM), WaterAid (a British NGO based in London), the Swedish International Development Agency (SIDA), the German Technical Cooperation Agency (GTZ), and the Danish Agency for International Development (DANIDA). Our closest governmental partners are the ministries of water development, health, and culture and social services. These ministries have technical know-how, but are not equipped to deal with the social and cultural aspects of planned water and sanitation systems. This is where KWAHO comes in. We support the government of Kenya's ministry of water development initiatives by providing sociological input such as training, conducting surveys, and promoting community involvement, while the ministry provides the physical development—the engineering and actual construction of the water delivery system. In addition, the government of Kenya has entered into partnerships with numerous other NGOs and local communities, and KWAHO has played a liaison role here.

And of course we are in partnership with the local people. Experience in Kenya has shown that when the potential beneficiaries of a water supply project are not themselves involved in running and maintaining the scheme, it is likely to end long before the pump itself breaks down. So we have developed the idea of community management, as opposed to community participation. It is our business to help people manage—not just participate in—their own affairs, to have the ultimate authority and responsibility for decision making about the use of available resources and day-to-day operations related to water supply and sanitation. We do this by employing a strategy we call "integrated community management systems." Under this strategy, a community is involved in the conception, planning, design, implementation, maintenance, and evaluation of the work. Our main thrust is to promote community ownership. Ownership is crucial if you are in the business of community management.

Our partnership with the people of Kenya is permanent, but eventually

KWAHO will become independent of donor support. Already we are moving in this direction by providing our services to the government on a consulting basis. We realize that we cannot be supported forever; donors are getting tired, and we are also feeling increasingly demeaned by the process. The best thing we can do is eventually to have a wonderful, long, loving divorce.

Over the last fourteen years, we have developed and tested a methodology that we call HUMASA. The word is an acronym made up of the first two letters of three Kiswahili words: *huduma* (services to humankind), *maji* (water), and *safi* (safe drinking). Using the HUMASA methodology, KWAHO has managed to grow in size from a single coordinator in 1980 to a staff of 152 today, so there is every indication that this methodology is effective and will be workable through the 1990s and beyond.

Briefly, the HUMASA methodology is based on these principles:

- that a healthy and productive community is a prerequisite to the economic development of a nation;

- that communities themselves know the solutions to their own problems;

- that women are the latent motivating force for change in local communities, and their empowerment to participate is a prerequisite for the success of any community-based project;

- that local-level grassroots organizations are crucial for sustainable development (including water projects);

- that with well-coordinated, consistent support from agencies for financial, logistical, and local institutional capacity building, communities are capable of pulling themselves out of the cycle of poverty; and

- that through participatory training programs, communities are capable of building their own intellectual base for addressing issues relating to their environment.

The HUMASA approach aims to provide women with the opportunity to engage in income-generating activities during their free time. After they are finished securing safe water in their villages, we ask them, what is it that you want to do with your free time? Do you want to make more babies? Do you want to install affordable solar-powered machinery in the village? What is it you want to do? And we help them do whatever is possible.

At the same time, alongside these projects, we have also introduced health education materials. These are published in Kiswahili, which is the national language, and also in Luo, which is the language of western Kenya, around Lake Victoria. We have also published in English. Our extension workers, popularly known as water for health assistants or WAHAs, sit down with women's groups and help them to use these materials.

Historically, KWAHO's main concern has been to realize safe water and sanitation for Kenya's rural areas, where most of the Kenyan people live. During its ten years of existence as an NGO, the organization has initiated water and sanitation projects in all eight provinces of Kenya but one. A project we undertook in Kwale, a poor, rural district on the coast, south of Mombasa, populated by almost half a million people, exemplifies KWAHO's work in rural areas (see Ogana 1989). Water was in short supply in Kwale. The area suffers seasonal droughts; its wells, deep enough to be dangerous to water-drawers (mostly women and girls), were too shallow to provide water reliably all year round; the water was often impure, causing a wide variety of chronic illnesses; and in the average household in Kwale someone had to fetch water eight times daily, often carting heavy containers two miles or more each way in the process. When wells in the district dried up, this distance was increased. The only alternative, purchasing water, strained household budgets—when there was water to purchase.

In 1984, in cooperation with the ministry of water development and with support from the World Bank, UNIFEM, and SIDA, KWAHO started a pilot program in Kwale district intended to provide safe water to some fifty thousand people in fifty villages. Dangerous wells were covered over, the water ministry drilled one hundred new boreholes, and KWAHO helped community members to install new handpumps. The villagers were involved in the project from the beginning. In the planning stages, they identified their needs and priorities and helped choose the locations for their new water points. Later, they formed water committees responsible for operations and maintenance. Eventually, they assumed full responsibility for their new facilities. Today, with the help of over twenty community-based KWAHO extension workers, all women, they provide security for the water sources, maintain and clean the pumps, and handle all finances.

The results have been dramatic: a 50 percent reduction in the number of cases of diarrhea and vomiting in the villages with new, safe water sources, less illness of other kinds, far less walking, and greater ease in drawing water to the surface. The pilot project was so successful that it was expanded to cover the whole of Kwale district, with a population of approximately 700,000 people.

Recently, KWAHO has begun to expand its once exclusively rural focus by venturing into peri-urban areas, with a view toward helping city dwellers to improve their water, environment, and sanitation situation. Where water and sanitation are concerned, peri-urban settings present quite different problems from rural ones. For example, the pit latrine systems that have been developed over the years are appropriate for areas where there is plenty of land to construct new latrines when old ones have been filled up, but in peri-urban areas any empty bit of land is needed for living space first and foremost—with or without regard to sanitation amenities. It is also the case that clean, safe water may be harder to access in peri-urban settings because these settlements are usually informal and illegal, and in any case these communities tend not to be tightly knit (see Kinley 1992:17).

The Kibera peri-urban project is a good example of KWAHO's new peri-urban initiatives. Kibera is located on the outskirts of Nairobi, and consists of some eight squatter settlements with a population of about 200,000 people—fifteen or twenty thousand people per square kilometer. Sanitation is poor; there are too few pit latrines, no garbage collection, poorly maintained wastewater drains, and an inadequate supply of clean water. Children in particular suffer in Kibera; whereas the infant mortality rate in Kenya is eighty-three per thousand live births, in Nairobi, mostly because of peri-urban settlements like Kibera, it is ninety-two per thousand.

KWAHO is currently engaged in a number of activities in Kibera. It has installed eleven water storage tanks, which enable the women of Kibera to buy water at wholesale prices and then sell it inexpensively to community residents. This helps the saleswomen to realize income, and makes safe water more available in the community. KWAHO has also been assisting female weavers to modernize their craft and market their wares, thereby enhancing their income and raising their standard of living. Elderly residents of Kibera visit a KWAHO center for meals, recreation, a new awareness of personal hygiene and environmental sanitation, and income-generating advice. And fourteen ventilated, improved pit latrines have been constructed for demonstration purposes. Finally, when community residents raised the problem of a lack of unoccupied land on which to construct new latrines to replace filled ones, KWAHO arranged for an "exhaust van," a vehicle that removes wastes from filled latrines.

KWAHO has succeeded in its primary objective, to support local communities' efforts to gain access to safe water, sanitation, and the health improvements these can bring. In the future, in addition to providing communities with the opportunity to secure an adequate supply of safe water, KWAHO will continue to encourage community development so that local people can establish enterprises funded and run completely by themselves. We at KWAHO have found it very useful indeed to sit with people, to talk with them, to plan with them, to work with them, to succeed with them, and also at times to fail with them. By taking an advisory role only, and by encouraging communities to make all their own decisions, KWAHO has been able to lead people from behind.

Notes

The editors thank David Kinley of the World Bank for his contributions to this chapter.

1. There is little evidence that Kenya will soon achieve population stability (Jordan et al. 1994:53). When the country's demographic situation is graphed, the pyramid that emerges—a broad base representing the many people under the age of fifteen tapering to a needle-thin tip representing the very few people over the age of sixty-five—is a classic portrait of population growth. —Ed.

References

Jordan, Terry G., Mona Domosh, and Lester Rowntree. 1994. *The Human Mosaic: A Thematic Introduction to Cultural Geography.* 6th ed. New York: HarperCollins.

Kinley, David. 1992. "Kenya: Bringing Village People into Planning." *Source* 4(1):14–18.

Ogana, Winnie. 1989. "Kenya: The Water That Brings New Life." In *Against All Odds: Breaking the Poverty Trap.* Ed. Donatus de Silva, 112–30. Washington, D.C.: Panos Institute.

Chapter 8

Indoor Air Pollution, Household Health, and Appropriate Technology

Women and the Indoor Environment in Sri Lanka

Emma Crewe

E nergy is necessary for human survival, and running a household demands large amounts of it. Part of the energy required comes from
fuel, which for half the people in the world means biomass fuels—wood,
charcoal, dung, or agricultural residues. These fuels provide heat for cooking in most of the economically poor countries of the South, where a typical cookstove consists of three stones covered with mud or clay to form a
U-shape. Biomass fuels are also used for space heating, lighting, drying
crops, and keeping insects at bay. Such fuels are usually much cheaper
than the kinds of fuel on which the North relies, but they are time-con-
suming to collect, often in short supply, and highly polluting when not
burned efficiently.

Another kind of energy needed to run a household is human energy, as
vital a resource as fuel, although one that is easily and frequently overlooked. People who cook and heat with biomass fuels—almost entirely
women—must invest huge amounts of their own energy, not to mention
time and often money as well, in procuring and using these fuels. In parts
of Gujarat, India, women routinely spend four or five hours a day gathering fuel, and in areas of sub-Saharan Africa, most notably the Gambia,
they regularly walk from midday to nightfall in search of wood
(Dankelman and Davidson 1988:69).

When biomass fuel is burned in a poorly ventilated house, the pollution
it produces is distributed throughout the house via smoke, contributing to
a wide range of adverse health conditions including chronic obstructive
lung disorders, associated heart diseases, lung cancer, impaired fetal development, eye infections, and acute respiratory infections (ARI). ARIs
alone are the biggest killer of children in the countries of the South, annually taking the lives of four to five million children under the age of five; in

terms of disability-adjusted life years (DALYs), acute respiratory infections cause an annual loss of 119 million DALYs versus 117 for diarrhea and intestinal worm infections (World Bank 1993:91).

A woman cooking with wood or dung in an unventilated room is exposed to the equivalent of more than a hundred cigarettes a day. The need to reduce indoor air pollution from cooking fires is so urgent that it has been identified, in a recent World Development Report, as one of four priority areas for protecting the environment (World Bank 1992:2). The 1993 World Development Report states: "reducing indoor air pollution from very high to low levels could potentially halve the incidence of children's pneumonia." Moreover, "Comprehensive improvement in indoor air quality in the developing countries might avert a loss of 24 million disability-adjusted life years each year by reducing the burden of acute respiratory diseases by 15 percent and of respiratory tract cancers by 10 percent" (World Bank 1993:92).

A related health consequence of using biomass fuels, typically in open fires or unshielded stoves, is injury from burns, scalds, and fires. This greatly concerns women because it is their babies and small children, hovering around the fire while their mothers work, who are usually the victims. The accuracy of the German proverb "the kitchen kills more than the sword" is unimpeachable.

Cooking, and the many chores related to it, can take a rural woman in Africa, Asia, or Latin America between two and twelve hours a day. Most women who work in the kitchen spend at least a quarter of every day there, in addition to the time they spend outside the house acquiring fuel. Often a women must seek help with the task of collecting large quantities of wood, dung, or other fuel. It is usually her children, particularly her daughters, who provide it, which may keep them away from school. Fuel collecting is a physically demanding chore with negative consequences that are both specific (for example, it can cause exhaustion and back injuries) and general (it can restrict the collector's involvement in other activities). In areas where fuel is in short supply, usually because of deforestation brought about by land clearance for agriculture or commercial timber operations, fuelwood collection is particularly burdensome.

Faced with a fuel shortage, a woman may turn to inferior, smokier fuels, particularly dung. This is an environmental problem in itself, since dung is more safely and effectively used as a fertilizer. She may cook food for less time, or boil less of the water her household uses. She may serve her family more leftovers from the meal before or the day before, or purchase more expensive, ready-made foods. She may prepare fewer meals—perhaps only one rather than two or three meals a day—or cook less food per meal. These coping strategies can have a disastrous impact on nutrition for all household members, but especially for the woman herself, since she is already likely to be malnourished and overworked. If she lives in a rural area, she must spend more and more of her time collecting fuel as it becomes more scarce. If she lives in an urban area, she must purchase increasingly expensive fuel with money that could be better spent on other needs.

Poor health as a result of dependence on dwindling supplies of biomass fuels potentially affects half the world's population. The problem, however, is often neglected. People concerned about environmental issues usually focus instead on problems associated with high technology encountered in the public domain, such as global atmospheric pollution, nuclear waste, and occupational hazards in factories. Certainly these deserve our attention, but in much of the world, including rural areas of Africa, Asia, and Latin America, the less visible dangers related to the use of biomass fuels in the domestic domain are both more immediate and more widespread. When pollution experts do study the indoor environment, they tend to concentrate on problems associated with tobacco smoke or gas stoves in Europe and North America. Yet a gas stove releases only one-fiftieth of the pollution emitted by a wood-burning stove.

What accounts for the widespread neglect of the negative health and environmental impacts of biomass fuel use in poor households? It is not that the hazards associated with biomass-burning stoves affect only a small number of people; kitchen workers are the second biggest occupational group in the world, after farmers. At least a half billion—probably a billion—women work in kitchens; the fact that the number is unknown reflects how little research has been done in this area. Neither is it the case that the environmental hazards associated with unsafe stoves are being ignored for lack of solutions; fifteen years of work in the field of household energy have shown that successful or potentially successful technology interventions are readily available—mainly simple technologies emanating from the appropriate technology (AT) movement.[1]

Appropriate technologies respect the environment, conserve resources, and allow local people to make decisions affecting their lives. Thus, rather than promoting foreign kerosene stoves dependent on an expensive fuel that usually has to be imported, advocates of AT would recommend that existing stove-making technologies be upgraded to make stoves safer and more fuel efficient. Industries for the manufacture of more efficient stoves have been established in a number of countries, most notably China, India, Kenya, and Sri Lanka. Yet despite the fact that viable solutions exist, the international development agencies have reduced, and in many cases abandoned, biomass energy development at the household level.

The main reason why household energy management, indoor air pollution, and other health consequences of unsafe kitchens are receiving so little attention is that the managers of energy resources in households are almost always women. In all cultures women's status tends to be lower than men's, which often means that neither women's household problems nor the technical expertise they can bring to bear on these problems are taken seriously enough. Moreover, household work everywhere is unpaid, invisible, low-status work which is not included in national economic statistics. Yet the enormous amount of time it takes a woman to do this work has significant implications for the health of her entire family.

The successful creation of a stove industry in Sri Lanka demonstrates that appropriate technologies can alleviate health problems associated with household energy. In Sri Lanka rural women spend up to eight hours a day preparing meals for their households, typically on three-stone cookstoves. These stoves burn wood, the major source of fuel energy for the 94 percent of Sri Lankan people who cannot afford other, more costly fuels such as electricity or kerosene. Most Sri Lankan stoves in use today burn fuel relatively inefficiently, produce high levels of smoke, and are, at best, only partly shielded. They cause all the health problems associated with similar stoves used elsewhere in the South, from air pollution to injuries to the diverse detrimental effects of biomass fuel acquisition.

In 1979, a Sri Lankan grassroots organization, Sarvodaya, began trying to improve the basic U-shaped Sri Lankan stove in consultation with villagers and with assistance from Intermediate Technology Development Group, an international private voluntary organization with offices in Asia, Africa, Latin America, and the United Kingdom. Initially, male villagers dominated the stove improvement process, as they were accustomed to having a greater say than women in the development of new technologies. Once women were given the opportunity to test various stove prototypes in their homes, however, they began to use their cooking and fuel management expertise to suggest modifications. Technicians who had left a new stove in a woman's kitchen for a few weeks would return to hear her complain that it cracked too easily or was difficult to light, or that it didn't accommodate her cooking pots adequately. Design improvements would follow.

After a protracted process of research development, the most popular new design proved to be a simple, two-piece clay liner held together with mud. One piece, large and cylindrical, shields the fire and holds a cooking pot above the flames. The fire is fed through a hole in its side. Attached to this is a tunnel-shaped piece through which the air passes. Connected to it is a separate disc of clay that supports a second cooking pot. To install the new stove, the pieces are assembled and cemented together with mud, ash, clay, and straw. Called the Sarvodaya stove, this design results in improved combustion, better heat retention, and 20 to 40 percent reductions in both fuel consumption and time spent cooking.

As newly designed stoves began to be used in Sri Lankan homes, the project attracted the attention of the government. In 1984, in response to a government-sponsored report on the rapid rate of deforestation in Sri Lanka, the ministry of power and energy began promoting the new stoves as a means of conserving woodfuel energy. Through an extensive government network, women began buying Sarvodaya stoves by the thousands. There was one problem, however: the distribution system relied on subsidies which were provided by the Dutch government. Determined to establish a sustainable way of making fuel-efficient stoves accessible without outside funding, the ministry of power and energy decided to work through existing markets for ceramic products. For this they needed a more portable stove, one that could easily be sold through local shops and wholesalers. Again the project's implementers sought advice from stove users—this time two hundred women who tested various models and whose opinions and suggestions were collected in a household survey. The majority chose an adapted, portable version of the original Sarvodaya pottery stove. This model, called the Anagi stove, uses roughly a third less fuel, saves a third of the time spent cooking, and produces less smoke than traditional stoves and open fires.

Making pottery stoves requires only a very small capital investment and no new skills; artisans can begin production after only a few days of instruction. To make the stoves, potters (both men and women) find local clays—often two or more varieties which, when blended, produce a durable finished product—and knead these together with water. They then use potter's wheels to fashion the stove's parts, which are fitted together when semidry. Finished stoves are allowed to dry fully before being fired in kilns.

The new stoves began to be distributed through stalls, markets, and ceramic retailers in 1988. Each costs less than the local equivalent of U.S.$2, an amount that is returned to the purchaser in the form of savings on fuel (for those who buy their fuel) within three months. The ministry of power and energy and, since 1990, a private voluntary organization called Integrated Development Association have publicized the stoves by demonstrating their advantages in schools, hospitals, and villages, and by explaining how they work on the radio and television, in posters and leaflets, and on billboards. It is estimated through large-scale surveys that 50 to 60 percent of Sri Lankan women currently know about the stoves, mostly due to this energetic publicity campaign. The most effective advertising, however, has been the recommendation of those who have already bought stoves. To ensure that its advertising focuses on the stove's prioritized benefits and that the design continues to be favored, project staff continually survey the cooks' responses. Most women report that the stove's most valuable feature is that it frees up their time, so this benefit is stressed by stove sellers.

So far, even though the improved stoves have won remarkable popularity—over half a million are in use—the stove program has failed to meet its original goal of energy conservation. The effect of the program on combatting deforestation has been at best only marginal, since trees are cut in Sri Lanka not so much for fuel as to clear land for agriculture and to provide timber for the construction industry. And although the program has successfully raised the average income of potters, most of the financial benefits so far have been reaped by a relatively small number of male potters.

Nevertheless, the program has conveyed significant health and environmental benefits on Sri Lankan women and their families. First and foremost, the improved stoves have reduced the burdensome workload of Sri Lankan women. The time spent in cooking has decreased, a benefit that is highly valued by women who previously spent up to eight hours a day in food preparation. Since the new stoves require less fuel to produce the same amount of heat as is given off by traditional stoves, some women have also been able to reduce the amount of time they spend acquiring fuel. Sri Lankan cooks have also found that the new stoves save cleaning time; since they emit less smoke, they leave less soot and tar to be scrubbed from cooking pots. A lighter workload not only contributes to women's health in itself, it also increases opportunities for women and other family members to achieve better health by allowing them more time to rest, visit clinics, attend school, prepare more nutritious food, or earn more money.

Second, thanks to improved combustion, the new stoves have helped to alleviate health problems caused by airborne pollution. Although the direct impact on health of using the new stoves has not yet been measured, benefits surely include reductions in the incidence of lung diseases, eye infections, and acute respiratory infections through lower smoke emissions (World Health Organization 1991). Women and children are the primary beneficiaries of these improvements.

In addition to alleviating women's workload and reducing indoor pollution, the new stoves undoubtedly convey more direct health benefits on Sri Lankan women and their families. Increases in the amount of food cooked, in the thoroughness with which food is cooked, or in the amount or frequency of water boiling should lead to lower risks of undernutrition, ailments caused by undercooked foods, and water-borne diseases such as diarrhea, dysentery, and cholera.

Users of the new technology have reported ancillary benefits as well, thanks largely to the efforts of extension workers who have taken advantage of their stove promotion role to make householders more conscious of safety, hygiene, diet, and adequate ventilation. During their visits to households, they have stressed the importance of boiling water, introduced householders to the components of a balanced diet, and explored possibilities for better ventilation. Some stove promoters, for example, have suggested installing wooden racks above fireplaces. These are useful for drying crops, wood, and clothes, and also serve to keep these items away from the flames and thus reduce the risk of accidental fires. Stoves with chimneys are more expensive and difficult to maintain, so promoters have recommended instead that hoods be placed over stoves to catch any remaining smoke and direct it outdoors, or that stoves be placed near windows, allowing smoke to escape. Thus the new technology appears to be serving as a springboard not only to reducing indoor air pollution but also to improving people's health and living conditions generally. Meanwhile the stove industry thrives, with ever more potters requesting training in stove-making.

The success in Sri Lanka has not yet been matched in all countries that depend upon biomass energy. One reason is that the emphasis technicians put on fuel efficiency, at the cost of women's priorities, has often resulted in low acceptance of new stoves. In mountainous areas of Nepal, Fiji, and Guatemala, for example, space heating is more important to women than fuel conservation, so well-insulated, fuel-efficient stoves are not popular (Gill 1987:138). Another reason why appropriate stove technologies may be resisted is the continuing imbalance in gender relations in many parts of the world. Smith attributes the failings of technology in general to male dominance. Appropriate technology, like capital-intensive technology, tends to be promoted by men, who adhere to androcentric values that dictate that "men have the technical skills and make the technical decisions" (Smith 1983:66). Certainly appropriate technology on its own cannot transform women's social and political position, despite its positive effect on their relative control over resources and decision making. Finally, even the Sri Lankan stove program has not benefited the most resource-poor women, because the stove, although cheap at around U.S.$1.50, is beyond their financial means.

In the long term, clean alternatives to biomass fuels, such as those provided by new solar or micro-hydro technologies, will no doubt become available in Africa, Asia, and Latin America. However, without the political will to promote them, the majority of people in the South—particularly poor people—will have no alternative but to rely on wood, dung, or other biomass fuels. But the technology they will use can, at least, be improved if they wish. Perhaps the most immediately obvious benefit of the new stove technology is the reduction in indoor air pollution. Broadly speaking, however, its most significant contribution is that women who use it can now spend much less of their time on cooking, fuel collecting, and other stove-related chores. The implications of this for the health and well-being of both women and their children are incalculable.

Notes

The author and the volume editors thank Peter Young and Peter Watts of Intermediate Technology Development Group, United Kingdom, for their helpful comments on a draft of this chapter.

1. Begun in the 1960s by E. F. Schumacher, "appropriate technology" not only encourages the use of culturally appropriate, low-tech devices, but also embodies the philosophy of helping the poor to help themselves rather than simply transferring equipment or ideas from North to South. In his now-classic book, *Small is Beautiful*, Schumacher (1974) argued that high technology is beyond the financial reach of economically underdeveloped countries; it steals rather than generates job opportunities; and the work it provides is usually dehumanizing and undignified. Exporting it from North to South is socially and environmentally damaging, causes maintenance problems, and induces dependency. Four principles devised by Schumacher continue to guide the AT movement's promotion of low-cost technology: development should benefit those in greatest need; workplaces should be capital-saving rather than capital-intensive; production methods should be simple, so that skills required can be accessible to all; and production should rely mainly on local materials.

References

Dankelman, Irene, and Joan Davidson. 1988. *Women and Environment in the Third World: Alliance for the Future.* London: Earthscan Publications.

Gill, Jas. 1987. "Improving Stoves in Developing Countries: A Critique." *Energy Policy* 15(2):135–43.

Schumacher, E. F. 1974. *Small is Beautiful: A Study of Economics as if People Mattered.* London: Abacus.

Smith, Judy. 1983. "Women and Appropriate Technology: A Feminist Assessment." In *The Technological Woman: Interfacing with Tomorrow.* Ed. Jan Zimmerman, 65–74. New York: Praeger.

World Bank. 1992. *World Development Report 1992: Development and the Environment.* New York: Oxford University Press.

————. 1993. *World Development Report 1993: Investing in Health.* New York: Oxford University Press.

World Health Organization (WHO). 1991. *Epidemiological, Social and Technical Aspects of Indoor Air Pollution from Biomass Fuel.* Report of a WHO consultation. Geneva.

Part IV

Environmental Politics: Grassroots Activism and the Search for Environmental Justice

Photo credit: D. Kakkak

Indigenous Environmental Network 1993 Conference
Sac & Fox Nation, Stroud, Oklahoma, USA

Part IV

Introduction

Industries often produce hazardous wastes as by-products. Some countries with strict regulations governing the disposal of these by-products export these hazardous materials to less strictly regulated countries (CIR 1990). The payment offered by exporters often makes it difficult for the potential receivers of these hazardous wastes to resist. A related problem is the migration of "dirty" industries out of developed nations, where labor is often more expensive and environmental protection regulations more strict, into less developed, less expensive, less strictly regulated nations (LaDou 1991). The goods produced are returned to the developed world, leaving unwanted by-products behind. In neither case are local residents generally well informed about the effects, short- or long-term, of living near dirty industries or toxic industrial by-products.

Both in the United States and elsewhere, the same pattern can be discerned: communities that can be differentiated from others on the basis of socioeconomic status or ethnicity are more likely than other communities to be located near hazardous waste dumps, polluting industries, landfills, waste treatment facilities, or other dangerous, environmentally harmful, or aesthetically undesirable projects (Bullard 1993). There is ongoing debate about whether this kind of discrimination is economic or intentionally racist. Either way, the result is the same: healthy surroundings for some groups at the expense of others.

In the United States in the early 1980s, representatives of African American, Indigenous, Latino, and other groups began to organize, both internally and collaboratively, to protest this kind of discrimination in their communities and to fight for the right to a healthy environment. Today their efforts, known as the environmental justice movement, are drawing increasing attention to the human rights aspects of what had once been treated as primarily economic decisions on the disposal of toxic wastes and the siting of dirty industries.[1]

The agenda of the environmental justice movement includes working toward four goals: (1) a more equitable distribution of undesirable industries among those who use the products of these industries; (2) new regulatory measures; (3) stricter enforcement of existing industrial regulations; and (4) insistence on wider access to information about the present and planned locations of polluting industries, their products and by-products, and their impact on physical and cultural environments. In general, the groups that advocate for environmental justice are more ideologically inclusive than other grassroots environmental protection organizations, since they view problems of social exploitation as inseparable from the exploitation of the natural world.

Part IV explores the history and contemporary reality of the fight for environmental justice through the personal experiences and observations of representatives of three different groups in the United States: Appalachian farmers, Indigenous peoples, and urban African Americans. The situations described by the chapter authors cover a wide range of environmental problems, but their stories are linked by the view that environmental equality should be a basic human right.

Appalachian Farmers

Human-made environmental problems are more difficult to address than those caused by objective, external threats such as climatic events or particular disease vectors. This is because such problems are rooted in people's self-interests, and resolving them often requires choosing between diametrically opposed values. Industry, for instance, may raise the income of some, but at the same time its by-products may have detrimental effects on the health of others. When they attempt to stop polluting industries and insist on environmental justice, groups organized around issues of community safety or environmental protection may be ignored or disparaged, even at the local level; and in extreme cases, they may face harassment, violence, or death. In some cases, the greatest sources of harassment are other members of environmental activists' own communities, who fear losing their jobs more than they fear environmental threats to their health and safety.

The difficulty of resolving the environmental problems of one group to the perceived detriment of another is illustrated in chapter 9, by Kentucky farmer, community organizer, and environmental justice advocate Larry Wilson. Wilson describes the efforts of citizen-activists to bring a life-threatening health problem, a water supply polluted by industrial effluents, to the attention of the appropriate authorities.

Indigenous Peoples

Many Indigenous peoples around the world question the pace and direction of industrialization, and particularly economic development, which in their view has led not to "progress" but instead to the degradation of their local environments, economies, cultural and spiritual lives. Health and socioeconomic indicators for Indigenous peoples worldwide reflect, in part, the long-term negative public health and social impacts of poorly planned development projects, many of them undertaken to meet the economic goals and consumption levels of non-Indigenous people.

In the United States, Indigenous communities, perhaps because of their special status as government protectorates, have often had government land-use decisions imposed upon them. Some, for example, have become repositories for hazardous wastes produced during weapons development by the United States military and its contractors, with a myriad of adverse health consequences. In response, Indigenous peoples in North America are joining forces with others to insist that misuse, abuse, and disrespect of land, water, air, and people cannot be tolerated. In chapter 10, Indigenous women activists Nilak Butler and Winona LaDuke describe the fundamental differences in values between industrial societies and societies with traditions of dependence on natural resources. These are distinctions that can help us reshape our attitudes, perceptions, and policies regarding the relationship of human beings with the natural world. The chapter focuses on some of the consequences of attempts to impose human rules on natural conditions, including violations of the cultures and human rights of Indigenous peoples by the widespread practice of dumping nuclear and toxic wastes on or near their lands.

Urban African Americans

Some proponents of environmental justice assert that communities of people of color in the United States have been specifically targeted as sites for unwelcome development, and that this is a continuing vestige of the sub-human treatment of individuals based solely on skin color (Bullard 1993). While there has been considerable movement in the direction of racial equality in the United States since the abolition of slavery, in environmental matters, communities of people of color have often been excluded from the decision-making process. As a result, this kind of community is more likely than others to find itself host to a municipal waste incinerator or other hazardous waste facility (Bullard 1993).

In chapter 11, civil rights and environmental activist Vernice D. Miller presents her view of "environmental racism." She traces the planning decisions that culminated in the placement of a waste treatment plant in a once-pleasant urban community of color, and details the detrimental effects of the plant on the community and the response of its citizens. Miller argues that the ability of communities to shape and control their own environments should be considered a basic human right, and suggests that if environmental racism is to be deterred, members of communities of color must be full and active participants in both the planning and execution of industrial projects. They must have full access to relevant information and sources of empowerment, and equal roles in the making of decisions and policies.

Together the three chapters in Part IV show how powerfully and eloquently the case for environmental justice can be made by those who strongly believe they have suffered the lack of it. Collectively, the chapter authors highlight several points. First, people living in unhealthy environments, often those who in the past have lacked the economic and political power to avert environmental damage, may be the best qualified to raise public awareness about environmental health problems, mobilize community support and participation, identify the causes of these problems, and begin the search for solutions. Second, organizing and speaking out, even in the face of strongly entrenched political and economic interests, are often essential elements in combatting environmental injustice. Third, on environmental matters there is often a communications gap between local people and outside professionals. Communications between these two groups could be improved if professionals would listen to people at the community level and speak clearly with them. Finally, the chapters collectively highlight the concept of environmental justice as the motivating ideology behind a constructive new approach to environmental problems.

Note

1. Added impetus for the movement grew out of the First National People of Color Environmental Leadership Summit, held in Washington, D.C., in October 1991.

References

Bullard, Robert D. 1993. *Confronting Environmental Racism: Voices from the Grassroots.* Boston: South End Press.

Center for Investigative Reporting (CIR) and Bill Moyers. 1990. *Global Dumping Ground: The International Traffic in Hazardous Waste.* Carson, CA: Seven Locks Press.

LaDou, Joseph. 1991. "Deadly Migration: Hazardous Industries' Flight to the Third World." *Technology Review* 94(5):47–53 (Massachusetts Institute of Technology).

Chapter 9

Fighting Toxic Waste Dumping in Kentucky

Larry Wilson

I come from an area in southeastern Kentucky, in the central Appalachian coalfields, a very rural area, very mountainous, which has been depressed and suppressed for many years. Our greatest claim to fame was that's where President John F. Kennedy discovered poverty in 1960. We were isolated until 1960, and then through a lot of federal grant programs—the infamous "donors"—roads were built and the rest of the world discovered us. We thought they were building the roads to help us, but they built them so they could get the coal out a little better.

We're in the Kentucky Fifth Congressional District, the most rural congressional district in the United States. It's second in poverty behind the South Bronx, it has the highest illiteracy rate in the United States (over 50 percent of the people are functionally illiterate), and it has the highest percentage of unemployment in the United States. A recent University of Kentucky survey showed that we have 56 percent unemployment. I could go on and on, but that gives you the picture.

I want to tell you a little about my home community. In 1980, I was farming on the banks of Yellow Creek. When I say "farm," don't get any grandiose ideas . . . we had eight acres, four of which you could drive a tractor across, if you had a tractor to drive. I was raising dairy goats and vegetables. And in the summer of 1980, there was a drought. At the time, all of us along Yellow Creek, a population of about one thousand people, were getting our drinking water from private wells. And my well went dry. But before I watered my animals from Yellow Creek, I called the city to ask about the water. In eastern Kentucky, a creek should run clear, but this creek looked bad, purple and brown. The city said there was nothing in the water that would hurt anything. So I bought a pump and put it into Yellow Creek. I watered all of my animals, and in ninety days they were all dead—thirty-six hogs, thirteen registered dairy goats, seven cows, two hundred chickens, and various rabbits and other animals.

It didn't take long to trace the problem. The water in that creek was the color of leather. The problem was that a leather-tanning company

107

upstream was dumping three-quarters of a million gallons of waste per day into a municipal sewage treatment plant. The chemical waste from the tannery had destroyed the treatment plant by killing the bacteria and corroding the metal parts. The plant was totally inoperable, so what was coming out of that plant was raw municipal sewage mixed with industrial waste—and it was being dumped into Yellow Creek. Later we saw some EPA daily monitoring reports that showed that what was coming out of the treatment plant was more toxic than what was going in.

My neighbors were facing similar problems. I got together with a couple of them and we decided to form a group, Yellow Creek Concerned Citizens. We organized a meeting and seven people showed up. We talked for a couple of hours, and decided to meet again. At this next meeting we had twelve or fourteen people. Now, thirteen years later, we're still active and we have over 450 people that are dues-paying members of our organization, out of a population of one thousand. It all happened by word of mouth.

The Yellow Creek Concerned Citizens decided to call the problems along Yellow Creek to the attention of the local government, so something would be done about it. That's all you have to do, right? Go tell them what the problem is. We have great environmental laws and we have great health laws, and that'll take care of it. It didn't work that way.

I went to the city council meeting in my little town of ten thousand people. There was a veterinarian on the city council, and I told him that I'd lost thirty-six hogs because they drank out of Yellow Creek. And I'll never forget his response. He said, "Mr. Wilson, can you prove that those hogs didn't have a heart attack?" So we kind of lost our faith in veterinary science.

We decided to do our own health survey, and it wasn't long before we found out there were more problems than just the hogs dying. You know, what'll kill a hog will kill a person. So we started looking at problems. We went door to door, and we found what we thought was twice the number of pregnancy problems and reproductive problems that we should have. We found what we thought was twice the average incidence of leukemia among our children. We found over ten times the expected rate of cancer, overall. We found central nervous system problems. We found liver problems, gastrointestinal problems, kidney problems. But nobody would listen, because our survey wasn't a professional survey. It was biased because we had done it ourselves. We couldn't get anybody to take us seriously. We couldn't get any of the medical profession, no one from the public health profession, no one from the universities, no government agency to take us seriously. They actually accused us of having something to gain by proving that we were dying—as if we wanted to know that.

So we took this information to our U.S. representative. He said, "Aha, we can prove you wrong," and he called in the Centers for Disease Control. They did a leukemia survey, and they proved us wrong—we didn't have twice the average incidence of leukemia, we had 4.75 times the average. And that was one of the lesser problems.

They refused to look any further, and said that our population base was so small that our findings were statistically insignificant and therefore no action was necessary. They calculated that there was only a 3 percent chance this could have happened randomly. And they said there had to be less than a 3 percent chance it could happen randomly before they would take action.

Let me give you a little tour through our valley to show you exactly what I'm talking about. It's a small valley; there's not over fifteen or twenty houses. Most of the people who live in them are related to me. As you first come into the valley, my first cousin lives there. They lost their daughter at thirty-two from cancer. The next house was a schoolteacher; he died in his sixties of cancer. The next is another first cousin—they don't have a problem yet, but across the road from them is the house of a good friend where one of the daughters died from cancer—she was in her twenties—and the mother died from cancer. Then you come to another house where the gentleman died of cancer. Across the road is my aunt and uncle. He has cancer of the prostate; she just had a breast removed with cancer. Next there's my parents' house. My father died of pancreatic cancer, my mother currently has cancer. Next there's my house. My oldest daughter just had a baby. Something went wrong, and we had to rush her to the hospital at the University of Tennessee. We almost lost her. My youngest daughter just lost a baby. My son has central nervous system damage. He can't see. We think it's from heavy metal poisoning. The next house is my cousin . . . he just had a lung removed because of Wagner's disease, an immune system problem. His wife has colon cancer. I think I'll stop there.

We tried to talk to the doctors and nurses at our local health department. We called them and asked to be put on the agenda for their next meeting. The way it works in Kentucky, the chief executive officer of the county—we're kind of archaic, they still call the executive officer a county judge, but he's not a judge, he's an administrative person—is the chair of the board of health. So we called the judge and asked him when the next meeting would be. He said he didn't know. We asked him if we could find out, and he said "No, the administrator of the health department sets meetings as necessary, so call him." So we called the administrator of the health department and he said "I don't know when we're going to meet; I just call meetings whenever the judge tells me to." So we went into a public court meeting where the judge was presiding, and asked him formally for a meeting date. He promised he would set one and let us know. Later he called us and told us when the next meeting would be held. We went to the meeting; nobody was there. Finally he sent a message over saying it had been canceled.

A few days later, we found that they'd had the meeting, but they'd moved it to a different part of town to avoid us. Why? The tanning company was inside the city limits, so it was the city's responsibility to treat the wastes, but they were ignoring it because the tanning waste didn't affect people living in the city, only people outside the city limits. And for political reasons the board of health wouldn't oppose anything the city government or the tanning company was doing. To make a long story short, it took us three months just to attend a public health meeting, even though by law these meetings have to be held once a month and they're supposed to be announced publicly.

When we finally got through to some of the local doctors and showed them some of the data we'd gathered, they agreed that Yellow Creek should be posted against all water contact. We didn't get any help from the city council. The Yellow Creek Concerned Citizens raised the money, bought the signs, and put them up by themselves. Then we went to the city council to ask them to stop the sewage treatment plant from receiving waste from the tannery because they couldn't treat it. And things got very heated. They told us to go home and shut up, that it was none of our business, that we didn't live in the city limits, we only lived downstream from the city, and for us not to cause trouble because we would cost four hundred jobs at the tanning company.

So we started really making a lot of noise. We felt that was the only way we could get attention. We went to the state, we went to the U.S. Environmental Protection Agency (EPA). We worked for three years with the city and the EPA, and in the end we signed a plan, called a consent decree, we could all live with. The EPA assessed fines. At one time they fined the city and tannery two million dollars, but the city said it couldn't pay, so the city and the EPA negotiated. Together they lowered the standards in the consent decree so the city could meet them, and they lowered the fines too. The city still hasn't paid a dollar in fines. That was about ten years ago.

When we started really speaking out, strange things started happening. A friend and I were driving down the road and the windshield of my pickup truck disintegrated. The state trooper picked up the wadding out of a twenty-gauge shotgun from between my legs. My wife's brake lines were cut. My oldest son was kicked off the local football team, and told "If you can get your father to shut up, you can play football for us again." My daughter was followed home from work every day. Another friend was shot at. His car was shot up pretty badly. Another one had the lug nuts on his truck loosened so when he went across a railroad track it fell apart. Our family dog was poisoned. I got a phone call afterward, saying, "Have you found your dog?" Well, I had—it was in the yard, dead. And the fellow said "Just keep in mind that what happened to your dog could happen to one of your children."

Yellow Creek is only one little community and one story, but it isn't unique. People in communities just like Yellow Creek have been subjected to similar harassment. There has been arson, there have been assassination attempts and car bombings. At a public meeting in Arizona, community activists were stun-gunned by the police for protesting.

About 1985, we heard about a place called the Highlander Research and Education Center in Newmarket, Tennessee, about a two-hour drive from us. Highlander had been very, very active in community education and community empowerment during the civil rights movement. Dr. Martin Luther King went through a workshop there. So did Andrew Young, Rosa Parks, and several others. They invited us to come to their workshops, and we started going.

At the time I was working for the board of education in my hometown. A board member came up to me and said, "Have you decided to keep your mouth shut yet?" And I said no. He said, "Well, then we don't need you to work here anymore." And so he fired me. Shortly thereafter, Highlander offered me a job. That was in 1985, and I'm still there. They offered me a job because they felt sorry for me. I've been around ever since.

What we do at Highlander is work with communities like Yellow Creek. We try to encourage people, help them realize that they can think for themselves, that they can do things. Along Yellow Creek, for example, our groundwater was so contaminated we couldn't take a bath in it. You would come out with grey slimy stuff on you. We managed to get the American Red Cross to haul drinking water to us. They hauled drinking water to us for two years. We drank it out of plastic milk jugs. We carried water for miles and miles. We had one five-hundred-gallon tank to serve a fourteen mile stretch of creek and about one thousand people for two years. Meanwhile, we wrote our own grant to the state of Kentucky, an imminent threat grant, and we got a water line from a mountain lake to come down through the community. No one else would do it. We researched how to do it ourselves without outside help. We negotiated contracts for land the pipeline would cross. We negotiated with the railroad to be able to cross their tracks several times. We learned how to do it ourselves.

Right now, we are in touch, through Highlander, with over four hundred communities. Our workshops over the last three years have been attended by over a thousand people from forty-five states and fifteen countries. All of these folks, the great overwhelming majority of them, are from communities like Yellow Creek. Ours isn't an isolated story.

What we're learning from this is that we have to do for ourselves, because there seems to be a big, big gap between us and the public health professionals. We have to bridge that gap. A lot of people come in and offer to help, but they want to help on their terms. They want to define the problem. They want to study the problem. They want to design a solution to the problem. And then they want us to help implement their solution. But often it's people in the local communities who know best what their problems are.

We speak different languages, you know. There was a biologist from one of the universities in North Carolina who came through to study the aquatic organisms in Yellow Creek. And we were sitting around at a friend's house talking to her, and she was trying to get a historical data base because the creek at that time was dead, there was nothing in it. The Department of Fish and Wildlife inspected five miles of Yellow Creek and didn't find a thing. And she said, "Did you ever have any hellgrammites in the creek?" Everybody looked at each other and said, "Nope." We had never heard of hellgrammites. A couple of hours later we were talking about how we used to fish in the creek and what we used for bait. And one of the fellows said, "Well, I always liked those grampuses, but they're not in there anymore." And she said "What's a grampus?" And he started describing it to her. She said, "Oh, that's what I was calling a hellgrammite." We knew what was in that creek, but she was getting faulty data because we weren't communicating.

So at the community level we might not speak the technical language of the scientific community. But we can think. And we know our problems. And we have a right to say something about our problems. What we need is assistance, not supervision. We don't need to be spoon-fed information. And we shouldn't be expected to speak the language of the scientific community. They should be expected to speak our language, and to take us seriously.

Take the health survey. We know that we have way too many deaths from cancer, that there's something wrong, that the rate of cancer is too high. We know that. But the scientific community says "Sorry, there aren't enough of you for us to get a good fix on it." So we can't prove whether anything's wrong or not. What is wrong is that we are tied to a certain methodology. We treat it like a god. Let's develop the methodology. Let's listen to the local people. You know . . . when people are dying, they're dying. When they're dead, they're dead. And it's wrong. Nobody has the right to do this to other human beings.

We also have to realize that this is a political and economic problem. We've got to quit trying to treat the symptoms. We've got to try to prevent the problem. And we can do that only by recognizing that it is a political and economic problem and by taking the risk of speaking out. As long as we're motivated by money and power, the problem will never go away. And what's happening in other countries, and especially in the southern countries, is happening to some extent here in the United States. Go look at the Native peoples and look at the black belt. Look at the African American communities, look at the Latino communities and look at the Appalachian communities. We are being wiped out. It's a form of genocide for all of us.

Note

For additional information and publications, contact the Highlander Research and Education Center or the Clearinghouse on Hazardous Wastes (see Resource Organizations at end of book).

Chapter 10

Economic Development and Destruction of Indigenous Lands

Nilak Butler and Winona LaDuke

There are many parts of the world where Indigenous peoples represent a significant part of the population and control a significant proportion of land within those countries. While our issues in North America are very different than in other parts of the world, at the same time there are certain commonalities. The commonalities have to do with sustainable ways of living, and the unsustainability of what we view as industrial society and the impact of that unsustainability on our communities.[1,2]

In Canada, north of the fifty-fifth parallel (the fiftieth parallel in the eastern provinces), the majority population is Native, and occupies approximately two-thirds of the Canadian landmass. In northern Canada, for example, the Inuit territory (Nunavat) is about five times the size of Texas. In North America, there are seven hundred Native communities; two hundred of these are in Alaska and eighty in California alone.

Native peoples in the United States once constituted 100 percent of the population and controlled 100 percent of American lands. Today they represent approximately 1 percent of the population and control less than 4 percent of the land base in the United States. As Native peoples, we look at the issue of population from the distinct vantage point of communities that face extinction. Industrial society has caused the extinction of about two thousand Indigenous nations in the Western Hemisphere in the five hundred years since the invasion.

In terms of numbers, it has been estimated that in 1492, there were 112,554,000 Indigenous people in the Western Hemisphere. By 1980, the number was only 28,264,000 (Venables 1990). And in the past 150 years this society has caused the extinction of more animal species in all the years since the Ice Age. When we talk about how we all collectively need to live, we need to address the issue that a society that causes this level of extinction is not sustainable.

One has to take a historical view of what are considered "expendable populations." There has been a historical view that people of color are primitive people, and people from developing countries are more expendable

113

than people from industrial countries. That somehow we are viewed as people who will come into the fold of industrialization. That somehow, over time, industrial society will turn us from primitive into civilized people, and that there will be some casualties along the way. It is possible that not only is this a racist view, but it is also a view which has been used to justify genocide in our case. We need to change these views of our communities.

The experience of extinction and destruction is not just historical, it is still occurring. For example, in the Brazilian rainforest an average of one Indigenous nation per year has become extinct since 1900. Seventeen Indian nations in the United States were declared extinct by the Bureau of Indian Affairs 1½ years ago. From my own perspective, and from the perspective of many Indigenous people, these are systemic issues, not isolated events.

Native lands are sites of every kind of environmental destruction that exists: logging, pesticides, and the entire "nuclear cycle," as it is called. Native peoples are both the miners and the miners' canary—the little caged bird that miners used to lower down into a mine and whose survival or death would indicate whether or not the mine was safe for human beings. We are the test site, the fuel processing site, the garbage dump.

Native peoples are being asked to play "Let's Make a Deal." If they accept deposits of high level nuclear waste because they're impoverished, they are told it is "economic development" for their community. There is an environmental crisis of major proportions in our communities. Many Native peoples believe that, because of our historic and present relations with the United States and Canadian governments (a colonial relationship in which much of what occurs in our territories is intended not to benefit us, but someone else), we are a microcosm of the larger environmental crisis facing the continent.

We would like to discuss the differences in values between Indigenous and industrial societies. There are certain beliefs that unify many Indigenous peoples. One is the understanding that each one of us comes from Mother Earth. She is a living being, not an exploitable commodity. Just as the earth is so much water and so much land, so are our human bodies. What she is, so are we also.

As human beings, we all share responsibility for the future. We are here today because people suffered and struggled against odds that are very hard for us to imagine. In turn, we have to look forward to future generations. When we consider the nuclear waste issue, it is frightening. For 12,500 generations are going to have to deal with the legacy of our time. That is a terribly heavy responsibility.

There are two views that permeate the world today. The division is not between left and right, or between capitalism and communism. In our perspective, there is an Indigenous or land-based society, and an industrial society. The conflict between these two ways of living has been the basis of the conflict that has been going on in the Western Hemisphere for the past five hundred years.

The issue of consumption, from our perspective, is not a North–South issue. Instead we would suggest that the middle is consuming both the North and the South. The Arctic is being consumed at an accelerated rate. The Free Trade Agreement with Canada has only increased the level of mining, logging, clearing, and dam building in the North. And our communities bear the burden of this consumption.

The level of consumption of industrial society causes constant intervention into other people's countries and other people's lands. Any society that consumes 30 to 40 percent of the world's resources, with only 5 percent of the world's population, requires constant intervention into other people's territories and lands. It is meaningless to talk about human rights or social conditions without talking about the fundamental levels of consumption in this society, which are the cause of interventions, development programs, and exploitation of other people's lands and resources.

The casualty is that our communities face extinction. I believe these are some of the issues for societies all over the world to recognize. For a long-term view, we must see the relationships between cultural diversity and biological diversity. We need to see that cultural monocropping is as dangerous as biological monocropping over the long term. It simply is not sustainable.

I'd like to talk with you about sustainability in our way of living and in our view of the world, because I believe these can offer something for those of you who are in policymaking positions, and for those of you who live in the industrialized world. I would suggest to you that Indigenous societies are the only societies that have lived sustainably for thousands of years. Industrial societies cannot document having lived sustainably. Indigenous peoples believe natural law is preeminent, it is the highest law. It is higher than law made by nations, states, or municipalities. It is our experience that not to live in accordance with this natural law is to be foolish. To make nature live by your rules is not a sustainable way to live.

People divert and change rivers, flood communities, and change the natural face of the land. And many people make arrogant assumptions about altering natural law. You really can't do much negotiating with natural law. Natural law is the power of the volcano giving birth to new land, natural law is the hurricane, natural law is not always kind, gentle, or easy.

Natural law is based on thousands of years of observation. Some of our observations are that most things that are natural are cyclical. That's why there are the tides, the phases of the moon, the seasons. That which is alive, that which is natural, is cyclical. All things around us have spirit and stand alone—and they are reckoned with as such in our interaction with the natural world. When we harvest, we always give thanks to that which we harvest, for giving itself to us. We recognize that we are totally reliant upon keeping a balanced relationship with the earth, and taking only what we need, leaving the rest, and giving back when we harvest. These are some tenets of sustainability which we practice.

It is our contention that these tenets are very different from industrial practices. In industrial society, we are taught about human domination of nature, that human law is higher than natural law. That humans have a God-given right to all that is around them. And instead of the natural order having its own standing, it is viewed in terms of its utilitarian value to humans. This is a different set of values.

The Hopi will tell you that the Black Mesa coalfield is alive, it is the lungs of Mother Earth. The Arizona public service company will tell you it is valued at U.S.$20 per ton, its value is in relationship to the power plant to which that coal is delivered. That is the value of that coalfield and that land.

The conflicts between industrial and Indigenous world views have manifested themselves in terms of holocausts. Our experiences today are very much based on history being carried forward into today's reality, and this is true for Indigenous peoples around the world. We have our own intact environmental systems, economic, political, land tenure, and health institutions. These are all institutions that become prey for the predatory systems that come into our territories—to those who come to bring us "development."

What follows are a few examples of the long-term public health and social implications of development programs coming into Indigenous communities.

About two-thirds of the uranium resources in the United States are on Indian reservations, as well as one-third of all western low-sulfur coal. We also have the dubious honor of being host to the single largest hydroelectric project in North America—the James Bay. All these projects are viewed as "progress" and are billed as bringing development to our communities. In our experience, these projects do not bring progress, instead they bring devastation.

I can give you examples that illustrate just a few of the problems. The first is about uranium mining. The production of uranium or yellowcake from uranium ore usually requires the discharge of significant amounts of water and the disposal of significant amounts of radioactive material. Uranium mill tailings, the solid wastes from the uranium milling stage of the cycle, contain 85 percent of the original radioactivity in the uranium ore. One of these products, Radium 226, remains radioactive for at least sixteen thousand years.

In 1975, 100 percent of all federally produced uranium came from Indian reservations. That same year there were three hundred and eighty uranium leases on Indian lands, as compared to four on public and acquired lands. By the 1980s, these U.S. mines had closed down to open in Canada. Now virtually identical figures exist for Canada, which is the number one producer of uranium in the world, followed by Australia. Worldwide, it is estimated that 70 percent of uranium reserves are contained on Indigenous lands (Organization for Economic Cooperation and Development 1988).

Spurred on by the advice of the Bureau of Indian Affairs and promises of jobs and royalties, the Navajo Tribal Council approved a mineral agreement with the Kerr McGee Corporation in 1959. In return for access to uranium deposits and a means to fulfill risk-free contracts with the U.S. Atomic Energy Commission, Kerr McGee employed mostly Navajo men as uranium miners in the underground mines. Wages for the nonunion miners were low, and worker safety enforcement exceedingly lax. By 1959 radiation levels at the operations were estimated to be ninety to one hundred times above tolerable levels (Sorenson 1978, Pearson 1975).

Seventeen years later, most of the easily retrievable ore had been exhausted, and the company began to phase out the mines. By 1975, eighteen of the one hundred and fifty Navajo miners who had worked in these Kerr McGee mines had died of lung cancer. By 1980, twenty more had died of the same disease, and ninety-five more had contracted respiratory ailments and cancers (Samet 1984). The incidence of miscarriages, bone, reproductive, and bladder cancers, birth defects, leukemia, and other diseases associated with uranium mining also accelerated (Shields and Goodman 1986).

As it departed from the Shiprock area of the Navajo Nation (in the "four corners" region of the United States, the intersection of Arizona, Utah, New Mexico, and Colorado), Kerr McGee abandoned approximately seventy-one acres worth of uranium mill tailings on the banks of the San Juan River, the only major waterway in the arid region. As a result, radioactive contamination spread downstream. Southeast of the facility, the Churchrock uranium mine discharged eighty thousand gallons of radioactive water from the mine shaft annually into the local water supply.

In July 1979, the largest radioactive spill in United States history occurred at the United Nuclear uranium mill near Churchrock on the Navajo reservation. The uranium mill tailings dam at the site broke under pressure and 100 million gallons of sludge flooded the Rio Puerco River. The company had known of the cracks in the dam for two months before the incident, but no repairs had been made (Shuey 1988, Hinschman 1987). The water supply of seventeen hundred Navajo people was irretrievably contaminated, and subsequently over one thousand sheep and cattle ingested radioactive water.

By 1980, forty-two operating uranium mines, ten uranium mills, five coal-fired power plants, and four coal strip mines were in the vicinity of the Navajo reservation. Fifteen new uranium mining operations were under construction on the reservation itself. Although 85 percent of Navajo households had no electricity, each year the Navajo nation exported enough energy resources to fuel the needs of the state of New Mexico for thirty-two years.

The birth defect rate in the Shiprock Indian Health Service area is two to eight times higher than the national average, according to a study supported by the March of Dimes (McLeod, Hayes, and Switkes 1985).

There are many other examples that can be told about uranium mining. There are also many that relate to toxic waste dumping. In the past few years, over forty-five Indian communities have been approached by waste companies offering multimillion-dollar contracts in exchange for the right to dump or incinerate on Indian lands. East of San Diego alone, over eighteen *rancherias* (small Indian communities) have been approached as possible dumping grounds for garbage and toxic wastes. One community that has already been impacted by a toxic waste dump is the Akwesasne Mohawk reservation.

The Akwesasne Mohawk reservation spans the United States/Canadian border, and is home to approximately eight thousand Mohawk people. Through the center of their territory flows the St. Lawrence River, the waterway of their people. For generations, the Mohawk have relied upon the river for fish, food, and transportation. Today, the river is full of poison.

On the American side in 1983, the U.S. Environmental Protection Agency (EPA) designated the area as one of the top Superfund sites in the United States. The General Motors Massena Central Foundry, adjacent to the reservation, is possibly the most significant polychlorinated biphenyl (PCB) dump site in North America. The chemical is known to cause brain, nerve, liver, and skin disorders in humans and cancer and reproductive disorders in laboratory animals. Five PCB-saturated lagoons, and a number of sludge pits dot GM's 258-acre property.

According to the EPA, 50 parts per million PCBs is classified as hazardous waste. Sludge and vegetation at the bottom of Contaminant Cove, at the conflux of the Grasse and St. Lawrence Rivers, have been documented at 3,000 parts per million. A male snapping turtle was located with 3,067 parts per million of PCBs in his body (Akwesasne 1991).

A project known as the Akwesasne Mothers Milk Project is carrying out a study of breastmilk, fetal cord, and urine samples of Mohawk mothers on the reservation. A total of 168 women are participating in the study. The primary organizer of the project, Katsi Cook Barreiro, is a practicing midwife who has delivered many children on the reservation. "I've got myself four one-hundredths parts per million of mirex (a flame retardant) and 84 one-thousandths parts per million PCBs in my body," she explains. "The analysis of Mohawk mother's milk shows that our bodies are, in fact, part of the landfill" (LaDuke and Foushee 1988).

Studies of Inuit breastmilk in the Hudson Bay region of northern Canada indicate that Inuit women have levels of PCB contamination higher than those recorded anywhere else in the world. The maximum PCB concentration considered "safe" by the Canadian government is $1\frac{5}{10}$ parts per million. A Laval University study in 1988 discovered much higher samples (one-third of all nursing mothers in that year). Some samples were recorded at $14\frac{7}{10}$ parts per million. The average concentration of PCBs in breastmilk in Quebec is $\frac{5}{10}$ parts per million.

According to an Inuit spokesperson, Mary Kaye May of the Kativik Regional Health Council, the findings brought "fear and great sadness" to the village. It is assumed that the higher levels are attributed to the Inuit diet of fish and marine mammals which are known to concentrate PCBs in the food chain. The PCBs have appeared in the Arctic food chain in recent years, largely attributed to atmospheric distribution of heavy metals, toxins from southern industries, and from abandoned military, radar, and communications installations utilizing PCBs.

While the toxic contamination of infants is of great concern to the Inuit, there are no viable alternatives. "If the women stop breastfeeding," Mary Kaye May continues, "and with the cost of baby formula at $17 a can, we will face a frightening number of cases of infant malnutrition."

Ninety-five percent of the Native land base has been destroyed in some of these communities. Two-thirds of the land of the Cree of Moose Lake in Northern Manitoba was flooded by dams put in by Manitoba Hydro. Manitoba Hydro took 634 people who were living in outlying areas in hunting camps. They gave them "progress" and moved them into a housing project. Today, they continue to live in the housing project and for some reason, the government can't understand why, 90 percent of the people are on welfare and have substance abuse rates that affect about 90 percent of the population living in that village. These are circumstances that result from colonialism—a process in which your land base, your economic institutions, and your ability to sustain your community are destroyed.

What people talk about is the soul-destroying effects of development projects. Jim Tobacco, the chief of one of these villages says, "There is a very hostile attitude in our communities. Young people are always beating each other up. My people don't know who the hell we are any more. We live month to month on welfare. Today we are poor and Manitoba Hydro is rich."

These are the circumstances our communities now face, and the human impact is something public health professionals encounter. These are issues that are caused by poorly planned development projects and development programs that serve someone else's communities, and do not serve ours. They are issues of environmental racism, but they are also fundamentally structural issues of this society. They are the issues we have inherited as Indigenous peoples.

So some of the issues and questions that are posed to you as public health professionals are how do you address these issues over the long term? We need to reconsider the idea of acceptable risk levels in the absence of any hard data. We don't believe there is any acceptable risk level for any of these energy projects that come into our communities. We also do not believe we should be guinea pigs for uranium mining, hydroelectric dams, or mercury contamination in our communities.

Very clear public health connections exist for people living close to the land, in subsistence-based economies. One of the problems many Indigenous communities face is that we see many health effects almost instantly, but industrial society is preoccupied with twenty or thirty years of testing. A lot of our populations are heavily impacted by the time they have finalized all their tests. A lot of our communities say: "We could have told you that and saved you a few million dollars." The public policy implications of trying to rethink this problem and take action present some of the challenges.

We have some underlying concerns about a lot of research that occurs in our communities because many researchers and research institutions are more interested in the research than in the people themselves. We are often faced with being seen as the objects of research and not as people with valid human rights or rights to just continue living our lives. One of the underlying conflicts and issues for many Indigenous communities is the right to continue their existence without being intruded on by industrial societies.

We suggest that the fundamental issue we must all collectively address is the issue of recovering our relationship to natural law. The challenge is to bring this society, which consumes at such an insatiable level, and has so much influence in the world, back in order with natural law. We need to bring it back to the extent that we can support local communities and our struggles to rebuild sustainable economies and find fundamental ways to change public policy so that long-term sustainability is readdressed.

We have to challenge our materialistic consumption that creates and manufactures needs that are taking from our communities and developing countries. As human beings we have universal needs. We need clean air, clean water, clean food, shelter, and one another's companionship. If you think each year you must have the newest and latest television or computer you are not thinking in holistic terms. Where did the mineral resource come from to build these machines? What were the working conditions and health conditions of the people who extracted those resources and at the factory where all these little pieces are put together? Where does the power come from to run this equipment? What did we have to do to get this power?

For Indigenous peoples, natural law is the highest law. And natural law includes people working together for change. That is also power. There is a strong Indigenous network being built here on this continent, and there are a lot of emerging organizations that tend to be community-based, grassroots groups. They usually have little in the way of funding or paid staff, but they are accomplishing incredible feats in their communities. They don't have people with scientific degrees. But they are stopping the toxic incinerators in their neighborhoods. People are tired of being the targets.

How can non-Indigenous groups best work with or support Indigenous groups? Partnership agreements need to be developed. In partnership agreements it is not a question of anyone, myself included, going into another Indigenous community and telling them what to do. It is taking time to listen, to learn, and then focus in on what the people there decide are the priorities.

In some communities there are no telephones, no paved roads, and no running water. And the nearest telephone might be fifty or eighty miles away. Other areas are urban based and steeped in high technology. Support means understanding where you are and what the important issues are. And there is a lot of expertise within the communities.

In our Indigenous environmental networking, we have had a conference for each of the past four years. This has been held in a different area of the United States each year. We raise funds for presenters and participants to be able to come, to share information, and to work toward identifying experts within our communities. Some of the knowledge is very old, some of the knowledge has been carried for generations. And some of the knowledge is new, like how to test water, how to test for radioactivity, and how communities can receive these kinds of trainings. We have over seventy groups as members of the Indigenous Environmental Network.

There are cases where Indigenous peoples have successfully defended their homelands. For example, the Innu people in Labrador successfully defeated the siting of a NATO base in their territory, after a decade of litigation, rallies, and civil disobedience. The Northern Cheyenne, who now face a new series of coal developments, have successfully defeated and opposed coal strip mining on their reservation for almost three decades.

The White Earth Anishinabeg from northern Minnesota successfully fought the siting of a nuclear waste repository on the reservation. The nuclear waste dump was proposed for the headwaters of the Mississippi River. The Native Hawaiian people, after four decades of struggle, stopped the bombing of their sacred land, Kaho'olawe, by the American military. It was, until then, the only national historical landmark regularly shelled with artillery.

The Navajo people, Kaibab Paiute, Oglala Lakota, and others successfully opposed the siting of hazardous waste incinerators and dumps on their reservation lands, in spite of millions of dollars of jobs and "benefits" promised to the people. The Cree of the Moose River have thus far stopped the proposal for twelve dams in the River basin, and now the government says it will not go ahead with any dam construction without Native consent. And in November of 1994, the new government of Quebec announced the cancellation of the James Bay Hydroelectric Project Phase II at Great Whale. This was a result of almost a decade of grassroots organizing, coalition work, litigation, and legislation.

These, and many others, are examples of Native peoples successfully resisting the destruction of their land and lives. There are also many examples of communities rebuilding traditional economies, social structures, and ways of life. Indigenous peoples remain on the front lines of the North American struggle to protect our environment. We understand very clearly that our lives, and those of our future generations, are totally dependent on our actions, and in our rebuilding our communities.

Notes

This chapter is based on a presentation by Nilak Butler at the 1993 NCIH conference, a presentation by Winona LaDuke at the 1994 NCIH conference, and a paper prepared by Winona LaDuke, 1992, "Indigenous Environmental Perspectives: A North American Primer," *Akwe:kon Journal* 9(2) (Ithaca, New York).

1. The United Nations' Decade of Indigenous People (1994 to 2004), launched in December 1994, should draw attention to the problem of ensuring the basic human rights of Indigenous peoples throughout the world. Many of these rights relate to self-determination, territorial integrity, security of land, and cultural integrity. —Ed.

2. While there is no universally agreed upon definition of Indigenous peoples, this term is commonly used internationally to describe the original inhabitants of traditional lands who maintain traditional values, culture, and ways of life. The population of Indigenous peoples worldwide is reported to be over 500 million. *The Gaia Atlas of First Peoples* identifies Indigenous peoples in every continent and over two hundred nation states. (Brascoupé 1992:9). —Ed.

References

Akwesasne Mothers Milk Project Success Story. Presented at the Global Assembly of Women and the Environment, Miami, Florida. November 1991. Published in *Global Assembly of Women and the Environment Proceedings*, Volume I. WorldWIDE Network, 1991.

Brascoupé, Simon. 1992. "Indigenous Perspectives on International Development." *Akwe:kon Journal* 9(2) (Ithaca, New York).

Burger, Julian. 1990. *The Gaia Atlas of First Peoples*. London: Gaia Books, Ltd.

Hinschman, Steve. 1987. "Rebottling the Nuclear Genie." *High Country News*, 19 January. Cited in *Struggle for the Land: Indigenous Resistance to Genocide, Ecocide and Expropriation in Contemporary North America*. Ed. Ward Churchill. Monroe, Maine: Common Courage Press, 1993.

LaDuke, Winona. 1985. "Native America: The Economics of Radioactive Colonialism." *Review of Radical Political Economics* 15(3).

————. 1992. "Indigenous Environmental Perspectives: A North American Primer." *Akwe:kon Journal* 9(2) (Ithaca, New York).

LaDuke, Winona, and Lea Foushee. 1988. "Nuclear Native America." Research paper of Indigenous Women's Network. Unpublished.

McLeod, Christopher, Randy Hayes, and Glenn Switkes. 1985. "Four Corners: A National Sacrifice Area?" *Workbook* 10(2) (Albuquerque, NM: Southwest Research and Information Center).

Organization for Economic Cooperation and Development (OECD). 1988. Nuclear Energy Agency Joint Report with the International Atomic Energy Agency.

Pearson, Jessica S. 1975. *A Sociological Analysis of the Reduction of Hazardous Radiation in Uranium Mines*. Washington, D.C.: National Institute for Occupational Safety and Health, National Health Service. Cited in *Struggle for the Land*.

Samet, M. J., et al. 1984. "Uranium Mining and Lung Cancer Among Navajo Men." *New England Journal of Medicine* 310:1481–4.

Shields, Lora Magnum, and Alan B. Goodman. 1986. "Outcome of 13,000 Navajo Births from 1964–1981 in the Shiprock Uranium Mining Area." Cited in Ward Churchill, "The Native Ethnic amid Resource Development." *Environment* 28(6):13–17, 28–33.

Shuey, Chris. 1988. "The Puerco River: Where Did the Water Go?" *The Workbook* 11:1–10. Cited in *Struggle for the Land*.

Sorenson, J. B. 1978. "Radiation Issues: Government Decision Making and Uranium Expansion in Northern New Mexico." San Juan Regional Uranium Study, *Working Paper* no. 14, Albuquerque. Cited in *Struggle for the Land*.

Venables, Robert. 1990. "The Cost of Columbus—Was There a Holocaust?" In *View from the Shore: American Indian Perspectives on the Quincentenary*. Cornell University: Akwe:kon Press.

Chapter 11

The Environment and Human Rights in West Harlem

Vernice D. Miller

I 'm from New York. The place where I live, a neighborhood called West Harlem, occupies the western part of the greater Harlem community. For many, many decades—almost a century, in fact—Harlem was the cultural center of the African American community in the United States. At one time it contained the largest concentration of African Americans in the country.

My community borders the Hudson River, a mighty and majestic river that separates the states of New York and New Jersey. Over the last twenty years, the Hudson has become incredibly polluted, due to unchecked industrial development and population growth. In fact, in the 1970s and '80s, parts of the river, particularly near New York City, were considered dead; they could support neither plant nor animal life because the levels of pollution from industrial and human waste were so high. The human waste problem was particularly acute because of the rapid rate of growth of New York's population. On the west side of Manhattan, where the majority of the city's commercial and some of its industrial development have occurred, we have a population of about 600,000 people, but during business hours we have a population of 2.5 million people, and every day they produce more waste. Up until 1986, all of the waste they produced flowed right into the Hudson River.

The city of New York decided that it needed to do something about this problem. Actually, the city had decided something needed to be done as long ago as 1931. The first federal protocol in the United States dealing with sewage treatment was not put forward until 1943, so you can see that New York was well ahead of the federal government in this regard; its decision to develop a sewage treatment or pretreatment system actually far predated any comparable initiative on the part of the federal government. The idea was to create and link together a number of facilities to treat the raw sewage that was coming from individual homes and industries, and then put that treated effluent back into the Hudson or take it to a landfill to be dumped. So the city decided to build a number of sewage treatment plants.

123

But in fact, like everything else in New York City, the idea got caught up in the bureaucracy of city government, and it took thirty years before a plan was actually developed. First the planners talked about building eighteen waste treatment facilities along the banks of the Hudson River. Then they talked about building twelve, then seven, then two, and finally only one, to treat the sewage from the west side of Manhattan. That one facility was supposed to be built in a neighborhood called the Upper West Side, a community that is demographically and socioeconomically similar to Georgetown in Washington, D.C.

But at the same time the city had some very forward-looking plans for the cultural as well as the commercial development of the Upper West Side, and the city planners decided that a sewage treatment plant in that part of the city would probably not be a good fit with the kind of development they had in mind. One of their plans was to build the Lincoln Center complex. If you've been to New York and gone to the Metropolitan Opera or the New York City Ballet, you've seen Lincoln Center. Another plan, currently in the development stage, is for a huge megadevelopment called the Riverside South complex that Donald Trump is getting ready to build. In effect, this complex will bring 5,700 additional units of housing to a neighborhood that is probably already the most overdeveloped in the city of New York.

So in their forward-looking wisdom, the city planners said "Well, we shouldn't put our sewage treatment plant on the Upper West Side; we should put it somewhere else." They sought another community where they could put the facility, and they found my community, West Harlem.

Most of what you've heard about Harlem is probably negative, but at one time, it was a place where people wanted to live. Residents looked out on the Hudson River, they had a view of the beautiful Palisades, they were surrounded by beautiful architecture, they were centrally located. West Harlem used to be a very desirable place to be, and people who lived there fought for decades to keep it that way. Today, like most settings in which the vestiges of racial segregation remain, West Harlem is a mixed-income community. There's a very vibrant middle and upper middle class. The neighborhood that I live in is a historic district where the average home sells for a quarter of a million dollars. But like most communities of color in the United States, my neighborhood is surrounded by pockets of poverty. Communities like mine aren't usually monolithic; they're neither very, very poor nor very, very rich. Thanks to gerrymandering—the creation of political districts and well-defined community boundaries that, in this case, reinforce racially-segregated residential areas—they tend to be a little of everything.

This is the community in which the city planners decided to build the sewage treatment plant, officially called the North River Water Pollution Control Plant. It went on line in 1986 (thirty years after the planning started), and it is designed to treat 170 million gallons of raw sewage a day. That is an awful lot of sewage, as you can imagine, and it has an incredibly foul odor, as you can probably also imagine. This plant lies only a couple of hundred feet from where I live, along with thousands of other people. It's right across the highway from us, and the only thing that buffers us from the sewage smell is the smell from the exhaust pipes of cars going through our community every day. So as you can see, we're catching it in many different ways.

Of course the residents of West Harlem intensely opposed the siting of this foul-smelling plant in their community. As a result of their opposition, the state and the city of New York came up with a mitigation measure: they created a park, the Riverbank State Park, on top of the plant. The process that resulted in the siting of the plant in West Harlem had been exclusionary—outside the realm of public participation—but the construction of the park, which was designed primarily by the West Harlem community and cost nearly $130 million dollars to build, was a battle that the community sustained. The park opened in May of 1993. It's one of the largest recreational facilities in New York City, and the rate at which New Yorkers use it has been astronomical. The problem is that the pollution and odors emanating from the plant have not abated. In fact, to the extent that the park brings people closer to the source of the plant's emissions, we have more of a problem now than we did before the park was built. Right at the bottom of the emission stacks are a children's carousel, a toddler playground, and a restaurant. In various spots throughout the park, you can smell sewage more strongly than you can across the street.

The sewage treatment plant isn't West Harlem's only environmental problem. The area also has seven of the eight municipal bus depots for the county of Manhattan, and several highways intersect the community at some point. We have the highest infant mortality rate in the Western world—higher than many developing countries—and just one hospital. So, as you can see, West Harlem is no longer a safe, pleasant, aesthetically pleasing place to live.

Those of us who live in the midst of this environmental mess wonder why our community was targeted for this particular kind of development. We are not, nor have we ever been, politically impotent. The second African American ever elected to the United States Congress, post-Reconstruction, was elected from Harlem. One of the most powerful current members of Congress, the second-ranking Democrat on the House Ways and Means Committee, is from Harlem. David Dinkins, who was the Mayor of New York from 1989 to 1993, was a resident of West Harlem for thirty-six years, and began his political career there. So we are not without political voice. We have always been a very vibrant and politically active community.

Why then was our community targeted for locally unwanted land uses? Clearly it wasn't because of any perceived political impotence. It wasn't land values, nor home values, nor the academic achievement of the people who live there. We believe it was purely because of the racial composition of the people who live there. So it's not true that communities that lie adjacent to hazardous waste facilities are always poor, politically powerless communities. In truth, there are many upper-income and middle-income communities of color that have become host sites for hazardous or municipal waste facilities, particularly in urban centers. Indeed, most of the municipal waste facilities in cities seem to find their way into such communities (Bullard 1993). West Harlem, while it's no longer a pleasant place to come home to, is by no means the worst, compared with the environmental degradation suffered on a daily basis by other communities of color throughout this country and in the developing world.

What has happened, both in this country and others, is that certain populations have been deemed expendable. Lives have actually become currency in market-based economies. A value has been placed, for example, on the lives of those of us who live in the United States, based on how equal we are to other people in other parts of the world. And the lives of people in other parts of the world have been defined as being of less value than those of people who live in the United States of America. I've learned a tremendous amount from our brothers and sisters in developing countries about their efforts to grab hold of policy, particularly environmental and development policy, as they go forward into the next millennium. They're trying to get a grip on the philosophy that the United States and other Western countries have put forward into the global discourse, that any and all development is good development. Well, I live in a community that proves this is just not true. It's one of many communities suffering from this unchecked kind of growth and industrial policy that is not balanced by any consideration of the value of human lives and ecosystems that cannot be replaced.

What is required of us who are involved in the global struggle for human rights? How can we help to shape the future of the human rights movement, to define the future of international and national policy? First, we must not allow national borders to prevent us from joining together to bring basic human rights and environmental justice to one and all. Second, we must not allow issues of race, class, and gender to be separated from the overall quest for equality and justice. And finally we must not allow issues of environment, population, and development to be decoupled, either in local or in global discourse. We cannot, for example, separate economic growth from human needs and ecological needs. We've got a tremendous amount of work to do, but we've got to do that work in a holistic context. We may be dealing in different parts of the hemisphere, but we're definitely dealing with the same problems and the same issues.

Postscript

In 1992, six years after the North River Water Pollution Control Plant went on line, West Harlem Environmental Action and the Natural Resources Defense Council, along with eight individual plaintiffs from the West

Harlem community, sued the city of New York for the cost of repairing the damage that the plant had caused to the local environment (Pérez-Peña 1994). The suit was settled rather than fought and won in court, but at the same time the environmental activists achieved a significant victory: the city agreed to contribute $1.1 million to the residents of West Harlem to help alleviate the environmental problems—from foul odors to upper respiratory infections to the obstruction of their view of the Hudson River—caused by the plant. The money was put into a trust fund, the North River Fund, from which it would be administered by West Harlem Environmental Action and the Natural Resources Defense Council.

References

Bullard, Robert D. 1993. *Confronting Environmental Racism.* Boston: South End Press.

Pérez-Peña, Richard. 1994. "City Settles Suit on Odors at Harlem Site." *New York Times*, 5 January.

Part V
Creating Responsive Institutions

Patan, Nepal

Part V

Introduction

A myriad of institutions are helping people identify and solve their own problems, and develop sound sustainable solutions to many of the world's most pressing health and environmental concerns. These institutions include community-based organizations, private and nongovernmental organizations (NGOs), private businesses, foundations, national and international agencies, as well as local, regional and national governments. Despite these efforts, however, millions of people throughout the world continue to live in unsafe and unhealthy environments.

While sustainable health and environmental improvements in communities require the commitment and active participation of people at the local level, input from outside the community is usually needed to help solve complex problems. In some cases, solutions, and strategies to implement solutions, have already been developed. However, the chapters in Part V explore situations that are more complex and for which external assistance is often needed. Institutions from outside the community may be called upon to provide technical assistance, capital, or materials to supplement local expertise. The chapters in Part V contain examples of strategies and approaches for creating institutions that are responsive to the health and environmental needs of local communities.

While there is no one definition of a "responsive" institution, one common characteristic is a solid human and financial resource base, or the knowledge and ability to gather together the resources needed to fulfill the mission and goals of the institution. Responsive institutions are typically proactive, forward-looking institutions that attempt to anticipate future problems while reacting to immediate and pressing concerns. In addition to the chapters in Part V, many other chapters in this book provide examples of responsive institutions. These include the municipality of Cali, Colombia (chapter 1), the Cooperative Housing Foundation (chapter 2), the Violence Prevention Coalition (chapter 3), the Environmental Health Project (chapter 5), the Katibougou PMI-Maternité (chapter 6), the Kenya Water for Health Organization (Chapter 7), the Intermediate Technology Development Group and Sarvodaya (chapter 8), the Highlander Research and Education Center (chapter 9), many of the grassroots organizations and networks mentioned in chapter 10, and West Harlem Environmental Action (chapter 11).

A number of themes unite the chapters in Part V, including: (1) the need for responsive institutions to help communities learn how to solve problems in an interdisciplinary manner; and (2) the need to help communities develop solutions that connect basic health needs and pressing environmental issues in an integrated and synergistic way. To have the most profound, long-term, and sustainable impacts, responsive institutions often focus on capacity-building. This generally means strengthening skills and capacity to identify and work toward solving present and future problems. Many local communities, as well as government agencies, at the local, regional, and national levels, benefit most from the institutional strengthening and capacity-building that are important aspects of outside technical assistance from responsive institutions.

Integrating Population and Environmental Conservation

Chapter 12 explores the problems faced by rural communities in developing countries as they struggle to achieve a sustainable balance between population growth and environmental conservation—a task that is increasingly difficult in the face of the level of exploitation of natural resources that is necessary to support that same population growth. The chapter describes two projects—one primarily an environmental conservation effort and the other a family planning initiative—currently taking place in Uganda. By combining their skills and resources, representatives of these two projects are finding that their environmental conservation and family planning messages and services can reach more people, in new and more effective ways.

The two projects are being carried out with the assistance of CARE, a large international NGO. Strengthening the capacity of local communities and government agencies to respond to particular problems, and promoting community-based environmental management—through which communities learn to make their own decisions about how to safeguard the productivity of their environment—are important aspects of CARE's work in Uganda.

Fostering Community Involvement and Capacity Building

An estimated 100 million people are at risk of contracting Chagas disease—a vector-borne disease considered one of the most serious health problems in Latin America. Chapter 13 describes the Chagas Disease Control Program of the Bolivian Secretariat of Health (SOH) and the Community and Child Health (CCH) Project—a nationally-organized effort that is making significant progress in developing effective approaches to this environmentally linked public health problem. The SOH/CCH Chagas Control Program has been providing technical assistance and in-country expertise to local participating communities.

Chapter 13 describes this multi-institutional and multidisciplinary effort which uses a broad management approach to Chagas disease control.

This approach emphasizes community-based, integrated vector control through education, community involvement, housing improvements, and limited application of insecticide. The program has found that active community involvement enhances program components such as home and environmental improvements and vector and disease surveillance. It also has been found to result in public health benefits that go beyond more limited program goals.

Developing Strategies for Sustainable Development

Chapter 14 explores the concepts and principles of primary environmental care (PEC), a community-based approach to help alleviate poverty and halt environmental degradation. PEC integrates three essential elements: (1) meeting basic health and livelihood needs; (2) empowering people and communities for decision making and action according to what they identify as their priorities; and (3) ensuring protection and sustainable use of natural resources in and around communities.

A number of organizations are actively pursuing the PEC approach, including the United Nations Children's Fund (UNICEF). The chapter provides examples from UNICEF's experiences with the PEC approach and describes some of the many challenges that remain in successfully applying this approach. Three issue are of major importance in further development of PEC: (1) maintaining the active participation of women and children in environmental education and community action; (2) building confidence within communities to better meet priority needs; and (3) developing mechanisms to sustain innovative initiatives at the local level as well as ensuring that these efforts are adapted and extended into other areas—in other words, that they are widespread enough to make a difference on a large scale.

Taken together, these chapters provide insights into useful and appropriate roles for responsive institutions whose aim is to assist communities, as well as governments, to come to terms with and try to solve complex public health and environmental problems. The chapters also explore issues related to achieving sustainable development. One of the themes of these chapters is that in order for development to be sustainable, outside institutions need to be responsive to people's felt needs—whether at the local or national level. As illustrated in these chapters, capacity-building and intersectoral coordination are often the most critical elements in developing long-lasting solutions to pressing public health and environmental problems.

Chapter 12

Linking Population and Environmental Conservation Activities in Southwestern Uganda

Jennifer Jael Nahalamba Mukolwe,
Therese McGinn, and Cynthia L. Carlson

The southwestern corner of Uganda, the country lying west of Kenya in East Africa, is bordered on the west by the huge central African country of Zaire (formerly the Congo) and on the south by Tanzania and tiny Rwanda. With its beautiful mountains, cool climate, plentiful rainfall, and fertile soils, southwestern Uganda has been described as "the Switzerland of Africa." Its rich, dense forests, characterized by extraordinary biodiversity, are home to the mountain gorilla, an endangered species much sought after by researchers and tourists alike.[1]

Over the last half-century, the population of southwestern Uganda has grown considerably. Part of this growth has been due to an influx from neighboring Rwanda of refugees who began to flee their country in the 1940s.[2] But the area's rapid population growth is primarily a product of its high fertility rate, which in turn can be attributed, at least in part, to traditional practices and beliefs such as early marriage and the high cultural value placed on large families. In addition, there has been very little voluntary out-migration. Southwestern Ugandans do not like to move; most would rather stay in their own communities.

The combination of high fertility and limited out-migration has meant greater and greater population pressure on natural resources. In the twenty years between the 1971 and 1991 censuses, the population of the three districts of the southwest in which CARE is working (Kabale, Kisoro, and Rukungiri Districts)[3] rose from 647,000 to 995,000 people. These districts are only 5,250 square kilometers in area, 4,900 of which are land mass; the remainder is water. Population density has also increased, from 132 to 201 persons per square kilometer; in some communities, density is as high as 500 persons per square kilometer—among the highest in Africa. The region's population growth rate of 2.7 percent implies that the population size will double in about twenty-six years. While growth rates of this magnitude are not uncommon in Africa, southwestern Uganda's total fertility rate (TFR) of 7.8 in 1989 (Kaijuka et al. 1989) is extremely high by any standard. For example, the 1992 TFR of low-income countries (excluding China and India) was 4.9 (World Bank 1994).

Ninety-five percent of the people of southwestern Uganda are subsistence farmers. Like most such farmers in Africa (and the rest of the world), the Ugandan farmers mainly produce food for their families, but—since they need cash to buy the things they do not produce—they also sell some of their produce locally, and process food for sale (such as banana beer and hot lunches for laborers). What have these farmers done in response to the increasing strain that their growing numbers have placed on local resources? Principally they have cleared more land in order to survive. Between 1954 and 1991, for example, the size of Bwindi Impenetrable Forest, a hilly, tropical forest in southwestern Uganda, declined by 27 percent, from 400 square kilometers to the current 321. Today in Bwindi Forest there are cultivated crops in places where once there were only trees. Even swampy areas are now under cultivation; lush, extensive marshlands that existed in the local area through the 1930s have disappeared.

An important reason why the local farmers must constantly clear new land is their inheritance system. In southwestern Uganda, as in most African communities, a farmer cultivates his land in order to support his family, and at his death the land is distributed equally among his sons. The sons, in turn, use their shares of land to support their own families, and at their deaths bequeath it to their sons. Within a generation or two, a plot of land that once sustained one family must now provide food for several, and through the years the plots of land on which families must depend become smaller and smaller. Eventually, sons will inherit pieces of property too small to sustain their families, forcing them to clear additional land for cultivation.

Farmers have also responded to the problem of population growth by attempting to increase the output of their land. This has resulted in overcropping, now a serious problem. Farmers used to take care when sowing sorghum, for example, that their plants were properly spaced. Today they try to get as much food out of their plots as possible, so they sow generously and let whatever has germinated grow, without regard to spacing. Fallow periods are now shorter, meaning that soils become depleted of nutrients sooner.

As early as the 1940s, the government tried to promote more intensive agriculture through the use of contour *bunds*, hillside embankments designed to control erosion. The program was not a great success, however, for two reasons. Most important, land used for bunds could not be used for cultivation. On small plots, particularly, farmers were unwilling to remove so much of their land from production. Second, the erosion between bunds causes fertile soil eventually to build up around them. Farmers would break the bunds down and distribute the fertile soil around their plots. Since bunds require considerable effort to build, farmers often did not rebuild them.

In addition to putting more land under cultivation and attempting to intensify agricultural production, some farmers—those who could neither expand their acreage nor increase their agricultural output—left the area because their plots of land were too small to feed their families. Periodically since the 1940s, the government of Uganda has attempted to intervene by promoting voluntary resettlement to other areas of the country. During the 1940s and 1950s, for example, farm families in the southwest were told they could find land in districts further to the north. Unfortunately, these farmers were moved into warm areas, rife with mosquitoes—a very different climate and environment from that to which they were accustomed. Both the migrants and their animals soon began to suffer from malaria and other diseases. Some of the resettled farmers returned to their homeland, and subsequently other area residents who were considering emigrating refused to go. Ultimately, the resettlement program had little effect on the population problem. Officially it still exists, but little use is made of it.

Until 1967, the problem of limited natural resources in southwestern Uganda was compounded by the fact that no modern family planning program was in place, either through the government of Uganda or through nongovernmental organizations (NGOs). In that year, the Family Planning Association of Uganda (FPAU), an International Planned Parenthood Federation (IPPF) affiliate, opened a clinic in Kabale town and hired a fieldworker to cover the three districts. However, because of the local people's very limited knowledge about family planning, plus meager resources and a small staff, FPAU had a very limited reach.

The government of Uganda has encouraged local and international NGOs to support its efforts through collaborative and/or complementary activities in all development sectors. CARE has been doing this since 1968, when it first opened its doors in Uganda. After ceasing operations during a particularly turbulent period in the mid- to late 1970s under Idi Amin Dada's rule, CARE was among the first international organizations to be welcomed back into the country in 1979. The organization's current work in Uganda includes projects in agriculture, water and sanitation, primary health care, and AIDS prevention, as well as the conservation and population activities discussed below. CARE's focus is more often regional than national; in Uganda, its activities are concentrated in the northwestern and southwestern parts of the county.

CARE's mission in southwestern Uganda is to work with communities to improve residents' health and socioeconomic status and, at the same time, to help them manage their environment sustainably. To achieve this, CARE undertakes program interventions in the areas of environmental conservation and reproductive health, including family planning. It also collaborates with both government and nongovernmental organizations, including the ministries of health, agriculture, natural resources, and tourism, wildlife and antiquities; district civil authorities; the Uganda Agroforestry Research Network for Africa (the regional affiliate of the International Council for Research in Agroforestry, which has one of its three Ugandan research sites in Kabale); FPAU and its Kabale office; church health facilities in the area; and local community groups.

CARE's environment project, called Development Through Conservation (DTC), began in 1988. Its goal is to improve the quality of life through natural resource conservation among farm families living in communities around Bwindi Impenetrable Forest and another local tropical moist forest, Mgahinga. The project strategy has three components: institutional strengthening of local and government natural resource management capabilities; changing attitudes, knowledge and practices about natural resource conservation; and improving the productivity of farms and forests in the project area.

Family planning was not a component of the DTC project, but discussions of conservation, land use, and land shortages between farmers and CARE staff naturally turned to questions of family size and birth spacing, and farmers and their families frequently asked project staff for family planning information and services. DTC staff, with limited knowledge themselves of these subjects, were unable to offer much help. Since this important need was not being met, CARE joined with Uganda's ministry of health in 1992 to establish the Community Reproductive Health Project (CREHP), with several goals: strengthening the capacity of local authorities to initiate and maintain high quality reproductive health services in clinics and in communities, increasing knowledge and changing attitudes about family planning among the population, and improving women's health and status through increased access to, and use of, family planning and other reproductive health services.[4]

Under the new project, clinic staff are trained to educate and counsel clients and to provide family planning and reproductive health services, largely unavailable prior to the project. They also assure that basic equipment and commodities are available and that the services are integrated with other clinic services and activities. To extend services outside the clinics, volunteers chosen by their communities are trained and supervised to raise awareness about family planning, inform the community of the services available, provide nonprescription contraceptives, and refer clients to the clinics. An underlying purpose of the project is to work with the ministry of health to strengthen its internal management systems so that these expanded services are well run and maintained.

Both projects have recently carried out surveys that have illuminated southwestern Ugandans' environmental and family planning concerns and the links between them. In 1992, CREHP conducted a random sample baseline survey of 787 female and 672 male respondents of reproductive age in the project area (Turyasingura et al. 1992). Of the total number of respondents, about 71 percent of the women and 65 percent of the men were married and about 20 percent of the women and nearly 26 percent of the men were single; all others were separated or divorced. The survey found that knowledge of modern contraceptives was relatively high, with two-thirds of the women (64.9 percent) and over half of the men (56.3 percent) able to name at least one method of contraception without prompting. Use of modern methods,[5] however, was extremely low, at just 2.9 percent of women and 4.1 percent of men.

Focus group discussions conducted by trained facilitators as part of the baseline research revealed a desire to control fertility. For example, the use of certain herbs believed to have a contraceptive effect is widespread. Breastfeeding is also widely practiced, although it was not clear whether its contraceptive effect is a motivating force. Certain rituals are thought to have a contraceptive effect: for instance, after a woman delivers, her mother-in-law may put a small pot or grinding stone at the foot of her bed to delay the next pregnancy. Others advocate hanging the dry umbilical cord in the roof of the house. Another recognized method involves temporary separation; after his wife gives birth, a husband takes a temporary job elsewhere.

The survey revealed that the ideal number of children is still high; most survey respondents (74 percent of women) said they wanted five or more children. However, ample birth spacing is traditionally valued, which helps in introducing modern family planning methods. The research showed attitudes toward family planning to be quite positive, despite a common assumption that in traditional societies such attitudes will be negative, especially among men. In-depth, semistructured interviews with 125 female and 80 male respondents who had indicated that they had heard of modern contraceptives in the larger survey revealed that only four percent of women and nine percent of men had unfavorable attitudes. High proportions of both women (82 percent) and men (88 percent) agreed that there should be a limit to the number of children a family should have. In focus groups with community residents conducted as part of the preparatory research, those who preferred "small" families of four to six children said that fewer children were easier to look after, and that parents would have enough land to distribute among them.

Some reservations were voiced regarding who should use contraceptives and under what circumstances. For example, the majority of respondents agreed with the statement that family planning methods should be used only by married people (66 percent of women, 75 percent of men), and disagreed with the statement that adolescents should be allowed to use contraception (62 percent of women and 75 percent of men). Some thought contraception should be used only or primarily for spacing children (67 percent of women and 56 percent of men), while others thought it would be better used after the desired family size was reached (57 percent of women and 69 percent of men).

The DTC survey of randomly selected communities in the project area was undertaken in early 1993, as a baseline for the project's second phase. A total of 402 interviews were conducted, 90 percent with male and 10 percent with female heads of households. The results suggested widespread recognition of the problem of land shortage in the area. Half the survey respondents said a shortage of land was one of their major problems, and 19 percent said it was a major obstacle to their successfully carrying out their main economic activity which, for 70 percent, was farming. Among families in which at least one member had moved away from the community, 37 percent cited land shortage as the major reason for leaving. Others complained of a shortage of food, closely tied to the land problem. Survey respondents recognized that their agricultural yields have gone down because of their shrinking land holdings, and that soil fertility has lessened due to overcropping and insufficient fallowing. Two-thirds of them reported that they had enough food to feed their families only some (34 percent) or most (32 percent) of the time.

The DTC survey also revealed that local communities rely heavily on forest products, despite government regulations protecting forested lands. Enforcement of these regulations has been uneven over the years, but in 1991, Bwindi was officially declared the Bwindi Impenetrable National Park, upgraded from its prior status of Reserve. Enforcement of regulations which prevent harvesting of any forest resources, except in certain pilot multiple use areas, was stepped up. Local residents' adaptation to this new situation was sometimes painful. For example, 26 percent of all respondents admitted that they had cut timber from Bwindi Forest for use in building their houses. People also reported that they collected dead wood or cut wood in the forests for use as firewood. Given the government ban, it is reasonable to assume that these activities are underreported. Some 16 percent of those who claimed they stopped cutting trees after 1991 acknowledged that their income has been reduced as a result.

In general, survey respondents indicated that they understood the value of natural resource conservation, but that their own needs were often incompatible with this goal. For instance, 62 percent agreed that it is important to conserve forests like Bwindi, but at the same time 70 percent felt that while conservation is important, their needs and those of their animals are even more so.

CARE has taken a number of steps to emphasize the links between natural resources and reproductive health needs in the area of the two projects, through activities with the projects' staffs, community and political leaders, and the communities at large. At the project level, the two staffs are developing joint educational messages and materials, such as dramas, audiocassettes, and slide shows to be used in their educational activities, prepared in Rukinga, the local language. The projects also conduct joint educational sessions for staff members. For example, twice a year, CARE's conservation extension agents receive education in family planning. They discuss the benefits of family planning and traditional child spacing practices, and learn about modern contraceptive methods, including the advantages and disadvantages of each method, how each is used, and where it can be obtained. They also learn how to incorporate family planning awareness into their conservation work, and where to refer those wanting further information or services.

In the communities, the projects aim to raise awareness of conservation and population issues and their linkages among influential community and political leaders and among members of community groups involved in conservation and population issues, such as women's groups, church organizations, and scout troops. For example, when the conservation project scheduled a week-long workshop for female group leaders to train them in better agricultural practices, representatives of the family planning project presented information on general health, family planning and its benefits, contraceptives, HIV/AIDS, immunizations, and other health issues. The relationship of family planning to conservation was discussed, and workshop attendees were informed of the services available through both projects—information they could take back to their communities. Follow-up is planned to determine whether awareness is, in fact, increasing in the community, and whether leaders are serving as sources of information.

The two projects also conduct joint sessions during regular government-sponsored political education workshops attended by community leaders and civil servants at different administrative levels (that is, village, district, or region). The district government has agreed that development issues should be added to the political education agenda, so CARE has been leading sessions on family planning and conservation. This provides an excellent opportunity to engage policymakers in discussions of the relationship between the needs of an ever-growing population and the limitations of natural and economic resources.

To reach the community at large with information on the linkages between population and conservation, the project uses a variety of approaches. In addition to training DTC staff in family planning, as noted above, the projects also train government conservation workers and volunteers from NGOs, churches, and other community groups. Likewise, reproductive health agents are taught how to educate, counsel, and refer those desiring further family planning information and services, and in some cases to distribute nonprescription contraceptives. They also receive information on the fundamentals of conservation, including the role of population growth in environmental degradation and how decisions made by families and communities affect their surroundings and long-term prospects. So far, some fifty CARE conservation staff and government natural resource workers have been trained in family planning education and referral; conversely, more than two hundred volunteer community-based reproductive health agents have received conservation information. While the principal functions of the workers do not change, the cross-training increases their recognition of the relationship between population and environment, encourages them to raise community awareness of the relationship, and makes them better able to refer those wanting additional information to the appropriate sources.

In carrying out the two projects' activities, CARE has learned two important lessons. First, because they fear losing their land to the national park, farmers in environmentally protected areas are suspicious of outside programs, especially those linked with the government. Such antagonism does not bode well for the success of either conservation or reproductive health activities. To avert potential conflicts, CARE promotes community-based environmental management. Through this process, which involves ongoing discussions among community residents, community leaders, conservation professionals, and now health professionals, a community makes its own decisions about how to safeguard its environment so that it will remain productive. The DTC project then helps the community implement the actions it has decided upon, contributing technical skills and other resources not otherwise available. As a result, the community better understands the purposes and advantages of such activities as mapping and different farming techniques, and actively participates in them.

The second lesson learned was that there already existed a very clear link between land shortage and family size in the minds of southwestern Ugandans. Population growth and large numbers of children are invariably raised as factors contributing to smaller farms, high crop density, and declining crop yields. CARE's projects therefore need not create this association; instead, they must strengthen it by promoting family planning as an environmental management strategy, and respond to it by ensuring that accurate and appropriate reproductive health information and services are available and accessible.

CARE's initial activities to link widely felt concerns about natural resource limitations and population growth have been well received and supported by the communities, the government ministries with which the two projects work, the CARE system itself, and donors.[6] At the moment, we are searching for ways to forge, study, and test more linkages among environmental and population activities, both within CARE and between CARE and other organizations focusing on similar problems. While it is still too early to draw conclusions about the success of the two projects in southwestern Uganda, the initial signs are hopeful, and we are seeking to determine whether combining the goals of environmental conservation and reproductive health will result in a more effective program than addressing them separately.

Planning for the next phase of both the DTC and CREHP projects, to begin in 1996, has started. Although they were planned largely independently of each other, and efforts were made to link them during their implementation, the new phase is being planned as a joint activity. The preparatory situation analysis focuses on household security rather than on conservation or health specifically, and may well result in additional project initiatives, such as income generation. Joint baseline and follow-up surveys and other project research focused on the independent as well as the synergistic effects of various activities will contribute to a better understanding of the practical value of linking population and environment ventures. Joint planning also permits institutional and management issues, such as staffing and reporting, to be addressed at the outset.

These efforts will enable CARE to assist the government of Uganda to come up with facts—"this is what has been tried, this is what seems to be working"—and, indirectly, to advocate for policy change. Within CARE, our experiences in Uganda will help us to develop a practical population and environmental strategy, and ultimately aid us in expanding our interventions in southwestern Uganda, the country as a whole, and other countries worldwide where we have programs.

Notes

The authors would like to acknowledge, with appreciation, the contributions to this chapter made by Kim Lindblade, University of Michigan population-environment fellow working with CARE Uganda.

1. One of CARE/Uganda's mandates is to assist the government in protecting Uganda's mountain gorillas, along with many other species of plants and animals.
2. During and after the Rwandan war of 1994, there was substantial movement in both directions across the Rwanda–Uganda border. The net effect of this movement on the size of the Ugandan population is, as yet, unclear.
3. In this chapter, "southwestern Uganda" refers to these districts, unless otherwise noted.
4. Both the Development Through Conservation (DTC) and the Community Reproductive Health (CREHP) projects serve Kabale, Kisoro, and Rukungiri Districts, although DTC limits itself to the parts of those districts immediately surrounding the forests.
5. Modern methods are defined as including oral contraceptives, injectables, foaming tablets, condoms, IUDs, and male and female sterilization.
6. The major donor for both projects is USAID. In the case of the DTC project, the funds come from USAID/Kampala; for the CREHP, central funds from Washington are channeled through CARE/Atlanta. Each project has support from other donors as well.

References

Kaijuka, Emmanuel M., Edward Z. A. Kaiji, Anne R. Cross, and Edilberto Loaiza. 1989. *Uganda: Demographic and Health Survey 1988/89*. Entebbe, Uganda, and Columbia, MD: Demographic and Health Surveys, Institute for Resource Development/Macro Systems, Inc.

Turyasingura, Godwin B., Christina Biryabarema, Frank Kaharuza, and Thomas Barton. 1992. "Baseline Survey for Community Reproductive Health in Southwestern Uganda." Kampala, Uganda: Child Health and Development Centre, Makerere University, and CARE Uganda.

World Bank. 1994. *World Development Report 1994: Infrastructure for Development*. New York: Oxford University Press.

Chapter 13

Chagas Disease Control through Community Action in Bolivia

Fanor Balderrama, Hernán Bermudez, Faustino Torrico, and Andrew A. Arata

D iseases transmitted by insects, ticks, and rodents are often referred to as vector-borne diseases. Many of the classical tropical diseases, including malaria, plague, yellow fever, dengue, filariasis, and Chagas disease, fall into this category. Despite decades of work to control these infections, many are showing resurgences as human populations enter into previously uninhabited areas, change ecological balances, and increase in crowded urban areas. Changes in land use and water management, such as irrigation for agriculture, increase breeding areas for the vectors and increase the likelihood for human contact, which in turn increases the risk of disease transmission.

Insecticides, long a major tool in vector control, are becoming less effective since the use of the same insecticides against agricultural insect pests has resulted in insecticide-resistant vector populations. This has been especially true in efforts to control malaria and other diseases common in rural agricultural areas. Other problems with prevention arise from the lack of human and financial resources to conduct vertical programs that require the spraying of all houses, or that depend on large-scale environmental management to reduce the breeding sites of the vectors. Vertical programs are centrally funded, planned, and implemented as a single disease-control operation.

There are no vaccines for malaria, filariasis, the trypanosomiases (African sleeping sickness and Chagas disease in the Americas), leishmaniasis, or schistosomiasis. The most serious form of malaria, falciparum malaria, has become resistant in many areas to chloroquine, a cheap and effective antimalarial. Alternative drugs, such as mefloquine and halofantrine, are more expensive, some have unacceptable side-effects, and some resistance has been noted to these drugs. For other diseases, the chemotherapies may be expensive or only partially effective. This is the case in Chagas disease, in which drug therapy is only effective during the first, or acute, phase. After the acute phase, it is ineffective and no specific treatment exists.

143

The economic impact of vector-borne diseases can be very severe. Direct costs (treatment and prevention) and indirect costs (loss of productivity) may consume between 15 to 20 percent of the annual income of an individual African household (Ettling, Chitsula, and McFarland 1993). Chagas disease is estimated to cost Brazil approximately U.S.$5 billion a year because of absenteeism and another U.S.$250 million for treatment. In Bolivia where the population is much smaller, but more heavily infected, the losses due to Chagas disease are estimated at U.S.$100 million per year.

Some vector-borne diseases, such as yellow fever, produce epidemics with high mortality. Others, such as Chagas disease, result in serious disabilities, with the major effects on the circulatory and intestinal systems. Malaria may occur either in epidemic form, or in areas of high endemicity in which mortality is highest in nonimmune infants. The World Health Organization (WHO) estimates that in sub-Saharan Africa alone, one to two million children die each year from malaria and/or from the resultant anemia. Filariasis (caused by small round worms) produces elephantiasis by lymphatic blocking, and in one form, onchocerciasis, causes blindness. Over half of Africa is endemic for onchocerciasis, also known as river-blindness, causing people to abandon the rich riverine lands near where the black-fly vectors breed, feed, and transmit the disease.

WHO and the Pan American Health Organization (PAHO) consider Chagas disease the most serious parasitic disease in Latin America, and the main cause of heart disease in the region. Chagas is the fourth most serious health problem in Latin America (after respiratory and diarrheal illnesses and HIV infection), as measured by years of life lost, adjusted for disability. Chagas disease occurs only in the Western Hemisphere, where it can be found from Mexico to Argentina, with a few cases reported in the United States. An estimated 100 million people are at risk, and 16 to 18 million are infected in seventeen countries in the Americas.

The rates of Chagas disease infection found in Bolivia are far higher than those in any other Latin American country. It has been estimated that 22 percent of the Bolivian population is infected with Chagas disease, compared to 12 percent in Paraguay, 11 percent in Chile and Panama, 4 percent in Brazil, and 3 percent in Colombia and Peru (Schmunis 1994). The prevalence of positive serology for *Trypanosoma cruzi*, the parasite that causes Chagas disease, in blood donors is estimated to be 25 percent in Bolivia; between 6 and 7 percent in Argentina and Paraguay; and between 1 and 3 percent in Chile, Brazil, Venezuela and Peru (Schmunis 1994).

The Chagas Disease Control Project in Bolivia, sponsored by the Community and Child Health (CCH) Program of the U.S. Agency for International Development (USAID) has taken a preventive approach to vector-borne disease control. Improving people's living conditions is the focus of this approach, which depends upon people's active participation, as described in this chapter. Health education is also essential in Chagas disease programs, where the interval between infection and the development of chronic symptoms may be fifteen to twenty-five years. To be successful and economically sustainable, community participation is required at all levels and stages of the control effort.

The Republic of Bolivia, located in central South America, is a land-locked nation that shares frontiers with five other South American nations: Brazil, Paraguay, Argentina, Chile, and Peru. Bolivia is the fifth largest country on the continent. Its major cities are La Paz, the administrative capital, Sucre, the official and judicial capital, Santa Cruz, and Cochabamba.

Geographically and ecologically, Bolivia has three clearly defined regions: the mountains and high plains, or *Altiplano*; the valleys, or *Yungas*; and the lowlands, or *Llanos*. Approximately 80 percent of Bolivia's population resides in the highlands or valleys. Urban and peri-urban residents comprise about 36 percent of the total population, which was estimated to be 7.5 million people in 1992. Sixty-four percent of the population lives in widely dispersed rural areas.

In Bolivia, Chagas disease occurs primarily in the valleys, plains, and forests lying between altitudes of 300 and 3,500 meters above sea level. Roughly 83 percent of Bolivian territory lies within this endemic zone. Forty-seven percent of Bolivia's population resides in endemic areas, placing close to 3.5 million Bolivians at risk, or already infected, with *T. cruzi*.

Chagas disease is traditionally a rural disease, although it is increasingly being found in peri-urban areas. It is caused by a flagellated protozoan parasite (*T. cruzi*) and transmitted by "kissing" or cone-shaped bugs (or *vinchucas* in Bolivia). There are some fifty species of these insects of the subfamily *Triatominae* in Latin America—of which about twelve are efficient vectors. The most abundant vector in Bolivia is *Triatoma infestans*.

Chagas disease is perpetuated primarily by inadequate housing, and transmission occurs mainly in the home. Houses with cracked mud (adobe) walls and mud and thatch roofs provide ideal habitats for the insect vectors. The insects thrive in the cracks and crevices in the walls of the house, in thatch roofs, and in the corral walls and animal shelters adjacent to houses, feeding on the domestic animals as well, so that the whole residence becomes a small ecosystem supporting the disease cycle. The close proximity between houses and animal quarters, so common in rural Latin America, plays an integral role in the domestic cycle of the infection. The corrals and animal shelters are typically used for cattle, guinea pigs, and fowl. Domestic animals, such as dogs, cats, and guinea pigs, are reservoirs (sources of infection) for the parasites and also serve as food to increase the populations of the insects.

The clinical manifestation of Chagas disease occurs in three sequential phases: acute, latent, and chronic disease. Acute infection may vary from being without symptoms to being severe and fatal. The acute phase is recognized primarily in children, who typically develop fever, enlargement of the liver, spleen, and lymph glands. Mortality during this symptomatic phase is approximately 8 to 10 percent in Bolivia, and generally results from severe inflammation of the heart muscle, or severe meningitis. In nonfatal cases, symptoms usually last three to four months, during which time the children are at increased risk for diarrheal, respiratory, and other infections.

The latent phase is generally without symptoms. However, people in this phase of the illness can transmit the infection via vectors, blood transfusion, or placental transfer during pregnancy. Prenatal infection may result in abortion, low birth weights and congenital infections. From 5 to 15 percent of children born to infected mothers may themselves be infected at birth. Since such a high proportion of the population is infected, including women of reproductive age, this means Chagas not only affects adults, but is also an important childhood disease in Bolivia.

The chronic form of Chagas disease develops in at least 10 to 30 percent of infected people some ten to twenty-five years after the acute phase. In the chronic form of Chagas, heart muscle damage and cardiac rhythm disturbances are typical, and sudden death due to cardiac arrest is common. Chagas disease is said to be the most common cause of congestive heart failure in South America. Pathological changes may also result in swallowing and digestive disorders only treatable by major surgery, which is not a viable option in rural Bolivia.

In Brazil, where the disease has been well studied, Chagas disease seroprevalence (the presence of antibodies in the blood, indicating prior infection) is about 4 percent, compared to Bolivia's 45 percent. In the baseline study that initiated USAID's work in Bolivia, seroprevalence rates were 46 percent positive in Cochabamba, 61 percent in Tarija, and 78 percent in Chuquisaca.

We do not know for certain why the Bolivian infection rate is so high— it is over ten times the rate in Brazil. Certainly the poverty and poor living conditions provide an ideal environment for transmission and maintenance of the infection both in domestic animals and people. Also, however, Bolivia, and parts of Peru, seem to be the site of origin of this disease from which it spread to other parts of Latin America. We cannot prove this hypothesis, but we know the disease is ancient and that wild (and later domesticated) guinea pigs are heavily infected and may have brought the disease when they were introduced into the houses as food animals. The estimated annual cost of medical care due to the disease in Brazil is U.S.$250 million. Brazil loses an additional U.S.$5 billion a year because of absenteeism caused by Chagas disease. Chagas disease also represents a serious drain on the Bolivian economy to a level of at least U.S.$100 million per year. As such, Chagas disease prevention and control demands much greater attention in the area of national programs than it has received to date.

Chagas disease is named for Carlos Chagas, the Brazilian scientist who described the disease in 1908. More than one hundred and fifty wild and domestic mammals serve as reservoir hosts. Examples of reservoirs include armadillos, raccoons, opossums, wild rodents, dogs, cats, guinea pigs, rabbits, and goats.

The genera and species of triatomine insects, the *vinchucas*, that are the vectors of Chagas disease become infected by taking a blood meal from an infected host, and transmit the infection to the next host by contaminating the bite site with feces containing *T. cruzi*.

The prevalence of Chagas disease in Bolivia is highest in rural areas, where poverty, lack of education, and poor housing favor infestation by the triatomine bugs that carry *T. cruzi*. The changing demographic pattern in Bolivia has also produced large peri-urban populations. Immigrants from rural Chagas endemic zones are likely to transport vectors in their household belongings. Recent migrants tend to build housing similar to what they built in rural areas, thus increasing the likelihood of Chagas transmission. In a study (done by CCH) in Cochabamba, 30 percent of the peri-urban houses were infested by vectors. The most heavily infested were those that retained rural similarities, including lots of domestic animals. Intensification of *T. cruzi* transmission in such areas may also result from infections acquired by blood transfusion given the increased access to hospital care and the large proportion of paid seropositive rural donors infecting the blood supply system.

To better understand the emergence of Chagas disease in peri-urban situations, a special study was carried out in 1994 in seven barrios on the urban periphery of Cochabamba. Over 38 percent of residences were infested with *Triatoma infestans*, the vector. The high rates of infestation and infection in peri-urban areas is very disturbing, and will continue to be investigated.

Because there is no adequate medical intervention for Chagas disease, and no vaccine exists, vector control and elimination of vector habitats in and around houses are the only effective control measures. Given the lack of suitable medical interventions, the program has developed an integrated control approach consisting of community education, housing improvements, limited application of insecticides with low toxicity to mammals (including humans) for vector control, and operations research.

Community participation in previously organized efforts to control Chagas disease in Bolivia has been more passive than active. Most control efforts have followed the traditionally vertical malaria model by using government-sponsored insecticide spray teams, an approach that requires only that local people accept the periodic application of residual insecticides to their homes.

Historically, efforts to control Chagas disease in Bolivia were relatively isolated and limited in scope. Results from this project, and others, show that in Bolivia insecticide application alone is not adequate to reduce intense infestation levels encountered. Also, the poor housing makes spraying and other forms of insecticide application inefficient. Because of rugged topography and the lowest population density in South America, maintenance of vertical control programs is logistically difficult and expensive.

Recently, the role of community participation in Chagas disease control has become more dynamic, with increasingly active involvement by local community members in efforts to eliminate or reduce human–vector contact in rural homes. The Secretariat of Health (SOH) and the CCH Chagas Disease Control Program is a nationally organized effort that has made significant progress in incorporating community participation into Chagas disease control efforts.

The Bolivian Secretariat of Health, with assistance from the CCH project of USAID and the Centers for Disease Control (CDC), initiated a pilot vector control program in the three regions of the country where Chagas disease is most prevalent. Officially inaugurated in 1990, the Bolivian National Chagas Disease Control Program currently operates in the departments of Cochabamba, Chuquisaca, and Tarija. Between 46 and 80 percent of people in the test area are serologically positive for *T. cruzi*. Surveys have shown seroprevalence rates of 21 percent for children under one year of age; 34 percent for children one to four years old; 49 percent for children five to nine years old; 61 percent for ten to fourteen year olds; 75 percent for fifteen to forty-four year olds; and 87 percent for adults over forty-four years of age in the areas studied.

No other area of Latin America is so intensely infected by Chagas disease. Infants congenitally infected die at a rate of 50 percent due to Chagas. Children having severe acute infections often suffer malnutrition due to the lengthy febrile illness and frequently die from associated illnesses such as diarrhea, acute respiratory infections, and immunological disorders during this period. Parents, especially mothers, must spend significant amounts of time caring for children suffering from the acute phase of the disease.

Adults in the chronic phase are a large proportion of the population. For example, in an area where 50 percent of the population is infected, 30 percent of these will be expected to have symptoms. These adults suffer from general heart conditions, shortness of breath, inability to eat or defecate (if symptoms are intestinal). This means that productivity and the quality of life are heavily compromised for those who are ill, as well as the people taking care of them.

The overall objectives of this project have been to:

1. develop and test economically feasible control strategies based on epidemiological assessments, housing improvements, health education, and vector control; and

2. develop models for planning, costing, and implementing such strategies in affected areas.

The Bolivian Control Program is a multi-institutional, multidisciplinary effort that emphasizes community-based, integrated vector control through education, housing improvements, and limited insecticide application. Community education emphasizes the role of *Triatoma infestans* and household conditions in the transmission of Chagas disease.

Not all communities readily accepted participation in the program. Earlier government programs for rural improvement may have been unfulfilled, and questions of land tenure made some residents hesitant to become involved. For example, after national land reform several decades ago, precise boundaries and poorly documented land ownership caused concerns for some rural residents. However, following community meetings and workshops, confidence was gained, and the delivery of some building supplies increased participation. Family and neighborhood groups quickly formed to transform one house after another working in teams with the local promoters and artisans, and many exceeded the minimum housing improvements recommended. In areas where water systems were also installed, participation in housing improvement was easier, and people were enthusiastic.

Housing improvement uses a combination of local labor and materials in conjunction with training and program-donated building materials. The project relies on local construction materials. The Cooperative Housing Foundation (see chapter 2), at the request of the CCH Project, carried out a preliminary study on the type of cost-recovery/credit scheme that would be most appropriate in the study area. However, due to lack of resources to establish the needed capital funds, these efforts are not yet operational. Cost-recovery methods and access to credit for home improvements are important elements in a long-term Chagas control program.

After household improvements are completed, residual insecticide of low-mammalian toxicity is applied to all domestic and peri-domestic structures, but is repeated only where reinfestation is evident from a simple community-based surveillance system. In community surveillance, any live or dead vinchucas seen in the house are collected and put into a bag provided by the promoter, and marked with the date collected. These bags are picked up by the promoters who then schedule spraying for houses that need to be sprayed.

Community involvement begins early with the selection by the community of local people to be health promoters. Each promoter receives theoretical and practical training from program educators and eventually has responsibility for forty to eighty households. The promoter gains the confidence of household members, educates them about Chagas disease and its prevention, and motivates them to carry out control measures in their homes. The local promoters are paid a nominal local wage to compensate for other work they might have done. They serve as trainers whose role diminishes as others learn skills.

In Aramasi, a typical community in Cochabamba, houses are made of adobe with sod roofs and are usually about 300 square feet in size. The house is generally made up of a kitchen and one or two bedrooms. There is no electricity or household water connection. One in every four or five houses has an open well. Only 3 percent of the houses have sanitary facilities (latrines). Tarija is another rural area in the south, near the border with Argentina, which is somewhat more prosperous than Aramasi. In Tarija, 18 percent of the houses have latrines, 16 percent have piped water, and 56 percent have electricity. Promoters visit and inspect all the households in their areas.

The first phase of housing improvement is the destruction of irreparable structures, relocation of animal shelters and corrals away from the house, and the application of *revoque*, which is a layer of mud and straw smoothed onto all exposed adobe brick surfaces in all structures (including animal shelters and corrals) to seal the cracks and crevices that serve as the triatomine habitat.

All the home improvement work is done by family and friends who rotate from one house to another as work progresses until all the houses are completed. Locally trained promoters and construction personnel—a mason, a carpenter, and a roofer—assist the family groups. Once the family has completed this first phase, the promoter and a program-trained construction specialist oversee the subsequent housing improvements. During this second phase, roofing tiles are applied to protect improvements and improve insulation. The third phase involves further modification of walls and ceilings, with the application of *revoque fino*. The construction specialist assists homeowners with the installation of standardized windows (with screens) and doors. All modifications are carried out with local labor under the supervision of the local health promoter.

After home improvement, and usually at the same time as an initial insecticide application, promoters teach families practical ways to maintain a vector-free home, such as how to store goods, exclude animals from family living spaces, recognize signs of reinfestation—either live bugs, their molted skins or bloody fecal marks on the walls—and, if needed, how to reapply the insecticide. Surveys of knowledge, attitudes, and practices and other methods to better understand community beliefs have aided in the development of appropriate educational materials. In many areas these are produced in the local languages of Quechua and Aymara, in addition to Spanish.

Materials for use in community and school education programs focus on the important roles of women and children, maintenance of housing improvements, and household management to prevent conditions favorable to vector reinfestation. Emphasis is placed on community participation by analyzing local knowledge and beliefs about the disease and involving the community in education and decision making. Educational efforts are the basis for subsequent community-based surveillance activities. Health education is required to stimulate community participation and the likelihood of sustainability.

Often the symptoms of Chagas disease are well known, but they are attributed to mystical causes. Feverish or malnourished children are thought to be adversely affected by the odor of a dead animal. Sudden death is thought to be caused by bad air or with some aspect of a spirit. Cardiac arrest is considered the result of the person doing something bad, and the anger of Mother Earth demanding retribution and calling the person home. All of these beliefs involve a central knowledge of the symptoms of both acute and chronic Chagas. This makes education about the medical causes of these symptoms easier, because a basic knowledge about them is already present.

Since the operational phase began in 1991, approximately 3,100 houses in fifty-two different communities have been improved using locally trained promoters, educators, and artisans. Strong local interest and enthusiasm continue and the Bolivian government remains committed to the continuation and eventual nationalization of the program. Ongoing local interest and national political support suggest that this program is likely to continue beyond the pilot phase.

Costs to the program for building supplies, transportation of materials, and specialized labor (for example, carpenters and plasterers) were estimated to range from U.S.$250 to U.S.$350 per house in 1991. Increased reliance on local materials and labor has reduced program expenditures. In the Cochabamba pilot region, for example, the CCH program now spends approximately U.S.$140 per house; all other costs are borne by the owners. Depending on the nature of the housing improvements (for example, in Tarija, which is a richer province, home owners often add to the existing structure), the owner's share of the costs of renovation may exceed 50 percent.

Long-term sustainability will require the program to coordinate efficiently existing in-country resources and attract future assistance from donor agencies committed to extended support of health and community development projects and to establish appropriate credit schemes. Strategies to link Chagas disease control activities with other rural development projects such as potable water delivery or improvements in animal husbandry would enhance both community participation and the attractiveness of the program to potential international donors.

The model developed in the Bolivian Chagas Disease Control Project will not be cheap. It has been estimated that U.S.$75 million over fifteen years is a minimum figure; but the disease is costing Bolivia U.S.$100 million a year from lost productivity and early death. This is in addition to the heavy toll of the physical and psychological suffering of those who become ill or die, and the psychological and economic stress this causes for their families.

Participation of community members has inherent value because of its positive effect on the development of social relationships and community solidarity. Community involvement should not simply be considered yet another mechanism for controlling a particular health problem, or a means to lower operational costs in otherwise vertically structured programs, or as a process for returning the burden of unresolved health issues to local people. Rather the dynamic process of community participation represents a necessary strategy for community survival.

When applied to vector control programs, active community involvement not only enhances program components such as home and environmental improvements or vector and disease surveillance, but also results in accrued benefits for public health that exceed programmatic goals and endure well beyond the end of programs.

We are in a period in which donor and international agencies are reviewing priorities for the control of these diseases and in their assistance policies. Should vector-borne disease control be integrated with basic or primary health care systems? Should bilateral and multilateral assistance be targeted toward capacity building and health education rather than commodities? Are they providing the appropriate type of assistance?

Does disease control have to rely only on ministries of health? Could the agricultural sector be induced to help develop methods of cultivation that do not produce insect populations and thereby increase the risk of vector-borne diseases? What is the appropriate role of rural and municipal authorities in providing or assisting the development of housing, water supply, and sanitation that would exclude vectors or reduce their proliferation?

These are some of the questions that must be answered to develop a truly multisectoral preventive approach to disease control. As environmental health is the preventive arm of disease control, and has greater experience in multisectoral efforts, community participation, and health education, future programs should be designed to link environmental, health, and population issues.

The control of specific vector-borne diseases such as malaria, dengue, and filariasis may each require different approaches because of the ecology of the vector and the human populations. Sectors such as housing, agriculture, water and sanitation, and education must link their efforts with the health sector in appropriate ways to offer communities opportunities by which they can prevent these and other diseases.

Note

The authors would like to thank Paul Hartenberger, Ralph Bryan, Robert Tonn, Alvaro Muñoz-Reyes, Joel Kuritsky, Carmen Casanovas, Jorge Velasco, and Antonio Gomez who have contributed greatly to the ongoing work to control Chagas disease in Bolivia.

References

Bryan, Ralph T., Fanor Balderrama, Robert J. Tonn, and João Carlos Pinto Dias. 1994. "Community Participation in Vector Control: Lessons from Chagas Disease." *American Journal of Tropical Medicine and Hygiene* 50 (6, Suppl.):61–71.

Ettling, Mary B., Lester Chitsula, and Deborah McFarland. 1993. *Malawi: The Economic Impact of Malaria on Low-Income Households.* Vector Biology Control (VBC) Project *Report* no. 82239. Arlington, VA: VBC.

Human Development Ministry, National Secretariat of Health, Child, and Community Health Project. 1994. *Chagas Disease in Bolivia: The Work of the SOH/CCH Chagas Control Pilot Program.* La Paz, Bolivia: U.S. Agency for International Development.

Schmunis, Gabriel A. 1994. "*American Trypanosomiasis* as a Public Health Problem." In *Chagas Disease and the Nervous System. Scientific Publication* no. 547. Washington, D.C.: Pan American Health Organization.

Chapter 14

Primary Environmental Care: An Approach to Sustainable Livelihood

Deepak Bajracharya

The principal environmental concerns of millions of the poorest families on earth are the ever-present threat of disease, the loss of soil fertility in their fields, and the lack of such fundamental requirements for well-being as sufficient food, safe water, and adequate sanitation. Many people in developing countries depend directly on the local environment not only for their livelihoods but also for their very survival. Often they have little choice but to make use of whatever resources are within reach, ignoring—often knowingly—the adverse impact of their subsistence practices on the environment. In the long run, protecting the environment and correcting past environmental damage are necessary conditions for the satisfaction of people's basic human needs and continued well-being. But to protect the environment and put a halt to environmental damage, people must have alternative opportunities for making a living. To succeed, development activities must enable local people to secure their livelihoods and manage their resources more wisely and efficiently. Their participation and empowerment are necessary preconditions in the search for sustainable solutions.

Seventy-four percent of the poorest people in Latin America (35 million people), 57 percent in Asia (265 million people), and 51 percent in Africa (71 million people) live on marginal lands characterized by low productivity and high susceptibility to environmental degradation (United Nations Children's Fund 1994, Leonard 1989). In addition, some 850 million people, mostly in Africa, are threatened by desertification; another 500 million, living in highland regions around the world, are in jeopardy from soil erosion and deforestation; 200 million more, living in tropical forest areas, are affected by exploitation of forest and other resources; and over a billion people, living in the world's cities, lack garbage disposal and wastewater drainage facilities, and breathe air choked with suspended particulate matter (Durning 1989).

The poor are especially dependent on the optimal use and proper management of their environment. Yet it is they, more than any other group, whose lives and livelihoods have been the most severely threatened by resource degradation, especially in such ecologically fragile and vulnerable areas as arid and semiarid zones, mountain regions, tropical rainforests, and urban slums.

A community-based approach is essential to enable the poorest 1 billion people worldwide to strive for sustainable livelihoods. Primary environmental care (PEC) is advocated in this context as an appropriate strategy as it integrates three essential elements: (1) meeting basic health and livelihood needs; (2) empowering people and communities for decision making and action in accordance with their own priorities; and (3) ensuring protection and sustainable use of natural resources in and around communities.

Like primary health care (PHC), PEC focuses on alleviating the worst manifestations of poverty stemming from population growth and environmental degradation at the local level, rather than investments in higher-level problems demanding global or regional consensus or actions, or costly, highly technical solutions such as those required to address global warming, ozone layer depletion, or acid rain. PEC aims to enhance poor people's ability to manage their resources for improvement in areas such as health, nutrition, education, and water and sanitation. Applying the principles of PEC can also help incorporate active participation and empowerment of the poor in the search for alternatives and opportunities.

PEC was developed in 1990 as a strategy for poverty alleviation and to halt environmental degradation by the Working Party on Development Assistance and the Environment and endorsed by the Development Assistance Committee (DAC) of the Organization for Economic Cooperation and Development (OECD). It was inspired, in part, by the lessons learned from the successes and failures of primary health care, in which basic preventive and primary level health care are accorded a higher priority and a greater share of human, financial, and other resources than higher-level referral services and specialized medical care. In developing the PEC approach, the working group drew heavily on the international experiences, both successes and failures, of many different agencies and organizations over the last four decades (Directorate General for Development Cooperation 1990).

The following principles were identified as being among the most important for the successful implementation of PEC activities (Borrini 1991, Pretty and Sandbrook 1991, Pretty and Guijt 1992, Bajracharya 1994, Satterthwaite 1994).

- Local people and local communities must have the opportunity to identify, organize, and participate in development activities that facilitate the realization of their self-identified priorities.

- Local people and communities must be enabled to use natural resources, particularly land and water, in more creative ways by ensuring tenure rights to resources and by providing access to new information and financial resources.

- Local people and communities must be encouraged to build on their indigenous knowledge and awareness of the environment as they participate in the development of small-scale, low-cost, more productive, and more environmentally sound technologies.

- Government institutions and local functionaries must provide the political support and necessary services to encourage the process of community-based environmental management.

- Outside planning and implementing agencies (including government agencies, nongovernmental organizations (NGOs), university groups, and international organizations) must commit themselves to the facilitation and mediation of human resources development over the long term, by engaging people in dialogue at the local level, taking an adaptive and flexible approach, and accepting a longer time frame for support.

The PEC approach focuses on ways to improve conditions related to the availability and efficient use of food, fuel, and clean water, while at the same time conserving and protecting natural resources, both in terms of quantity and quality, for the well-being of children, women, and other members of poor communities. Priority attention is given to improving the availability and use of natural resources to reduce, for example, women's workload related to the procurement of food, fuel, and clean water.

Another category given priority attention in the PEC approach is pollution, in the form of biological pathogens and chemical pollutants in water, food, air, and soil that cause ill health and premature death, especially among children and women. PEC activities are directed at bringing about effective behavioral changes, at both the household and community level to alleviate such health problems as water-borne diseases attributable to polluted water or unsafe waste disposal, or airborne diseases caused by indoor air pollution due to smoke from burning coal and fuelwood and exacerbated by overcrowding and poor ventilation.

Examples from different parts of the world validate the soundness of the PEC approach and demonstrate further the potential for innovations and creativity by local people under diverse ecological, cultural, and political contexts (Bajracharya 1994, Davidson, Myers, and Chakraborty 1992, Pye-Smith, Borrini Feyerabend, and Sandbrook 1994, Satterthwaite 1994, United Nations Children's Fund 1992). The challenge that lies ahead is to sharpen the methodologies and tools for more effective implementation and to spread the lessons from successes and failures in local experiences to adjoining communities and neighboring districts and provinces. These concerns were reaffirmed with great conviction by more than one hundred and eighty participants who gathered at the International Symposium on Community-Based Sustainable Development, "In Local Hands," organized by the International Institute for Environment and Development (IIED) in July 1994.[1]

Adoption of PEC by UNICEF

As already noted, the most vulnerable and most severely affected victims of environmental and health-related problems are children and women. More than 13 million children under five years old die each year from easily preventable causes, and 400 mothers die for every 100,000 live births. Of 700 million children living in forty-three countries with very high child mortality rates, approximately a third are moderately or severely undernourished; about half have no access to primary school, basic health services, or safe water; and more than three-quarters lack access to adequate sanitation. Immunization coverage against DPT (diphtheria, pertussis, and tetanus), polio, and measles among children under one year of age, and tetanus among pregnant women, ranges only around 60 percent in these countries. Given these conditions, it is imperative that emphasis be placed on activities related to primary health care, immunizations, micronutrient deficiencies, household food security, basic education for all, and increased access to safe water and adequate sanitation facilities.

The linkage between these activities and the environment is clear from the Declaration and Plan of Action endorsed by the World Summit for Children in 1990:

> The child survival and development goals proposed for the 1990s seek to improve the environment by combatting disease and malnutrition and promoting education. These contribute to lowering death rates as well as birth rates, improved social services, better use of natural resources, and ultimately, to the breaking of the vicious cycle of poverty and environmental degradation. (United Nations Children's Fund 1990)

As described in the *State of the World's Children Report* for 1994 (United Nations Children's Fund 1994), low-cost opportunities to protect the health, nutrition, and education of children and women are the most immediately available and affordable ways to weaken the downward spiral attributable to poverty, population growth, and environmental degradation. The report postulated that the universal meeting of minimum human needs, the stabilization and possible reduction of population levels, and an overarching regard for environmental sustainability in the pursuit of economic growth should become the new central organizing principles of the post–Cold War world. This multifaceted challenge will demand technological, managerial, and political capacity and ingenuity from nations and the international community.

The adoption of PEC by the United Nations Children's Fund (UNICEF) is a strategic response to address these underlying global concerns. Following up on Agenda 21 recommendations,[2] the UNICEF executive board decision in 1993 emphasized that PEC be integrated in UNICEF-assisted programs in health, education, and water and sanitation. The idea is to draw lessons from past experiences where such integration was successfully carried out and to build in PEC as an explicit element in future program development. The approach is to supplement ongoing efforts of basic services delivery (to achieve survival, protection, and development of children and women) with capacity building of local people, especially the poor (to enable them to participate actively in programs based on their needs and priorities), and sustainable management of resources (to protect as well as promote their innovative and effective use for better livelihood).

Examples from UNICEF's Involvement

Rather than creating a separate, additional program, UNICEF is in the process of integrating the PEC approach into its ongoing programs in health, nutrition, education, and water and sanitation. In each case, finding an appropriate entry point for such integration is the key to implementation. The examples below are among many drawn from country programs where the PEC approach has already been tried, and where the potential exists to reinforce the PEC perspective more systematically.

Family Food Production in the Philippines. The Family Food Production Program (FFPP) in the Philippines began with a primary focus on severe malnutrition among children and women as the entry point. UNICEF, in partnership with the International Institute for Rural Reconstruction (IIRR), began by assisting the provincial government of Negros Occidental to implement bio-intensive gardens (BIG), a simple technology that relies on the use of 50-square-meter plots of land, together with organic fertilizers, natural pesticides, and indigenous seeds, to meet daily vegetable needs. Later, to help meet the cash and food needs of the families, the concept of the food lot module (FLM), which integrates components such as crops, livestock, fishponds and trees, on 1,000 square meters of land, was introduced. Children participated by establishing school nurseries for vegetable seeds and distributing seeds and seedlings in the community. Emphasis was also given to training for community organizing, technology updates, and forming family food production committees at the municipal level. This project has helped reduce malnutrition in children from 40 percent down to 25 percent in the communities where the project was introduced.

Poverty and Environment Project in Brazil. Drawing on indigenous knowledge of Amazonian conditions, this project promotes locally oriented development approaches that place top priority on meeting basic needs of the poor in ways that protect the environment. It mobilizes collaboration among state and municipal governments, local communities, and university researchers. Local efforts have concentrated on such activities as low cost treatment of water, agroforestry, income generation from recycling of garbage, and environmental education.

Making Veld Products in Botswana. A local NGO and research organization, Thusano Lefatsheng, has been supported by UNICEF and international NGOs since 1984 to purchase, process, and market indigenous veld products, specifically indigenous food and medicinal plants, commonly found in Botswana. The harvesting of raw materials is done by women during the agricultural off-peak season and has proven to be an important source of income over which women can maintain control. In 1993, this profitable enterprise became self-supporting. This provides a good example of an alternative livelihood strategy that is self-reliant and uses "drought-proof" local resources.

Activities to Reduce Women's Workload in Nepal. In Nepal, a broad range of activities was introduced in 1991 to mobilize local communities to help conserve the local environment, improve the household living environment, and reduce the workload of women. These activities were organized in conjunction with ongoing programs of the Production Credit for Rural Women (PCRW) and the Small Farmers' Development Programme (SFDP). The activities include community-based tree nurseries, small agroforestry schemes, village water supply systems, dissemination of improved stoves, and building latrines and compost pits. In addition, the project supports income-generation activities, creation of awareness about the local environment, and environmental improvements at the household and community levels.

Environmental Education in Madagascar. Environmental education has been combined with a number of activities in Madagascar as part of the primary school curriculum. With UNICEF's support, local NGOs and relevant government ministries (including those responsible for education, agriculture, water and forestry, animal production and fishery, and population and social affairs) have participated in the implementation of this integrated environmental initiative. Teachers and interested parents have been trained in school gardening and agroforestry techniques, as well as in the construction of latrines, improved cook stoves, and tree nurseries. The produce from the vegetable gardens has been used to supplement school meals or sold to purchase school supplies.

Child Survival and Development Program in Tanzania. This program, which reaches close to half of Tanzania's children, has succeeded in reducing severe malnutrition from levels as high as 10 percent in 1980 to between 0.5 to 2 percent today. The problem of malnutrition was given top priority in the course of community-level analysis and was approached in an integrated manner. It therefore emphasized household food security (including food and nutrition planning, agroforestry, crop promotion, and home gardening) together with infrastructure development, maternal and child health, child care and development, water and environmental sanitation, and income-generation activities. Factors affecting the success of the program have been the decentralized structure of institutions to support "bottom-centered" planning, local control of resources and decision making, multisectoral collaboration, and advocacy for support at the policy level.

Challenges in Integrating the PEC Strategy

To build on the foundation that already exists and to incorporate the PEC perspectives more explicitly into development activities like those of UNICEF-assisted programs, three interconnected issues are of central importance.

1. *Active participation of children and women in environmental education and community action.* Developing countries have more than 1.5 billion children below the age of fifteen, constituting about 38 percent of the total population. In countries of sub-Saharan Africa, the percentage is as high as 46 to 51 percent. Children's natural affinity for environmental issues as well as their concerns for a just, equitable, and sustainable world are often underestimated. Their untapped energy could form an essential force in the search for new and innovative strategies to attain better livelihoods today and to protect the earth for future generations.

Women constitute half of the human race, and are the primary managers of local environmental resources in many societies. In countries of Africa, they contribute as much as 80 percent of resource-related activities, including water collection, fuelwood gathering, domestic food processing, and agricultural food production for subsistence needs and increasingly for export. They are often the repository of valuable indigenous knowledge about resource management.

Recent experiences have shown possibilities of engaging students and teachers at schools, as well as young people outside of school, in ecological resource mapping and surveillance of community problems. This forms the basis for creating awareness about the environment—both the state of its degradation and the potential of alternative opportunities for a better livelihood. What could be pursued in conjunction with PEC is to use such experiences to identify activities that could be done at home and in the communities together with parents, grandparents, and other family members.[3] This intergenerational undertaking has tremendous potential in bringing about attitudinal and behavioral changes to alleviate the mounting problems of the environment and development. The difficulties may seem too complex and daunting. But the potential rewards, if there is a will to change, can be enormously satisfying. PEC methods need to explore ways of providing incentives that could lead to such fundamental changes.

2. *Confidence building in communities to meet priority needs.* UNICEF's experiences in different countries under varying conditions show that an emphasis on practical, measurable, and achievable goals can create unprecedented momentum and opportunities for public mobilization at the grassroots level as well as political support at the highest levels of government. To sustain the momentum, it is essential that cultural and ecological diversity be adequately reflected in setting up these goals, and that the local population, especially women, be involved in prioritizing these goals.

Such a process implies that the current resurgence of decentralization and democratization be oriented toward reinforcing the political will for sustainable social action, and giving greater attention to the plight of the poorest and most marginalized people. References have been made throughout this chapter to several possible entry points for concerted action. These include, for example, reduction of women's work load concerning water collection, fuelwood gathering, and food processing; generation of opportunities for alternate sources of income using underutilized resources in the community such as medicinal herbs, hydropower, solar and wind energy; introduction of relevant school curricula that would motivate students and teachers to reflect on the havoc created by environmental and other social problems; nonformal education to institute behavioral changes for better health, improved nutrition intake, and greater respect for nature.

Clear articulation of approaches and tools is needed in a number of critical areas, including the process for identifying problems and priorities in ecologically vulnerable areas, analyzing child survival indicators in these areas, locating and coordinating efforts with relevant NGOs, assessing related programs of government agencies and international organizations, and approaches for carrying out participatory appraisals and making choices about programs which are likely to have the greatest impact. A consolidated and collective approach that relies on inputs at local, national, and international levels will need to be developed in many areas.

A powerful tool for keeping up the momentum of community involvement is monitoring the progress made over time in achieving goals, using easily understood indicators that local people (including children and youth) can develop and measure on a regular basis. If the PEC perspective is to be incorporated successfully into the programming process of local as well as national and international organizations and agencies, including UNICEF, the linkage of environmental indicators and related process indicators to the goals of survival and development need to be clearly established. Relevant indicators might include: improvements in child growth and nutrition intake, reduction in women's time spent in collecting water or fuelwood, generation of additional income, or increases in agricultural production. Operational procedures and guidelines need to be made explicit for program planning, monitoring and evaluation, and formulating program strategies.

3. *"Going to scale" with community successes.* The biggest challenge for effective implementation of PEC is how to spread the lessons from successes and failures to other areas in a progressive way to make a significant impact on poverty alleviation and environmental improvement. Mechanisms must be found to sustain innovative initiatives at the local level while at the same time ensuring that such efforts are widespread enough to make a difference at the aggregate level. This has been a continuing concern and a major theme of the International Symposium on Community-Based Sustainable Development held in July 1994.

Experiences from area-based programs indicate that "going to scale" is, in general, not readily achieved when efforts are made to replicate successful innovations from one pilot area to other areas. This seems to be the case especially when the pilot area receives intensive external inputs in various forms, at the cost of paralyzing local initiatives and community participation.

The emphasis in PEC on the process of mobilizing community participation for local resource utilization and focusing on self-directed development is critical in order to overcome many of the constraints associated with externally driven efforts. However, there is a danger that this process can become too location-specific and the benefits of the experience can take too long to spread to other areas. PEC therefore needs a systematic focus on a related process that promotes extension and adaptation in adjoining communities and neighboring districts (Taylor-Ide and Taylor 1995). The following three interrelated elements at a country level are essential in such a process:

1. Identifying projects or initiatives where local people have managed on their own, possibly with catalytic support from outside the community, to introduce innovations that are appropriate within the social, cultural, and ecological context of the area.

2. Helping to make these communities epicenters of action-learning. For example, training can be conducted for people from other communities in community-to-community exchanges, to motivate and assist others in adapting these experiences to conditions in their own communities.

3. Utilizing social mobilization techniques to encourage national planners and policymakers, local authorities, NGOs, research institutions, and donors to assist families and communities in pursuing sustainable development efforts. This means increasing access to community extension workers, simplifying science-based interventions to be applied in the home by family members, and facilitating the transfer of techniques and methods from one community to another. It also means reexamining the different but complementary roles of community members, local authorities, government officials, NGO workers, experts and researchers, and donors, in order to facilitate self-directed action.

It is clear that the goals of PEC present a myriad of challenges. Among these is that the people who need the greatest attention are also the most politically and economically marginalized, and thus the hardest to reach. Cultural and ecological diversity must continually be taken into account, so that the process of empowerment and social mobilization reflects local priorities and capabilities, builds on local indigenous knowledge and local resources, and facilitates innovation to face the many challenges of these changing times.

There is heightened awareness of the environment in the world today, and of the need for action to counter the prevalence of increasing environmental degradation. PEC provides the opportunity to link this with development programs and give a new meaning to the fight against poverty. The task of moving toward a new paradigm of sustainable human development is enormously complex, but essential, to translate rhetoric about the environment into committed actions against poverty and environmental degradation.

Notes

1. This symposium was organized by the International Institute for Environment and Development (IIED) and sponsored by the Ford Foundation, as well as the governments of Italy, Switzerland, and the United Kingdom, and was organized in association with the World Conservation Union (IUCN), Oxfam U.K., Intermediate Technology Development Group (ITDG), Action-Aid, the Prince of Wales Business Leaders Forum, Friends of the Earth; World Fund for Nature U.K., and the Overseas Development Institute. See the list of organizations actively pursuing the PEC approach in the Additional Resources section.
2. Agenda 21 is the operational document on environment and sustainable development for the 21st century—one of the most important outcomes of the 1992 United Nations Conference on Environment and Development (UNCED).
3. For more details, see Espinosa and Hart 1994, Hart 1992, and Muntemba 1993.

References

Bajracharya, Deepak. 1994. "Primary Environmental Care for Sustainable Livelihood: A UNICEF Perspective." *Childhood* 2:41–55 (Denmark).

Borrini, Grazia, ed. 1991. *Lessons Learned in Community-Based Environmental Management.* Proceedings of the 1990 Primary Environmental Care Workshop, Siena, Italy, January 29–February 2, 1990. ICHM. Istituto Superiore di Sanità, Rome.

Davidson, Joan, Dorothy Myers, and Manab Chakraborty. 1992. *No Time to Waste: Poverty and the Global Environment.* Oxford: Oxfam U.K.

Directorate General for Development Cooperation. 1990. *Supporting Primary Environmental Care.* Report of the PEC Workshop, Siena, Italy, to the Working Party on Development Assistance and the Environment, Development Assistance Committee, Organization for Economic Cooperation and Development, Paris.

Durning, Alan B. 1989. "Poverty and the Environment: Reversing the Downward Spiral." *Worldwatch Paper* 92. Washington, D.C.: Worldwatch Institute.

Espinosa, Maria Fernanda, and Roger A. Hart. 1994. "Recommendations for Environmental Education and Girls' Education in Niger." Report of a mission for the United Nations Children's Fund. Niamey, Niger.

Hart, Roger A. 1992. "Children's Participation: From Tokenism to Citizenship." *Innocenti Essays* no. 4. International Child Development Centre, United Nations Children's Fund, Florence, Italy.

Leonard, Jeffrey. 1989. "Environment and the Poor: Development Strategies for a Common Agenda." Washington, D.C.: Overseas Development Council.

Muntemba, Shimwaayi. 1993. "Promoting Environmental Education for Sustainable Livelihoods in Eastern and Southern Africa." Report prepared for the Environment Section, United Nations Children's Fund, New York.

Pretty, Jules N., and Richard Sandbrook. 1991. *Guidelines for Aid Agencies on Sustainable Development at the Community Level: Primary Environmental Care.* Paris: Organization for Economic Cooperation and Development.
————— and Irene Guijt. 1992. "Primary Environmental Care: An Alternative Paradigm for Development Assistance." *Environment and Urbanization* 4(1):22–36.
Pye-Smith, Charlie, and Grazia Borrini Feyerabend, with Richard Sandbrook. 1994. *The Wealth of Communities: Stories of Success in Local Environmental Management.* West Hartford, CT: Kumarian Press.
Satterthwaite, David. 1994. "Children, Environment and Sustainable Development in the Third World." Report prepared for the Environment Section, United Nations Children's Fund, New York.
Taylor-Ide, Daniel, and Carl E. Taylor. 1995. *Community Based Sustainable Human Development: Going to Scale with Self-Reliant Development.* PEC Discussion Paper Series no. 1. Environment Section, United Nations Children's Fund, New York.
United Nations Children's Fund (UNICEF). 1990. *Declaration and Plan of Action of the World Summit for Children; and Convention on the Rights of the Child.* UNICEF, New York.
—————. 1992. *Environment, Development and the Child.* Environment Section, Program Division, UNICEF, New York.
—————. 1994. *The State of the World's Children Report.* Oxford: Oxford University Press.

Additional Readings

The following are suggested readings for those who would like more information about topics raised in this book. Readings for a number of chapters with overlapping subject matter have been combined in order to reduce repetition. Interested readers should also review the works listed at the end of each chapter, in the sections entitled "References," since those works are not repeated here.

Part I: Urbanization, Health, and the Environment

Chapter 1 and Chapter 2

Adams, Dale, and J. D. Von Pischke. 1992. "Microenterprise Credit Programs: Deja Vu." *World Development* 10:1463–70.

Arrossi, Silvina, Felix Bombarolo, Jorge E. Hardoy, Diana Mitlin, Luis Pérez Coscio, and David Satterthwaite. 1994. *Funding Community Initiatives.* London: Earthscan Publications.

Bartone, Carl, Janis Bernstein, Josef Leitmann, and Jochen Eigen. 1994. *Toward Environmental Strategies for Cities: Policy Considerations for Urban Environmental Management in Developing Countries.* Urban Management Programme *Policy Paper* 18. Washington, D.C.: World Bank.

Bradley, David, Carolyn Stephens, Trudy Harpham, and Sandy Cairncross. 1992. *A Review of Environmental Health Impacts in Developing Country Cities.* Urban Management Programme *Discussion Paper* 6. Washington, D.C.: World Bank.

Carroll, Thomas. 1992. *Intermediary NGOs: The Supporting Link in Grassroots Development.* West Hartford, CT: Kumarian Press.

Cooperative Housing Foundation. 1992. *Partnership for a Livable Environment.* Washington, D.C.

Environment and Urbanization. A journal available from the International Institute for Environment and Development, 3 Endsleigh Street, London WC1H 0DD, United Kingdom.

Hardoy, Jorge E., Diana Mitlin, and David Satterthwaite. 1992. *Environmental Problems in Third World Cities.* London: Earthscan Publications.

Hardoy, Jorge E., Sandy Cairncross, and David Satterthwaite, eds. 1990. *The Poor Die Young: Housing and Health in Third World Cities.* London: Earthscan Publications.

Hogrewe, William, Steven D. Joyce, and Eduardo A. Perez. 1993. *The Unique Challenges of Improving Peri-Urban Sanitation.* WASH Technical Report No. 86. Arlington, VA: Water and Sanitation for Health (WASH) Project.

Inter-American Development Bank. 1994. *Technical Guide for the Analysis of Microenterprise Finance Institutions.* Washington, D.C.

Jordan, Sara, and Fritz Wagner. 1993. "Meeting Women's Needs and Priorities for Water and Sanitation in Cities." *Environment and Urbanization* 5(2):135.

Lall, Vinay D. 1991. "Financial Strategy for the Urban Poor." In *The Urban Poor and Basic Infrastructure Services in Asia and the Pacific.* (3 vols.) A report on a seminar held on January 22–28, 1991. Manila, Philippines: Economic Development Institute, Asian Development Bank.

Leitmann, Josef. 1994. *Rapid Urban Environmental Assessment: Lessons from Cities in the Developing World.* Vol. 1: "Methodology and Preliminary Findings." Vol. 2: "Tools and Outputs." Urban Management Programme *Discussion Paper* no. 14. Washington D.C.: World Bank.

Letvitsky, Jacob, ed. 1989. *Microenterprises in Developing Countries.* London: Intermediate Technology Publications.

Mann, Charles K., Merilee S. Grindle, and Parker Shipton. 1989. *Seeking Solutions: Framework and Cases for Small Enterprise Development Programs.* West Hartford, CT: Kumarian Press.

Otero, María, and Elisabeth Rhyne, eds. 1994. *The New World of Microenterprise Finance: Building Healthy Financial Institutions for the Poor.* West Hartford, CT: Kumarian Press.

Prokopenko, Joseph, and Igor Pavlin, eds. 1991. *Entrepreneurship Development in Public Enterprise.* West Hartford, CT: Kumarian Press.

Rhyne, Elisabeth. 1992. "Financial Services for Microenterprises: Principles and Institutions." *World Development* 20(11):1561–71.

Small Enterprise Development. A journal available from Intermediate Technology Publications, 103-105 Southampton Row, London, WC1B 4HH, United Kingdom.

Solo, Tova María, Eduardo Perez, and Steven Joyce. 1993. *Constraints in Providing Water and Sanitation Services to the Urban Poor.* WASH Technical Report no. 85. Arlington, VA: Water and Sanitation for Health (WASH) Project.

Stren, Richard, et al. 1992. *An Urban Problematique: The Challenge of Urbanization for Development Assistance.* Toronto: University of Toronto, Centre for Urban and Community Studies.

United Nations Children's Fund (UNICEF). N.d. *Urban Examples: Prospective for the Future: Water Supply and Sanitation to Urban Marginal Areas of Tegucigalpa, Honduras.* Guatemala City: UNICEF/Guatemala.

The Urban Age. A journal available from The World Bank, 1818 H Street, N.W. Room S4-031, Washington, D.C. 20433

Varley, Robert C. G. 1995. *Financial Services and Environmental Health: Household Credit for Water and Sanitation.* Environmental Health Project (EHP) *Applied Study* no. 2. Arlington, VA: EHP.

Von Pischke, J. D. 1991. *Finance at the Frontier: Debt Capacity and the Role of Credit in the Private Economy.* Washington, D.C.: Economic Development Institute, World Bank.

Water Supply and Sanitation Collaborative Council. 1993. Report of the Working Group on Urbanization. Geneva, Switzerland.

Chapter 3

Curtis, Lynn A. 1985. *American Violence and Public Policy: An Update of the National Commission on the Causes and Prevention of Violence.* New Haven: Yale University Press.

"Forum on Youth Violence in Minority Communities: Setting the Agenda for Prevention: A Summary." 1991. *Public Health Reports* 106(3):225–77.

Franco, Agudelo, S. 1992. "Violence and Health: Preliminary Elements for Thought and Action." *International Journal of Health Services* 22(2):365–76.

Herzberg, Leonard J., Gene F. Astrum, and Joan Roberts Field, eds. 1990. *Violent Behavior.* Vol. 1. Great Neck, NY: PMA Publishing Corp.

Isaacs, Mareasa R. 1992. *Violence: The Impact of Community Violence on African American Children and Families.* Arlington, VA: National Center for Education in Maternal and Child Health.

Journal of the American Medical Association 267(22). 1992. Entire issue devoted to interpersonal violence.

Kellerman, Arthur. 1993. "Participation, Poverty and Violence: Health and Survival in Latin America." In *Reaching Health for All.* Edited by J. Rohde, M. Chatterjee, and D. Morley, 103–29. Delhi, India: Oxford University Press.

Kellerman, Arthur, Frederick P. Rivara, Norman B. Rushforth, and Joyce G. Banton. 1993. "Gun Ownership as a Risk Factor for Homicides in the Home." *New England Journal of Medicine* 329(15):1084–91.

Muckart, D. J. J. 1991. "Trauma—The Malignant Epidemic." *South African Medical Journal* 79(2):93–95.

National Committee for Injury Prevention. 1989. "Injury Prevention: Meeting the Challenge." *American Journal of Preventive Medicine* 5(3) (Supplement).

Prothrow-Stith, Deborah. 1991. *Deadly Consequences.* New York: HarperCollins.

Rosenberg, Mark. 1988. "Violence as a Public Health Problem." *Transactions and Studies of the College of Physicians of Philadelphia* 10(1–4):147–68.

Schwarz, Donald F., ed. 1992. "Children and Violence: Report of the 23rd Ross Roundtable on Critical Approaches to Common Pediatric Problems." Columbus, Ohio: Ross Laboratories.

Spivak, Howard, ed. 1994. "The Role of the Pediatrician in Violence Prevention." *Pediatrics* 94(4) (Supplement).

United Nations Centre for Human Settlement (Habitat). 1991. *Urbanization: Water Supply and Sanitation Challenges.* Nairobi.

The Urban Age 1(4). 1993. Entire issue devoted to urban violence.

Walker, Bailus, Jr., Norma Goodwin, and Reuben Warren. 1992. "Violence: A Challenge to the Public Health Community." *Journal of the National Medical Association* 84:490–96.

Wallace, Roderick, Deborah Wallace, and Howard Andrews. 1994. *AIDS, Tuberculosis, Violent Crimes and Low Birthweight in Metropolitan Areas: Public Policy and the Regional Diffusion of Inner City Markers.* New Brunswick, NJ: Rutgers University Press.

"Weapon Carrying Among High School Students—United States." 1990. *Morbidity and Mortality Weekly Report* 40(40):681–84 (Centers for Disease Control and Prevention).

Yunes, João. 1993. "Mortality from Violent Causes in the Americas." *Bulletin of the Pan American Health Organization* 27(2):154–67.

Ziwi, Anthony, and Antonio Ugalde. 1989. "Towards an Epidemiology of Political Violence in the Third World." *Social Science and Medicine* 28(7):633–42.

Part II: Implications of Industrialization for Health and the Environment

Chapter 4 and Chapter 5

Agency for Toxic Substances and Disease Registry. 1992. *Public Health Assessment Guidance Manual*. Atlanta, GA: Public Health Service, U.S. Department of Health and Human Services.

Aubel, Judi, and Mohamed Mansour. 1989. "Qualitative Community Health Research: A Tunisian Example." *Health Policy and Planning* 4(3):244–51.

Chivian, Eric, Michael McCally, Howard Hu, and Andrew Haines. 1993. *Critical Condition: Human Health and the Environment*. Cambridge, MA: MIT Press.

Debus, Mary. 1989. *Methodological Review: A Handbook for Excellence in Focus Group Research*. Washington, D.C.: Academy for Educational Development.

Finkel, Adam M., and Dominic Golding, eds. 1994. *Worst Things First? The Debate Over Risk-Based National Environmental Priorities*. Washington, D.C.: Resources for the Future.

Krueger, Richard. 1988. *Focus Groups: A Practical Guide to Applied Research*. Newbury Park, CA: Sage Publications.

Kumar, Krishna. 1987. *Conducting Group Interviews in Developing Countries. Program Design and Evaluation Methodology Report* no. 8. Washington, D.C.: U.S. Agency for International Development.

Minard, Richard, Kenneth Jones, and Christopher Paterson. 1993. *State Comparative Risk Projects: A Force for Change*. Burlington, VT: Northeast Center for Comparative Risk.

Paustenbach, Dennis J., ed. 1989. *The Risk Assessment of Environmental Hazards: A Textbook of Case Studies*. New York: John Wiley.

Project in Development and the Environment (PRIDE). 1994. *Comparing Environmental Health Risks in Cairo, Egypt*. Washington, D.C.: Chemonics International, Inc.

Scrimshaw, Susan, and Elena Hurtado. 1987. *Rapid Assessment Procedures for Nutrition and Primary Health Care*. Los Angeles: Latin America Center for Publications, University of California at Los Angeles.

Suárez, José, Jorge Oviedo Carrilo, Jorge Albán Gómez, Nelson Reascos Vallejo, Rodrigo Barreto Vaquero, and Ampara Gordillo Toban. 1992. *Medio ambiente y salud en el Ecuador*. Quito, Ecuador: Fundación Natura.

Symposia on Environmental and Occupational Health During Societal Transition in Central and Eastern Europe. Proceedings available from Barry S. Levy Associates, 128 Hollis Street, Sherborn, MA 01770.

U.S. Agency for International Development (USAID). 1990. "Ranking Environmental Risks in Bangkok, Thailand." *Working Paper*. Washington, D.C.: Office of Housing and Urban Programs, USAID.

Part III: Exploring Gender Roles in Environmental Management, Health, and Development

Chapter 6

Agarwal, Bina. 1991. "Engendering the Environment Debate: Lessons from the Indian Subcontinent." *CASID Distinguished Speaker Series* no. 8. East Lansing, MI: Center for Advanced Study of International Development.

Barrow, Christoper J. 1991. *Land Degradation: Development and Breakdown of Terrestrial Environments.* Cambridge and New York: Cambridge University Press.

Braidotti, Rosi, Ewa Charkiewicz, Sabine Hausler, and Saskia Wieringa. 1994. *Women, the Environment and Sustainable Development: Towards a Theoretical Synthesis.* London: Zed Books, Ltd.

Correa, Sonia. 1994. *Population and Reproductive Rights: Feminist Perspectives from the South.* London: Zed Books, Ltd.

Diamond, Irene, and Gloria Orenstein, eds. 1990. *Reweaving the World: The Emergence of Ecofeminism.* San Francisco: Sierra Club.

Dixon-Mueller, Ruth. 1993. *Population Policy and Women's Rights: Transforming Reproductive Choice.* Westport, CT: Praeger Publishers.

Hombergh van den, Helen. 1993. *Gender, Environment and Development: A Guide to the Literature.* Amsterdam: Institute for Development Research.

Johns Hopkins University Population Information Program. 1992. "Five Major Population Impacts." *Population Reports* 20(2):10.

Jiggins, Janice. 1994. *Changing the Boundaries: Women-Centered Perspectives on Population and the Environment.* Washington, D.C.: Island Press.

Koblinsky, Marge, Judith Timyan, and Jill Gay, eds. 1993. *The Health of Women: A Global Perspective.* Boulder, CO: Westview Press.

Leisinger, Klaus M., and Karin Schmitt. 1994. *All Our People: Population Policy with a Human Face.* Washington, D.C.: Island Press.

Mazur, Laurie Ann, ed. 1994. *Beyond the Numbers: A Reader on Population, Consumption, and the Environment.* Washington, D.C.: Island Press.

Moffett, George D. 1994. *Critical Masses: The Global Population Challenge.* NewYork: Viking.

Mueller-Dixon, Ruth. 1993. *Population Policy and Women's Rights: Transforming Reproductive Choice.* Westport, CT: Praeger Publishers.

Ofosu-Amaah, Waafas, and Wendy Philleo, eds. 1992. *Success Stories of Women and the Environment.* Vol. 2 of *Proceedings of the Global Assembly of Women and the Environment—Partners in Life.* Washington, D.C.: United Nations Environment Program and WorldWIDE Network.

Ofosu-Amaah, Waafas, and Wendy Philleo. 1993. *Women and the Environment: An Analytical Review of Success Stories.* Washington, D.C.: United Nations Environment Program and WorldWIDE Network.

Paolisso, Michael, and Sally W. Yudelman. 1991. *Women, Poverty and the Environment in Latin America.* Washington, D.C.: International Center for Research on Women.

Shiva, Vandana. 1988. *Staying Alive: Women, Ecology and Development.* London: Zed Books, Ltd.

Steady, Filomina Chioma, ed. 1993. *Women and Children First: Environment, Poverty and Sustainable Development.* Vermont: Schenkman Books.
United Nations Population Fund (UNPF). 1992. *The State of World Population.* New York: United Nations.

Chapter 7

Asit, K. Biswas, Mohammed Jellali, and Glenn E. Stout, eds. 1993. *Water for Sustainable Development in the Twenty-First Century.* Water Resources Management Series, no. 1. Oxford: Oxford University Press.
Cairncross, Sandy. 1992. *Sanitation and Water Supply: Practical Lessons from the Decade.* A United Nations Development Program (UNDP)/World Bank Water and Sanitation Program *Discussion Paper Series,* no. 9. Washington, D.C.: World Bank.
Kinley, David. 1987. "Handpumps Across the South." *Cooperation South* 2 (United Nations Development Program).
———. 1993. "Running Just to Stay in Place: Water, Health, and the Environment." *Choices* (December) (United Nations Development Program).
Mwangola, Margaret. N.d. "KWAHO's Experiences in Water and Sanitation, 1980–1990." Nairobi, Kenya: Kenya Water for Health Organization (KWAHO).
Narayan, Deepa. 1993. "Participatory Evaluation Tools for Managing Change in Water and Sanitation." *Technical Paper* no. 207. Washington, D.C.: World Bank.
Narayan, Deepa, and Lyra Srinivasan. 1994. *Participatory Develoment Tool Kit: Materials to Facilitate Community Empowerment.* Washington, D.C.: World Bank.
United Nations International Research and Training Institute for the Advancement of Women (INSTRAW). 1989. *Women, Water Supply and Sanitation: Making the Link Stronger.* Santo Domingo.
Water and Sanitation for Health (WASH) Project. 1993. *Lessons Learned in Water, Sanitation, and Health: Thirteen Years of Experience in Developing Countries.* Arlington, VA.
World Bank. 1992. *World Development Report 1992: Development and the Environment.* New York: Oxford University Press. See especially chapter 5, "Sanitation and Clean Water."
Yacoob, May, Eugene Brantly, and Linda Whiteford. 1994. *Public Participation in Urban Environmental Management. WASH Technical Report* no. 90. Arlington, VA: Water and Sanitation for Health (WASH) Project.
———, and Philip Roark. 1990. *Tech Pack: Steps for Implementing Rural Water Supply and Sanitation Projects.* Arlington, VA: Water and Sanitation for Health (WASH) Project.

Chapter 8

Agarwal, Bina. 1991. "Under the Cooking Pot: The Political Economy of the Domestic Fuel Crisis in Rural South Asia." In *Women and Environment.* Ed. Sally Sontheimer. London: Earthscan Publications.

————. 1992. "The Gender and Environment Debate." *Feminist Studies* 18(1):119–58

Ahuja, Dilip R. 1990. "Research Needs for Improving Biofuel Burning Cookstove Technologies: Incorporating Environmental Concerns." *Natural Resources Forum* 14:125–34.

Appropriate Technology. A journal available from Intermediate Technology Development Group, Ltd., 103–105 Southampton Row, London WC1B 4HH, United Kingdom.

Barnes, Douglas F., Keith Openshaw, Kirk R. Smith, and Robert Van der Plas. 1994. *What Makes People Cook with Improved Biomass Stoves? A Comparative International Review of Stove Programs.* World Bank Technical Paper no. 242. Washington, D.C.: World Bank.

Bhagavan, M. R. and Stephen Karekezi. 1992. *Energy Management in Africa.* London: Zed Books, Ltd.

Boiling Point. A journal available from Intermediate Technology Development Group Publications, Ltd., 103-105 Southampton Row, London WC1B 4HH, United Kingdom.

Braidotti, Rosi, Ewa Charkiewicz, Sabine Hauser, and Saskia Wieringa. 1994. *Women, the Environment, and Sustainable Development: Towards a Theoretical Synthesis.* London: Zed Books, Ltd.

Crewe, Emma. 1992. "Social and Economic Aspects of Stove Promotion and Use." *GLOW* (a publication of the Asia Regional Cookstove Program) 6:3–8.

Joseph, Stephen. 1990. "Guidelines for Planning, Monitoring and Evaluating Cookstove Programmes." Rome: Food and Agriculture Organization.

Kaplinsky, Raphael. 1990. *The Economics of Small: Appropriate Technology in a Changing World.* London: Intermediate Technology Publications.

Karekezi, Stephen, and Gordon A. Mackenzie, eds. 1993. *Energy Options for Africa.* London: Zed Books, Ltd.

Leslie, George B., and F. W. Lunau. 1992. *Indoor Air Pollution: Problems and Priorities.* Cambridge: Cambridge University Press.

Smilie, Ian. 1991. *Mastering the Machine: Poverty, Aid, and Technology.* London: Intermediate Technology Publications.

Smith, Kirk. 1987. *Biofuels, Air Pollution, and Health: A Global Review.* New York: Plenum.

Sontheimer, Sally. 1991. *Women and Environment.* London: Earthscan Publications.

Suliman, Mohamed. 1991. "Alternative Development Strategies for Africa." Vol. 2 of *Environment, Women.* London: Institute for African Alternatives.

United Nations Development Program/World Bank Energy Sector Management Assistance Program (ESMAP). A series of reports on household energy strategies. Washington, D.C.: World Bank.

Willoughby, Kevin W. 1990. *Technology Choice: A Critique of the Appropriate Technology Movement.* London: Intermediate Technology Publications.

World Health Organization. 1992. "Indoor Air Pollution from Biomass Fuel." WHO/PEP/92.3A. Geneva.

Part IV: Environmental Politics: Grassroots Activism and the Search for Environmental Justice

Chapter 9, Chapter 10, and Chapter 11

Bobo, Kimberly A., Jackie Kendall, and Steve Max. 1991. *Organizing for Social Change: A Manual for Activists in the 1990s.* Carson, CA: Seven Locks Press.

Bryant, Bunyan I., and Paul Mohai. 1992. *The Incidence of Environmental Racism.* Boulder, CO: Westview Press.

Bullard, Robert D. 1991. *Dumping in Dixie: Race, Class, and Environmental Quality.* Boulder, CO: Westview Press.

————. 1994. *Unequal Protection: Environmental Justice and Communities of Color.* San Francisco: Sierra Club Books.

————. 1994. *People of Color Environmental Directory.* Flint, MI: Mott Foundation.

Citizen's Fund. "Poisons in our Neighborhoods: Toxic Pollution in the U.S." Summary of EPA's Toxic Release Information, available from Citizen's Fund, 1300 Connecticut Avenue, NW, Washington, D.C. 20036.

Commoner, Barry. 1990. *Making Peace with the Planet.* New York: Pantheon Books.

D'Antonio, Michael. 1993. *Atomic Harvest: Hanford and the Lethal Toll of America's Nuclear Arsenal.* New York: Crown.

Fiffer, Steve, and Sharon Sloan Fiffer. 1994. *50 Ways to Help Your Community: A Handbook for Change.* New York: Doubleday.

Gaventa, John. 1988. "From the Mountain to the Maquiladoras." *Highlander Center Working Papers* no. 7. New Market, TN: Highlander Center.

Gaventa, John, Barbara Allen Smith, and Alex Willingham, eds. 1989. *Communities in Economic Crisis, Appalachia and the South.* Philadelphia: Temple University Press.

Gedicks, Al. 1993. *The New Resource Wars: Native and Environmental Struggles Against Multinational Corporations.* Boston: South End Press.

Goldman, Benjamin A. 1991. *The Truth About Where You Live: An Atlas for Action on Toxins and Mortality.* New York: Random House.

————. 1994. "Not Just Prosperity: Achieving Sustainability Through Environmental Justice." Washington, D.C.: National Wildlife Federation.

Goldstein, Eric A., and Mark A. Izeman. 1990. *The New York Environment Book.* Washington, D.C.: Island Press.

Haun, J. William. 1991. *Guide to the Management of Hazardous Waste.* Golden, CO: Fulcrum.

Helvarg, David. 1994. *The War Against the Greens: The Wise-Use Movement, The New Right and Anti-Environmental Violence.* San Francisco: Sierra Club Books.

Highlander Center, ed. 1992. *Environment and Development in the USA: A Grassroots Report.* New Market, TN.

Hofrichter, Richard. 1993. *Toxic Struggles: The Theory and Practice of Environmental Justice.* Philadelphia: New Society Publishers.

Human Rights Watch and Natural Resources Defense Council (NRDC). 1992. *Defending the Earth: Abuses of Human Rights and the Environment.* Washington, D.C.

Jaimes, M. Annette, ed. 1992. *The State of Native America: Genocide, Colonization, and Resistance.* Monroe, ME: Common Courage Press.

Johnston, Barbara Rose, ed. 1994. *Who Pays the Price? The Sociocultural Context of Environmental Crisis.* Washington, D.C.: Island Press.

Lappe, Marc. 1991. *Chemical Deception: The Toxic Threat to Health and Environment.* San Francisco: Sierra Club Books.

Lee, Charles. 1993. "Proceedings of the First National People of Color Environmental Leadership Summit." New York: United Church of Christ.

Mazmanian, Daniel, and David Morrell. 1992. *Beyond Superfailure: America's Toxics Policy for the 1990s.* Boulder, CO: Westview Press.

Merrifield, Juliet. 1989. "Putting Scientists in Their Place: Participatory Research in Environmental and Occupational Health." *Highlander Center Working Papers* no. 8. New Market, TN: Highlander Center.

Moser, Caroline O. N. 1989. "Community Participation in Urban Projects in the Third World." *Progress in Planning* 32:71–133.

Moyers, Bill. 1990. *Global Dumping Ground: The International Traffic in Hazardous Waste.* Carson, CA: Seven Locks Press.

Portney, Kent E. 1992. *Siting Hazardous Waste Treatment Facilities: The NIMBY Syndrome.* New York: Auburn House.

Race, Poverty, and the Environment Newsletter. A newsletter available from the California Rural Legal Assistance Foundation, San Francisco, California.

Shulman, Seth. 1992. *The Threat at Home: Confronting the Toxic Legacy of the U.S. Military.* Boston: Beacon Press.

United Church of Christ Commission for Racial Justice. 1987. *Toxic Waste and Race in the United States.* New York: United Church of Christ.

Wallace, Aubrey. 1993. *Eco-Heroes: Twelve Tales of Environmental Victory.* San Francisco: Mercury House.

Part V: Creating Responsive Institutions

Chapter 12

See listings under Chapter 6.

Chapter 13

Arata, Andrew A. 1991. *Environmental Assessment of the Bolivian Chagas Disease Control Program of CCH.* VBC Report no. 82236. Arlington, VA: Vector Biology Control (VBC) Project.

Ault, Steven K. 1994. "Environmental Management: A Re-emerging Vector Control Strategy." *American Journal of Tropical Medicine and Hygiene* 50(6, Suppl.):35–49.

Briceño-Leon, Roberto. 1990. *La casa enferma: Sociología de la enfermedad de Chagas.* Caracas: Fondo Editorial Acta Científica Venezolana.

Pan American Health Organization (PAHO). 1994. "Chagas Disease and the Nervous System." *PAHO Scientific Publications* no. SP 547. Washington, D.C.

Pinto Dias, João Carlos. 1987. "Epidemiology of Chagas Disease in Brazil." In *Chagas Disease Vectors.* Edited by Z. Brenner and A. Stoker. Boca Raton, Florida: CRC Press.

Pinto Dias, João Carlos, and Rosinha Borges Dias. 1982. "Housing and the Control of Vectors of Human Chagas Disease in the State of Minas Gerias, Brazil." *Bulletin PAHO* 26:117–28.

Schofield, Christopher J., and João Carlos Pinto Dias. 1991. "A Cost-Benefit Analysis of Chagas Disease Control." *Instituto Oswaldo Cruz* 86:285–95.

Valencia, Angel. 1990. *Investigación Epidemiológica Nacional de la enfermedad de Chagas*. La Paz, Bolivia: MPSSP.

Wendel, Silvano, Zigman Brener, Mario E. Camargo, and Anis Rossi. 1992. *Chagas Disease: Its Impact on Transfusion and Clinical Medicine*. São Paulo, Brazil: ISPT Brazil.

World Health Organization (WHO). 1991. *Control of Chagas Disease: Report of a WHO Expert Committee*. Technical Report no. 811. Geneva.

Chapter 14

Ekins, Paul. 1993. *A New World Order: Grassroots Movements for Global Change*. London and New York: Routledge.

Friedmann, John, and Haripriya Rangan, eds. 1993. *In Defense of Livelihood: Comparative Studies on Environmental Action*. West Hartford, CT: Kumarian Press.

International Institute for Environment and Development. 1992. "Primary Environmental Care—Building Participatory Approaches to Local Conservation of the Environment." Report to the New York Preparatory Committee, United Nations Conference on Environment and Development. London.

———. 1994. "In Local Hands: International Symposium on Community Based Sustainable Development." July 4–8, 1994, held at the University of Sussex at Brighton, Falmer, England. Selected conference papers. London.

Pretty, Jules N., and Richard Sandbrook. 1992. *Operationalizing Sustainable Development at the Community Level: Primary Environmental Care*. Report to the Working Party on Development Assistance and the Environment, Development Assistance Committee, Organization for Economic Cooperation and Development, Rome.

United Nations Children's Fund (UNICEF). 1993. "Children, Environment and Sustainable Development: UNICEF's Response to Agenda 21." Report prepared for the 1993 Executive Board Session. E/ICEF/1993/L.2. New York.

United Nations Children's Fund (UNICEF)/United Nations Environment Program (UNEP). 1990. *The State of the Environment, 1990: Children and the Environment*. New York: UNICEF and Nairobi: UNEP.

Resource Organizations

The following are resource organizations for readers who would like more information about topics raised in this book. Resource organizations for a number of chapters with overlapping subject matter have been combined in order to reduce repetition.

Part I: Urbanization, Health, and the Environment

Chapter 1 and Chapter 2

ACCION International
130 Prospect Street, Suite 202
Cambridge, MA 02139 USA

Cooperative Housing Foundation
8300 Colesville Road, Suite 420
Silver Spring, MD 20910 USA

Debt for Development Coalition
2021 L Street, NW, Suite 510
Washington, DC 20036 USA

Fundación Carvajal
(Carvajal Foundation)
Apartado Aéreo 6178
Cali
Colombia, S.A.

Grameen Bank
Mirpur Two
Dhaka, 1216
Bangladesh

Habitat International Coalition
3420 16th Street, NW, Suite 103
Washington, DC 20010 USA

International Institute for Environment and Development (IIED)
3 Endsleigh Street
London WC1H 0DD
United Kingdom

Urban Management Programme
*(United Nations Development Program/
United Nations Centre for Human
Settlements (Habitat)/World Bank)*
• *U.S. Contact:*
UMP Coordinator
Urban Development Division
The World Bank
1818 H Street, NW
Washington, DC 20433 USA
• *Main Address:*
UMP Coordinator
UN Centre for Human Settlements
P.O. Box 30030
Nairobi, Kenya

United Nations Environment Program
2 United Nations Plaza, Room DC2-803
New York, NY 10017 USA

Chapter 3

American Psychological Association
Commission on Violence and Youth
Public Interest Directorate
750 First Street, NE
Washington, DC 20002-4242 USA

The California Wellness Foundation
Violence Prevention Initiative
6320 Canoga Avenue, Suite 1700
Woodland Hills, CA 91367-7111 USA

Center to Prevent Handgun Violence
1225 Eye Street, NW, Suite 1100
Washington, DC 20005 USA

Children's Defense Fund
25 E Street, NW
Washington, DC 20001 USA

Department of Health Services
Violence Prevention Coalition
(Los Angeles County)
241 N. Figueroa Street
Los Angeles, CA 90012 USA

National Crime Prevention Council
1700 K Street, NW, Second Floor
Washington, DC 20006-3817 USA

Violence Prevention Research Program
University of California, Davis
1700 Alhambra Boulevard, Suite 106
Sacramento, CA 95816-7050 USA

Urban Management Programme
Regional Office for Latin America
and the Caribbean
Ed. Banco La Previsora
Av. Naciones Unidas 1084
Torre B., Dpto. 612
Casilla 17-17-1449
Quito
Ecuador

Violence Policy Center
2000 P Street, NW, Suite 200
Washington, DC 20036 USA

Part II: Implications of Industrialization for Health and the Environment

Chapter 4

The Armenian Assembly of America
122 C Street, NW
Washington, DC 20001 USA

Armenian National Committee of
America
888 17th Street, NW, Suite 904
Washington, DC 20006 USA

Center for Independent Ecological
Programs
Malaya Bronnaya 12, 12
Moscow 103104 CIS

ISAR: A Clearinghouse on Grassroots
Cooperation in Eurasia
1601 Connecticut Avenue, NW, #301
Washington, DC 20009 USA

Physicians for Social Responsibility
1000 16th Street, NW, Suite 810
Washington, DC 20036 USA

RAND/UCLA Center for Soviet
Studies
1700 Main Street
PO Box 2138
Santa Monica, CA 90407-2138 USA

Regional Environmental Center for
Central and Eastern Europe
Miklos ter 1
Budapest 1035
Hungary

U.S. Agency for International
Development
Bureau for Europe and the New
Independent States
320 21st Street, NW, Room 6724
Washington, DC 20523 USA

U.S. Environmental Protection Agency
Office of International Activities
401 M Street, SW
Washington, DC 20460 USA

Chapter 5

East-West Center
University of Hawaii
1777 East-West Road
Honolulu, HI 96822 USA

Environmental Health·Project
1611 North Kent Street, Suite 300
Arlington, VA, 22209 USA

Institute for Sustainable Communities
56 College Street
Montpelier, VT 05602 USA

Northeast Center for Comparative Risk
Vermont Law School
Chelsea Street
PO Box 96
South Royalton, VT 05068 USA

Resources for the Future
Center for Risk Management
1616 P Street, NW
Washington, DC 20036 USA

U.S. Agency for International
   Development
Office of Health and Nutrition
G/PHN/HN SA-18, Suite 1200
Washington, DC 20523-1817 USA

U.S. Environmental Protection Agency
Office of International Activities
401 M Street, SW
Washington, DC 20460 USA

Western Center for Comparative Risk
PO Box 7576
Boulder, CO 80306 USA

Part III: Exploring Gender Roles in Environmental Management, Health, and Development

Chapter 6

CARE
151 Ellis Street
Atlanta, GA 30303 USA

Centre for Development and
   Population Activities
1717 Massachusetts Ave., NW, Suite 202
Washington, DC 20036 USA

International Planned Parenthood
   Federation
902 Broadway, 10th Floor
New York, NY 10010 USA

International Women's Health Coalition
24 East 24th Street, 5th Floor
New York, NY 10010 USA

National Audubon Society
950 Third Avenue
New York, NY 10022 USA

Population Action International
1120 19th Street, NW, Suite 550
Washington, DC 20036 USA

Population–Environment Balance
2000 P Street, NW, Suite 210
Washington, DC 20036 USA

Population Reference Bureau
1875 Connecticut Avenue, NW, Suite 520
Washington, DC 20009 USA

Population Services International
1120 19th Street, NW, Suite 600
Washington, DC 20036 USA

The Population Council
1 Dag Hammarskjøld Plaza
New York, NY 10017 USA

Women's Environment and
Development Organization
Secretariat
845 Third Avenue, 15th Floor
New York, NY 10011 USA

Zero Population Growth
1400 16th Street, NW, Suite 320
Washington, DC 20036 USA

Chapter 7

Center for Environmental Research
Information
U.S. Environmental Protection Agency
26 West Martin Luther King Drive
Cincinnati, OH 45268 USA

Environmental Health Division
Pan American Health Organization
525 23rd Street, NW
Washington, DC 20037 USA

Environmental Health Project
1611 North Kent Street, Suite 300
Arlington, VA 22209 USA

IRC International Water and
Sanitation Centre
PO Box 93190
2509 AD The Hague
The Netherlands

Kenya Water for Health Organization
PO Box 61470
Nairobi
Kenya

Water and Environmental Sanitation
Division
United Nations Children's Fund
333 East 38th Street
New York, NY 10016 USA

Water and Sanitation Program
United Nations Development
Program/World Bank
The World Bank
1818 H Street, NW
Washington, DC 20433 USA

Water Environment Federation
601 Wythe Street
Alexandria, VA 22314 USA

Water Supply and Sanitation
Collaborative Council
World Health Organization
Community Water Supply
CH-1211 Geneva 27
Switzerland

Chapter 8

Asia Regional Cookstove Program
Jalan Kaliurang KM7
PO Box 19 Bulaksumur
Yogyakarta
Indonesia

East-West Environment and Policy
Institute
East-West Center
University of Hawaii
1777 East-West Road
Honolulu, HI 96822 USA

Energy Sector Management
Assistance Program
United Nations Development
Program/World Bank
1818 H Street, NW
Washington, DC 20433 USA

Environmental Health Division
World Health Organization
CH-1211 Geneva 27
Switzerland

Intermediate Technology
Development Group
Myson House
Railway Terrace
Rugby CV21 3HT
United Kingdom

Office of Radiation and Indoor Air
U.S. Environmental Protection Agency
401 M Street, SW
Washington DC 20460 USA

Program for Appropriate Technology
in Health
4 Nickerson Street
Seattle, WA 98109-1699 USA

Rocky Mountain Institute
1739 Snowmass Creek Road
Snowmass, CO 81654 USA

Solar Box Cookers International
1724 11th Street
Sacramento, CA 95814 USA

Union of Concerned Scientists
26 Church Street
Cambridge, MA 02238 USA

World Resources Institute
1709 New York Avenue, NW, Suite 700
Washington, DC 20006 USA

Worldwatch Institute
1776 Massachusetts Avenue, NW
Washington, DC 20036 USA

Part IV: Environmental Politics: Grassroots Activism and the Search for Environmental Justice

Chapter 9

California Rural Legal Assistance, Inc.
631 Howard Street, Suite 300
San Francisco, CA 94105 USA

Citizen's Clearinghouse for
Hazardous Wastes
119 Rowell Court
Falls Church, VA 22046 USA

Friends of the Earth
218 D Street, SE
Washington, DC 20003 USA

Greenpeace
1436 U Street, NW
Washington, DC 20009 USA

Highlander Research and Education
Center
1959 Highlander Way
New Market, TN 37820 USA

The National Toxics Campaign
1168 Commonwealth Avenue
Boston, MA 02134 USA

Natural Resources Defense Council
40 West 20th Street
New York, NY 10011 USA

Panos Institute
1717 Massachusetts Avenue, Suite 301
Washington, DC 20036 USA

Southwest Network for Environmental
and Economic Justice
PO Box 7399
Albuquerque, NM 87102 USA

•Office of Environmental Justice
•Office of Solid Waste & Emergency
Response
•Office of Pollution, Prevention, and
Toxics
U.S. Environmental Protection Agency
401 M Street, SW
Washington, DC 20460 USA
(Note: These are three separate offices
within the EPA.)

West Harlem Environmental Action
529 West 145th Street
New York, NY 10031 USA

Chapter 10

Akwe:kon Press
Cornell University
300-T Caldwell Hall
Ithaca, NY 14853 USA

American Indigenous Law and
Policy Center
College of Law
University of Oklahoma
300 Timberland Road
Norman, OK 73019-0701 USA

Diné CARE
10A Town Plaza, Suite 138
Durango, CO 81301 USA

Greenpeace
•1436 U Street, NW
Washington, DC 20009 USA

•568 Howard Street, 3rd Floor
San Francisco, CA 94105 USA

Indigenous Environmental Network
National Office
PO Box 485
Bemidji, MN 56601-0485 USA

•Alaska Regional Office
HCO 4 Box 9880
Palmer, AK 99645 USA

•Oklahoma Regional Office
PO Box 701796
Tulsa, OK 74170 USA

Second Inter-American Indian
Congress on Conservation and
Natural Resources
Casilla 14259
La Paz
Bolivia

UN Center for Human Rights
Office of Indigenous People
United Nations Plaza, Room S2914
New York, NY 10017 USA
*(For information about the UN Decade
of Indigenous People.)*

Indigenous Women's Network
P.O. Box 174
Lake Elmo, MN 55042 USA

Chapter 11
See listings under Chapter 9.

Part V: Creating Responsive Institutions

Chapter 12
See listings under Chapter 6.

Chapter 13
Centers for Disease Control
1600 Clifton Road
Atlanta, GA 30333 USA

Centro de Pesquisas "René Rachou"
Fundação Oswaldo Cruz
Avenida Agosto do Lima, 1715
Caixa Postal 1743
30190 Belo Horizonte
Brazil

Centro de Salud "Dr. Mario Fatala
Chaben"
Paseo Colon 568, 7 piso
1063 Buenos Aires
Argentina

Centro Nacional de Enfermedades
Tropicales (CENTROP)
Avenida Segundo Anillo
Esq. de Centenario
Santa Cruz
Bolivia

Proyecto de Salud Infantil y
  Comunitaria
(Child and Community Health Project)
Casilla 4910
Cochabamba
Bolivia
and
Calle Goitia Nos. 142-143
Casilla 14384
La Paz
Bolivia

Environmental Health Project
1611 North Kent Street, Suite 300
Arlington, VA 22209 USA

Instituto Boliviano de Biologia de la
  Altura (IBBA)
Casilla 824
La Paz
Bolivia

Instituto Nacional de Investigaciones
  Cientificas
POB 1141
Asunción
Paraguay

Ministerio de Salud de la Provincia
  de Córdoba
Departamento Atencion Primaria y
  Zoonosis
División Chagas
Santiago Cáceres 2085
5000 Córdoba
Argentina

Pan American Health Organization
525 23rd Street, NW, DPI
Washington, DC 20037 USA

Secretaria de Salud
Dirección Nacional de Epidemiología
Departamento Control de Vectores
Casilla 4331
La Paz
Bolivia

Universidad Central de Venezuela
Laboratorio de Ciencias Sociales
Apartado Postal 47795
Caracas 1040-A
Venezuela

Universidade de Brasilia
Núcleo de Medicina Tropical e
  Nutrição
Faculdade da Ciência da Saúde
Agencia Postal 15
Brasilia 70910
Brazil

World Health Organization
Division of Control of Tropical
  Diseases
20 Avenue Appia
CH-1211 Geneva 27
Switzerland

Chapter 14

Action Aid
MacDonald Archway
London N19 5PG
United Kingdom

Directorate General for Development
  Cooperation
Istituto Superiore di Sanità
Viale Regina Elena 299
00161 Rome
Italy

Enda Tiers Monde
4 & 5 Rue Kleber
BP 3370
Dakar
Senegal

Environmental Health Division
World Health Organization
CH-1211 Geneva 27
Switzerland

Friends of the Earth
218 D Street, SE
Washington, DC 20003 USA

Intermediate Technology
 Development Group
103-105 Southampton Row
London WC1B 4HH
United Kingdom

International Institute for
 Environment and Development
3 Endsleigh Street
London WC1H ODD
United Kingdom

Oxfam UK
274 Banbury Road
Oxford OX2 7DZ
United Kingdom

United Nations Children's Fund
UNICEF/DH-40C
3 United Nations Plaza
New York, NY 10017 USA

World Conservation Union (IUCN)
Avenue du Mont Blanc
CH-1196 Gland
Switzerland

World Wide Fund for Nature
The Panda House
Wayside Park
Godalming Surrey GU7 1XR
United Kingdom

Editors and Contributors

Bonnie Bradford, M.P.H., has been an international public health consultant to numerous agencies and organizations during the past fourteen years. She specializes in environmental health, housing and health linkages, water and sanitation, and peri-urban health issues in developing countries. Prior to entering the field of international public health, she was a community health educator in several Washington, D.C., community-based public health clinics serving low-income and minority clients. She completed her masters in public health at the School of Hygiene and Public Health at the Johns Hopkins University.

Margaret A. Gwynne's professional training (M.A., Ph.D.) is in social and cultural anthropology, with a particular focus on international health, development, and women's issues. In addition to her academic responsibilities in the department of anthropology at the State University of New York at Stony Brook, she has worked as an editor of books and academic journals; as a consultant on projects sponsored by the World Health Organization, U.S. Agency for International Development, private foundations, and consulting firms; and as a field researcher under research grants from the State University of New York and the Pew Charitable Trusts.

George Alleyne is director of the Pan American Health Organization (PAHO). Previously, he was assistant director, director of the Area of Health Programs Development, and chief of the Research Unit at PAHO. He received his M.D. at the University of the West Indies in Jamaica and completed specialty training in internal medicine in the United Kingdom.

Andrew A. Arata, Ph.D., is currently clinical professor of international health and development, Tulane School of Public Health and Tropical Medicine, and deputy director of the USAID-sponsored Environmental Health Project. He was formerly chief, Vector Genetics and Bionomics, WHO, Geneva; director at WHO/PAHO Center for Research and Training in Vector Biology and Control, Venezuela; and ecologist, WHO/PAHO Center for Human Ecology and Health, Mexico.

Deepak Bajracharya is currently the senior adviser for the Environment Section, Programme Division at UNICEF. He has a M.S. in environmental engineering from Stanford University, and a D.Phil. in science policy from the University of Sussex. He has acted as an advocate in national and international fora on issues related to participatory rural energy development, women and rural energy, rural institutions, and off-farm employment in mountain areas.

Fanor Balderrama, M.D., M.P.H., M.Sc. epidemiology, is on the faculty of medicine, Universidad de San Simón in Cochabamba, Bolivia. His M.P.H. is from the Institute of Tropical Medicine in Antwerp, Belgium; and his M.Sc. in epidemiology is from the Universidad del Valle, Cali, Colombia. He has done clinical work for several years in Zaire and Sudan and epidemiological and control work on numerous tropical diseases in Bolivia. He is currently technical coordinator of the USAID-sponsored CCH Chagas Control Program.

Hernán Bermudez, M.D., is on the faculty of medicine, Universidad de San Simón, Cochabamba, Bolivia. He has done postdoctoral work at the Institute of Tropical Medicine in Antwerp, Belgium, the University of Florida, and in Brazil. He has published widely on the disease vectors of malaria, Chagas disease, and leishmaniasis in Bolivia. He directs medical entomological work at the university and at the ministry of health entomological laboratory in Cochabamba.

Eugene P. Brantly Jr., M.S., J.D., is the Environmental Health Project's technical director for risk assessment and risk management, and also directs the International Environment and Natural Resources Program in the Center for International Development, Research Triangle Institute. At the Environmental Health Project, Mr. Brantly is responsible for adapting risk assessment procedures, priority-setting processes, and other methods used in environmental management in the United States for applications in developing countries. He has worked on projects in Central Asia, Ecuador, India, Indonesia, Senegal, and the United States.

Nilak Butler, Inuit, is the Nuclear Free Future–Indigenous Lands campaigner at Greenpeace, council member of the Indigenous Environmental Network, and board member of the Indigenous Women's Network.

Cynthia L. Carlson, M.P.H., has spent twelve years living and working in developing countries, nine of them in sub-Saharan Africa. Since receiving her M.P.H. from the Population and Family Health Division of the School of Public Health at the University of California, Los Angeles, she has worked as a coordinator for a British volunteer program in Mali, as a consultant to the ministry of health of Rwanda, and, from 1989 to 1994, as assistant country director in charge of programs for the international aid agency CARE, first in Rwanda and then in Uganda.

Emma Crewe, M.A., Ph.D., is currently a lecturer in social anthropology, School of African and Asian Studies, University of Sussex, United Kingdom. Formerly social scientist in the Operations Division of Intermediate Technology Development Group (ITDG), an international charity engaged in appropriate technology development for resource-poor people in the South, she earlier served with ITDG's Fuel for Food Programme.

Her specialties include international development, appropriate technology, and gender issues.

Caswell A. Evans Jr., D.D.S., M.P.H., formerly director of the County Health Services Division of the Seattle–King County Department of Public Health in Washington State, is currently director of Public Health Programs and Services, Los Angeles County, California. In this capacity, he is responsible for the administration of disease prevention, health promotion, and health protection services for more than 9 million area residents. Dr. Evans also serves as adjunct professor in the School of Public Health and the School of Dentistry at the University of California, Los Angeles.

Rodrigo Guerrero, M.D., Dr. P.H., formerly executive director of the Carvajal Foundation, Cali, Colombia; president of the Colombian Association of Medical Schools; and president of the Universidad del Valle in Colombia, is currently the mayor of Cali. Dr. Guerrero is a widely published specialist in epidemiology and population sciences. He is a member of Delta Omega Public Health Honorary Society and was a fellow of the Kellogg International Program in Health.

Kim Hekimian is currently a Ph.D. candidate in health policy and management at the Johns Hopkins School of Hygiene and Public Health. During the last three years, she has worked on public health issues in the former Soviet republics of Armenia and Georgia, with particular emphasis on infant feeding and postpartum hospital practices. She is also working on curriculum development for the public health program at the American University of Armenia.

Judith A. Hermanson has been Cooperative Housing Foundation's executive vice president for international programs since March 1992. Dr. Hermanson has a distinguished career in international development and has specialized for the past several years in the problems associated with urban development. She holds a Ph.D. in American studies from the George Washington University.

Lily P. Kak, Ph.D., is deputy director of the Asia Regional Program of the Centre for Development and Population Activities (CEDPA) in Washington, D.C. Originally from India, she holds a Ph.D. in anthropology from the State University of New York at Stony Brook, and has been a post-doctoral fellow at the Johns Hopkins University. Dr. Kak has done considerable evaluation research in the areas of family planning and reproductive health.

Theresa A. Kilbane joined the Cooperative Housing Foundation as country director in Honduras in July 1993. Ms. Kilbane has over fifteen years of experience working on urban community development issues, and has worked for the Urban Home Steading Assistance Board in New York City, CEDOPE in Mexico, and as a consultant to Honduran NGOs. She holds a B.S. in political science and a M.S. in urban planning.

Winona LaDuke, Mississippi Anishinabe, is the campaign director of the White Earth Land Recovery Project, a reservation-based organization, and a frequent writer on Native environmental issues. She also serves as a cochair of the Indigenous Women's Network (a continental and Pacific network of women active in their communities). She is environmental program coordinator of the Seventh Generation Fund and a board member of Greenpeace.

Therese McGinn, an independent consultant and specialist in population planning, has worked in family planning and reproductive health operations research and service delivery, primarily in Africa, where she lived for several years. She was deputy director of CARE's newly formed Population Unit from 1991–93, and now serves on the board of directors of the University of Michigan Population-Environment Fellows Program.

Vernice D. Miller currently serves as director of the Environmental Justice Initiative of the Natural Resources Defense Council. She is a graduate of Columbia University where she studied environmental policy and urban planning as a Revson Fellow. She cofounded West Harlem Environmental Action. Ms. Miller has also been a consultant for the United Church of Christ Commission for Racial Justice, and New York coordinator for the U.S. Citizens Network on the United Nations Conference on Environment and Development.

Jennifer Jael Nahalamba Mukolwe, who holds a master of science degree in community health from the University of Nairobi, Kenya, has worked for government, NGOs, and the private sector. After serving for nine years as program manager of the Maternal Health and Family Planning Program of Kenya's largest national women's organization, she worked for four years as program manager of the Family Planning Association of Kenya, an affiliate of the International Planned Parenthood Federation. Since March 1992, she has worked for CARE/Uganda as project manager of the Community Reproductive Health Project in southwestern Uganda.

Margaret Wuganga Mwangola, with a background in community development, is the executive director of the Kenya Water for Health Organization (KWAHO), which she joined in 1980. In 1993, Mrs. Mwangola received the NCIH Award for Service in International Health for "galvanizing women to bring clean water, improved sanitation, and a better life to rural Kenya, and for her efforts to heal the earth in ways that are tangible, visible, and sustainable."

Raymond Ocasio is currently a senior officer for Local Initiatives Support Corporation, a national intermediate organization in the United States that promotes and fosters community development and housing. Mr. Ocasio has been involved in housing and community development for more than twenty-five years, of which fifteen years have been in international activities. He has a M.S. in urban planning, and has advanced credit in public administration.

Waafas Ofosu-Amaah is a consultant on gender, environment, and sustainable development issues. She is currently working with the United Nations Development Program on the preparations for the Fourth World

Conference on Women, to be held in Beijing, China, in September 1995. She was formerly managing director of WorldWIDE Network, a nonprofit, international network of women concerned about environmental issues, where she directed the overall design and implementation of gender and environment projects and activities. Ms. Ofosu-Amaah has worked on various projects with the United Nations Environment Program and has consulted for the World Health Organization.

Marjorie B. Signer, a communications professional who holds a master's degree in journalism from Columbia University, has been a newspaper reporter and scientific editor specializing in health issues. She worked in south India for four years with a community-based development project, and is currently director of communications for the Centre for Development and Population Activities with responsibility for publications and public information.

Faustino Torrico, M.D., is on the faculty of medicine at the Universidad de San Simón in Cochabamba, Bolivia, and has done postdoctoral work at the Institute of Tropical Medicine in Antwerp, Belgium. He is a specialist in immuno-parasitology and heads the immunology diagnostic laboratory and practices clinical tropical medicine in Cochabamba.

Billie Phyllis Weiss, M.P.H., is a biologist and former director of the Violence Prevention Coalition of Los Angeles County, California. The author or coauthor of numerous papers on public health and a frequent public speaker on the subject of violence, Ms. Weiss currently serves as project director III for the Los Angeles County Department of Health Services' Injury Prevention and Control Project.

Larry Wilson, M.S., is currently the coordinator of the Community Environmental Health Program at the Highlander Research and Education Center, New Market, Tennessee, a nongovernmental organization that has played an active role in Southern people's struggles for justice and democracy since 1932. A dedicated community activist and formerly a farmer, Mr. Wilson was also director of environmental testing at Quality Laboratory in Kentucky. The concept of a "healthy environment" on a community level has been a central theme throughout his educational and professional career.

Index

Acute respiratory infection (ARI), 92–93
African Americans: the environment and human rights in West Harlem, 123–27; homicides among, 35–36; urban, 105
Air pollution: in Armenia, 53; in Quito, Ecuador, 68; residential, 75–76, 92–99
Akwesasne Mohawk Reservation, 118
Akwesasne Mothers Milk Project, 118
American Red Cross, 111
American University of Armenia, 57
Amin Dada, Idi, 136
Anagi stove, 96
Appalachian farmers, 104
Appropriate technologies (AT), 94–99
Armenia, industrial pollution in, 49–59
Asentamientos populares, 66, 68
Azerbaijan, 50, 51, 52

Barreiro, Katsi Cook, 118
Barrios marginales, 23–25
"Best Friends for Life" curriculum, 38
Bio-intensive gardens, 157
Biomass fuels, 75, 92–94, 97, 98
Birth control. *See* Family planning services
Bolivia, Chagas disease control in, 143–52
Bolivian National Chagas Disease Control Program, 148
Bolivian Secretariat of Health, 148
Botswana, making veld products in, 158
Brazil: Chagas disease control in, 144, 146; poverty and environment project in, 157–58
Bureau of Indian Affairs, 114, 116

Bwindi Impenetrable Forest, Uganda, 135, 137, 139

Cali, Colombia, programs for the urban poor in, 17–22
California State Department of Health Services, 39
Canada, 113, 115
Cancer, 2; high incidence of cancer in Armenia, 51, 55; high incidence of cancer in Kentucky, 108, 109; Navajo miners and lung, 117
CARE Uganda, 134–42
CEDPA, 79
Center to Prevent Handgun Violence, 38
Centers for Disease Control (CDC), 108, 148
Central America, 24
Chagas, Carlos, 146
Chagas disease control in Bolivia, 143–52
Chernobyl nuclear disaster, 54, 55
Children: birth defects, 117; Chagas disease infection among, 146; child survival and development programs in Tanzania, 158–59; infant and child mortality rates, 77, 79, 90, 125; participation in primary environmental care (PEC), 159; urban violence and, 36
Community and Child Health (CCH) Program, Bolivia, 144, 148, 149, 151
Community Reproductive Health Project (CREHP), Uganda, 137–38, 141
Community-based information, education, and communication (IEC), 79
Comparative risk assessment, 61
Consumption, issue of, 115
Contraceptive prevalence rate, 78

About NCIH

The mission of the National Council for International Health (NCIH) is to improve health worldwide by providing vigorous leadership and advocacy designed to increase the United States public and private sector awareness of, and response to, international health needs. NCIH facilitates national and international partnerships and stimulates private sector initiatives toward this end.

A private nonprofit membership association, NCIH includes individuals and organizations in the public and private sectors from all fifty states and over seventy-five countries worldwide who are committed to improving international health. NCIH leads the international health community in information dissemination, policy analysis, and health advocacy on current international health issues such as community health, women's health, child survival, environmental health, access to care, and AIDS. NCIH provides the largest forum in the United States for the international health community to discuss cutting-edge issues, generate new health initiatives, and influence international policies.

The NCIH concept of "global learning for health" is reinforced in this publication, since health and environmental problems are not unique to the developing countries, they are global. Sharing experiences enables us to better face the crisis of AIDS, the risk of new and emerging diseases, threats to child and family survival, environmental degradation, and increasing violence. Bringing health, environmental, and development organizations together is a vital step in the process of addressing these global issues.

For additional information, contact:
National Council for International Health
1701 K Street, NW, Suite 600
Washington, DC 20006 USA

Kumarian Press Books on International Development

Kumarian Press Books for a World that Works

For more information, contact:
Kumarian Press, Inc.
(203) 953-0214 tel / (203) 953-8579 fax
KPBooks@aol.com